PFS:FIRST PUBLISHER®3
MADE EASY

PFS:FIRST PUBLISHER®3

made Easy

Greg M. Perry

Osborne **McGraw-Hill**

Berkeley New York St. Louis San Francisco
Auckland Bogotá Hamburg London Madrid
Mexico City Milan Montreal New Delhi Panama City
Paris São Paulo Singapore Sydney
Tokyo Toronto

Osborne **McGraw-Hill**
2600 Tenth Street
Berkeley, California 94710
U.S.A.

Osborne **McGraw-Hill** offers software for sale. For information on software, translations, or book distributors outside of the U.S.A., please write to Osborne **McGraw-Hill** at the above address.

This book is printed on recycled paper.

PFS:First Publisher® 3 Made Easy

1234567890 DOC 99876543210

ISBN 0-07-881689-0

This book's for you Michael Stapp . . . and I know it's about time.

CONTENTS
AT A GLANCE

CONTENTS

ACKNOWLEDGMENTS

As always, John Levy's technical suggestions made this book 100% better (and more accurate) than it would have been without him.

Osborne/McGraw-Hill's Roger Stewart, Laurie Beaulieu, Judith Brown, Bob O'Keefe, Judy Wohlfrom, Stefany Otis, and Vivian Jaquette are the best people to work with. Ann Pharr's voice was always happy and soothing and made the deadlines seem calmer. You all are even nicer in person.

As always, my bride Jayne encouraged me, and my parents Glen and Bettye Perry were there to make it easier. My love goes to all three of you.

—Greg M. Perry

INTRODUCTION

Over the years, computer users like you have become very sophisticated, and so have your computing needs. Text-based word processors may not have the power that you need; desktop word processing is turning into desktop publishing, and you need more powerful programs to handle your publishing needs.

Unfortunately, with that increased power comes increased responsibility; many desktop publishing programs on the market are hard to understand and take a long time to master. Fortunately, First Publisher gives you that added power without demanding a time-consuming learning curve. First Publisher has the added bonus of costing much less than many other desktop publishing programs on the market.

Although the First Publisher system is easy to learn, this book makes that learning even easier and fun as well. You will walk through step-by-step examples of First Publisher's basics. Once you master the basics, you will tackle the advanced capabilities of the program by creating many different kinds of finished publications.

Most of the program commands are intuitive. Once you are acquainted with the design, layout, and menu system, you will be able to guide yourself through your own publications. You will become familiar with the consistent menu structure and file-selection features of First Publisher before finishing the second chapter.

FIRST PUBLISHER

First Publisher can handle the desktop publishing needs of just about every-one. Secretaries, managers, professionals, and students will all feel comfortable with the program. Some of the many features of the program are:

- A WYSIWYG ("What You See Is What You Get") feature that shows you a preview of your final printed document.

- Integration of the mouse and keyboard, which makes using the program fast and accurate.

- The ability to directly import ASCII text files, as well as those formatted by PFS:Write, PFS:Professional Write, or PFS:First Choice. All font information used in the original documents is retained.

- Up to 14 fonts that can be added to the First Publisher system at any one time.

- Freehand drawing capabilities with four line widths for the pencil-, box-, circle-, and line-drawing tools.

- A SNAPSHOT feature that allows you to import graphics from virtually any program.

- The ability to include up to four columns of text in one publication.

- Powerful art-manipulation features such as rotating and resizing.

- High-resolution (300 dots per inch) art images that can be placed any-where within a publication.

- Use of Bitstream scalable fonts to create better looking text.

ABOUT THIS BOOK

This book walks you through starting up the program, and then guides you through its features, from beginning to advanced. Both versions of First Publisher, 2 and 3, are explained in detail. You will create complete published documents by following the many exercises in Part II. There are plenty of figures and illustrations to let you verify your results.

Both novices and advanced users will find helpful tips and notes for the program's use scattered throughout every chapter. This book is more than just a guide; it is a stand-alone instructor that teaches you how to effectively use First Publisher.

HOW THIS BOOK IS ORGANIZED

This book is broken down into the following three parts:

Part I: Getting Started with First Publisher
Part II: Applications for First Publisher
Part III: Appendixes

The first section explains the keystrokes, commands, menus, and environment of the system. Both beginning as well as advanced features are described. The second part shows you how to lay out, edit, and preview publications for a variety of applications. The third section is a collection of appendixes that wrap up the final topics.

The contents of each chapter are summarized here.

Chapter 1, "What Is Desktop Publishing?," quickly gives you an introduction to hardware, software, and operating system concepts before delving into an overview of the desktop publishing environment. You will learn the basics of publication design and see the new features that were added to version 3 of First Publisher. The concept of fonts is explained. The chapter finishes with a look at how to start First Publisher.

Chapter 2, "The First Publisher Environment," describes the screen elements, side tools, menu selections, and use of the keyboard and mouse. You will get your first hands-on exposure to the publishing and layout screen of First Publisher.

Chapter 3, "Your Publication's Text," gives you the fundamental working knowledge for manipulating text from within First Publisher using the text overlay and clipboard. Importing text from other programs is fully described.

Chapter 4, "Your Publication's Art," shows you how to manipulate art. You also learn how to import screens from virtually any graphics program on the market. This chapter also explores version 3's ability to include high-resolution (300 dots per inch) art images inside a publication.

Chapter 5, "Printing Your Publication," acquaints you with First Publisher's page preview feature, which lets you see on the screen what your printed publication will look like. A draft mode produces output quickly, and the smoothed printing mode outputs a high-quality finished page.

Chapter 6, "The Publication Layout," gives you guidelines for good layout and design. You will create publications that look very professional using First Publisher's easy command and menu structure to manage the layout.

Chapter 7, "Advanced Font Support," describes how to add new fonts to First Publisher, providing your publications with a variety of typefaces. All sources of fonts, such as font cartridges, soft font files, and scalable Bitstream fonts, are explained.

Chapter 8, "Ruler Notation Used in Part II," is a short chapter designed to familiarize you with the ruler line notation used in the second part of the book. It will aid in creating the many publications described.

Chapter 9, "Single- and Multiple-Column Newsletters," instructs you on how to create newsletters. Newsletters can range from one to four columns, and the proper placement of art and text is critical. Because newsletters contain so much text, you will find that accurate baseline placement is essential.

Chapter 10, "Artistic Fliers," shows you how to create attention-getting fliers and announcements, with eye-catching art and little text. This chapter walks you through the creation of a flier and gives you additional tips for adding coupons and borders.

Chapter 11, "Invoices and Order Forms," helps you cope with invoices and order forms that offer a different set of challenges that the previous publications have not addressed. The lines and boxes of order forms and invoices require the special art tools that come with First Publisher.

Chaper 12, "Creating Letterheads and Business Cards," helps you save on printing costs by teaching you to produce your own stationery and business cards with First Publisher. Design tips for your company logo are included, and you will walk through several examples of placing the logo once it is created.

Chapter 13, "Business Reports," will help you to continue to use your spreadsheet and charting programs to create the tables and graphs that go into published business reports. This chapter shows you how to import those tables and graphs from other programs.

Chapter 14, "Restaurant Menus," guides you through the creation and layout of two different styles of restaurant menus. You must think ahead about future price and menu changes before finalizing your menus.

CONVENTIONS USED IN THIS BOOK

You will need to type several different kinds of keystrokes throughout this book. To distinguish between the book's text, the screen messages, and the keystrokes you must type, the following notation will be used:

- Names of keyboard keys are boxed, for example, (ENTER), (F1), and (END).

- A hyphen (-) between keys, as in (CTRL-HOME), indicates that you press the first key and hold it down while pressing the second, and then release both keys. (You have probably used the (SHIFT) key in this manner during regular typing.)

- Where you are asked to enter data, such as a letter, word, or block of text, the text is displayed in boldface, as in **newsletter,** or monospace, as in

`newsletter`

The command card at the end of this book will illustrate the use of many of these keystrokes and commands and can be removed and used as a quick reference for First Publisher.

WHY THIS BOOK
IS FOR YOU

You can easily understand the First Publisher concepts shown in this book, even if you only have a cursory grasp of computers. You do not have to be a programmer or an operating system guru to create eye-catching publications quickly and easily.

This book is aimed at beginning users of First Publisher. By following its many step-by-step examples, you are led through the fundamentals of the First Publisher program. You can stop along the way and compare your results to figures in the book to ensure success of the final document's appearance. Each publication created in this book is shown in its final printed form for your guidance when creating it.

First Publisher was designed to be an easy-to-use program. However, power and flexibility are not sacrificed for ease of use. Many so-called computer "power users" find that First Publisher creates publications that require far fewer commands and extensive keystrokes than other desktop publishing programs. If you are an advanced computer user and want to see what First Publisher can accomplish, you might want to flip through the last six chapters of the book to see the example publications.

Along with the text, figures, and step-by-step examples throughout the book, you will find tips and shortcuts to improve your publications and reduce the time needed to create them. You will be using First Publisher from the very first chapter to explore the world of desktop publishing.

GETTING STARTED WITH FIRST PUBLISHER

What Is Desktop Publishing?
The First Publisher Environment
Your Publication's Text
Your Publication's Art
Printing Your Publication
The Publication Layout
Advanced Font Support

First Publisher is a desktop publishing program that is easy and fun to use. This section gets you started by describing the fundamentals of desktop publishing, while teaching you the environment of the First Publisher system.

Part II will take you on a guided tour of several useful First Publisher applications. Before tackling the applications, read the following chapters to get yourself acquainted with versions 2 and 3 of First Publisher.

Stock Pick Paper

| Volume 3 | Bulls and Bears Review | December 10, 1991 |

Kicker

Technicians are Correct! The bears are back!!!!!!

Today marked the first occurence
of the down cycle that should span
some sever...
primarily
nicians, he
this fall in t
To the disma
it looks as t
taken the b

We are wit
move away
markets to
cash positi
interest ra
rocket; he
positions.

"I have bec
quite some
vice-pres
brokerage
if we have
cash, howe

Nex

In an ecc
many pe
figures

Edward
the com
rates

"We are
mortgag

"There i
The Fede

81332193

TJC Enterprises
10300 E. 81st Street
Tulsa, Oklahoma
74133

S I G N S

Sold to		Shipped to
Street & No		
City		
Customer's Order		

WHAT IS DESKTOP PUBLISHING?

Welcome to the world of desktop publishing and PFS:First Publisher. This chapter provides a preliminary review of desktop publishing concepts so you will feel right at home when you start First Publisher. Good luck on your journey to eye-catching quality publications.

Just a few years ago, publishing required expensive typesetting equipment and a team of professional printers. Mixing text and art on the page required considerable skill. Much of this skill was handed down from generation to generation, and publishing was considered more of an art than a science.

Desktop publishing puts this publishing power into the hands of virtually anyone with a microcomputer. Through the use of the computer's keyboard and mouse, integrating text and art is nearly effortless. The tremendous boom of desktop publishing speaks for itself; the desktop publishing market is expected to grow to more than five billion dollars by the mid-1990s. This growth is explainable when you realize that many organizations and individuals spend a considerable amount of money on some form of publishing: newsletters, invoices, fliers, letterheads, financial reports, manuals, and hundreds of other published productions. Publishing with a microcomputer not only lowers these costs, but also increases the freedom and control that a company has over its productions.

Desktop publishing is a term generally reserved for a microcomputer running some form of publishing package that fully integrates text and art and provides common layout tools for design. Companies that could not afford their own publishing departments, or could not justify the expense of outside publishing services, can now fully realize the advantage of publishing documents.

THE PROCESS OF DESKTOP PUBLISHING

Your word processor helps you create text like that shown in Figure 1-1. Word processors are tremendous tools for writers. Many of the new word

---

Is Rental Property a Good Deal?

Are you tired of giving so much money away in taxes, with nothing to show for your labor except a tax return? Rental properties give you the opportunity to save taxes, build equity, and help your economy! Sounds too good to be true?

We can show you how to accomplish buying single-family rental dwellings with little or no money down! Call, write, or come by and our friendly representatives will help you get started!

Property Consultants
9391 E. Yorktown Alley
Madison, MN 21555
(123) 555-4321

⚌ **FIGURE 1-1.** Text created with a word processor

processors include integrated spelling checkers and electronic thesaurus programs. The only drawback to using a word processor for your publications is that word processors can't manipulate art in the same efficient way as they do text. At best, drawing capabilities of word processors are limited to a few boxes and lines.

For art, you must use one of the many drawing programs to create pictures such as the one shown in Figure 1-2. Just as a word processor does not make you a better writer, a drawing program does not make you a better artist. It does, however, let you create pictures electronically with the computer's mouse and keyboard. Many of the drawing programs can read scanned images and create computerized pictures of the scanned art.

Before desktop publishing, when you needed to combine the text from your word processor and the art from the graphics program, you used scissors and glue. There were no software programs available that easily combined the two with a professional, typeset look and feel. Now, with desktop publishing software, you can manipulate the text *and* art to produce combined output such as that shown in Figure 1-3.

The process of desktop publishing is similar to the traditional methods of publishing. The following steps outline the process of desktop publishing.

FIGURE 1-2. A picture created with a drawing program

Is Rental Property a GOOD Deal?

Are you tired of giving so much money away in taxes with nothing to show for your labor except a tax return? Rental properties will give you the opportunity to save taxes, build equity, and help your economy!

Sounds
too
good
to
be
true?

We can show you how to accomplish buying single-family rental homes with little or no money down! Call, write, or come by and our friendly sales representatives will help you get started!

**Property Consultants
939 E. Yorktown Alley
Madison, MN 21555
(123) 555-4321**

FIGURE 1-3. Desktop publishing combines both text and art

Prepare Your Text Use a favorite word processor to write, edit, and proof-read your text. Nothing beats word processing for quickly and easily producing a manuscript. Once the text is just as you like it, save it to a disk file. For small publications, you may use the built-in word processor of the desktop publisher. This is recommended only for light text. The strength of the desktop publisher lies in its ability to lay out the page, not in manipulating text.

Prepare Your Art   Using a graphics program such as PC Paintbrush, draw the artwork that you want placed in the publication. Save the art to a disk file. Many art programs come with samples of *clip art.* You may also scan printed art to produce the graphics file needed for the desktop publisher. If you do not have a graphics program, your desktop publisher comes with samples of clip art.

Load the Desktop Publisher   Once you start the desktop publishing program, load your text and art directly into the desktop publisher's work area. If you need to make modifications to the text or art, you can do so within the desktop publisher. Lay out the art and text so they work nicely together. As you arrange the pages, the screen updates to show you these changes.

Print the Document   Send the published work to the printer. If minor changes and additions need to be made, you can easily do so from the desktop publisher.

   The desktop publisher has simple, built-in word processing and graphics capabilities that allow you to make minor modifications to your text and art. If you are not used to a drawing program, but still want to integrate art into your text, most desktop publishing software comes with several files of clip art that you might find useful for your own publications.

FIRST PUBLISHER'S DIFFERENCE

First Publisher is the first program to give advanced desktop publishing capabilities to beginners who do not want to learn professional typesetting but who need to do publishing. There are many popular desktop publishing programs on the market. Each of them has unique advantages and disadvantages. The strength of First Publisher is its easy-to-use interface, which lets you quickly prepare fliers, newsletters, menus, and other publications even if you do not have time to learn about typesetting and page layout. First Publisher also offers another advantage over many software products: it is fun to use and does not require a lot of complicated procedures to produce attention-getting output.

   First Publisher does not ensure that your output will look professional. It does, however, eliminate the tedious cut-and-paste process of laying out text and art squarely on the page. Electronic tools such as on-screen scissors, glue, ruler, pens, and erasers manipulate the art and text on the screen.

The *last* step of desktop publishing is sending the output to the printer. This is the key to its ease of use; text and art images are extremely easy to move, duplicate, and resize while they are still on the screen. First Publisher constantly updates the screen to show what you will see on the final printed page. This is known as *WYSIWYG* (pronounced "wizzy-wig") or "what you see is what you get," as shown in Figure 1-4.

Advance Planning is Still Important

Starting in Chapter 9, this book will give you detailed pointers on laying out text and art for specific types of publications. Many of you will want to jump in and immediately begin desktop publishing using these examples. Why not? That's the best way to learn. Thanks to First Publisher, you can begin producing documents without much preparation.

Figure 1-3 showed you a sample of what a desktop publisher can accom-

FIGURE 1-4. What you see on the screen appears on the printed page

plish. First Publisher gives you the ability to lay out your page to your liking. Before starting the program, you should give a little thought to how you want the final document to look.

Get a pencil and paper and draw a quick *thumbnail sketch* of what you have in mind for your publication before you walk to the computer's keyboard. Thumbnail sketches do not have to be elaborate. Think of them as guides to get to your final goal of a well-produced publication. Figure 1-5 shows you what four thumbnail sketches of the same document might look like. Even sketches as simple as these make for a better design plan, because you know where you are headed. Once you become familiar with First Publisher's page layout features, you will see how to access the thumbnail sketches supplied with First Publisher. These will help you get started with almost any format of publication you want to produce.

While learning First Publisher, feel free to experiment, mess up, correct errors, move art from one place to another, and so on. That is the best way to learn First Publisher, or any other program. However, keep in mind that planning in advance will *always* save you time when creating publications. Just as a builder needs a blueprint before picking up a hammer and nails, your work will go more smoothly if you draw a thumbnail sketch of your page before starting to put together the columns of text and art.

FIGURE 1-5. Sample thumbnail sketches

REMEMBER YOUR AUDIENCE Always keep your audience in mind when planning how your published documents will look. Newsletters are more "friendly-looking" if they have two or three columns with headings and titles in a larger typeface than the body of the text. Don't, however, mix too many typestyles on a page. Instead of a professional appearance, your page will look too "busy." Art mixed in here and there adds spice to a newsletter and breaks the monotony of the words.

 A general rule is never to mix more than three or four different typestyles and sizes on the same page.

A flier generally has more art and "white space" than a newsletter. With fliers, you do not have the captive audience you have with newsletters. Fliers generally try to grab the passerby's attention. If there is too much text, the flier never gets read.

Newsletters and fliers are just two examples of similar publications that end up looking totally different because of their intended audiences. If you ever forget your audience during the publication's design, your publication will never get read. Before going to your computer, think about these issues, as well as number of columns, amount of art, and so on. It is usually much easier to plan ahead a little than to change a publication once you lay it out.

FIRST PUBLISHER'S FEATURES

First Publisher offers advanced desktop publishing power usually found only in more expensive publishing programs. First Publisher provides many typestyles and sample clip art files while at the same time offering an easy-to-use, intuitive command structure; even a beginning publisher will quickly produce attractive documents. Before delving directly into the program, read the following sections to get a glimpse of how the program interacts with you to produce professional publications.

Working with Text

First Publisher offers many tools to organize your text into a final published document. If you are used to a particular word processor, you should use it to create and edit the text that will go into your publication. First Publisher can *import,* or transfer, text files saved directly within the following popular word processors:

DisplayWrite 1, 2, 3, 4	Microsoft Word 3, 4, 5
MultiMate 2 and higher	Office Writer 6, and higher
PFS:First Choice 1, 2, 3	PFS:WRITE
Professional Write 1, 2	Wang PC 2
WordPerfect 3, 4, 5	WordStar 3, 4, 5

If your favorite word processor is not listed, you can still import its files into First Publisher as long as you save those files in either of the ASCII text or DCA formats. Check in your word processor's reference manual to see how to do this.

You can also use First Publisher's built-in word processor to produce your text. First Choice offers many of the text-editing commands you will need — Insert, Delete, Justification, Move, and Copy, for example — and virtually every cursor-movement keystroke possible with any word processor on the market.

If you have a favorite word processor, by all means use it to create your text. Once you import that text into First Publisher, you can use First Publisher's editing commands to modify the text if you see changes you want to make. Once in First Publisher, you can begin to get an idea of how much text to leave or crop.

 First Publisher's built-in text-editing features are useful for adding captions and headings to your text and art. You might not know exactly what captions you need before you lay out the page with First Publisher, so save the typing of captions and headings until after you import the text created by your word processor.

FIRST PUBLISHER AND TEXT-ONLY DOCUMENTS Although First Publisher is especially good for integrating text and art on a page, you may want to use the program to create text-only fliers, handouts, and bulletins. First Publisher offers a wide range of typestyles and sizes. By effectively combining the right typestyles, you can create eye-catching output such as that shown in Figure 1-6.

Typefaces, Fonts, and Text Styles

With a word processor, you usually only worry about normal, boldface, underlined, and possibly italicized text. Desktop publishing opens up a new world of choices. Figure 1-6 shows you just a few of the many typefaces and

Summer Sale ! ! !

All swimwear on sale at reduced prices!!!

ONLY 2 days left !   H – u – r – r – y !

Don't miss this one!!!

The Swimming Trunk
6104 South Lake Drive
Longview, TX 19223

FIGURE 1-6. Using First Publisher to create various typestyles

sizes available in First Publisher. Before adding any text to a First Publisher publication, you must decide on the following factors:

- Typeface
- Type size
- Styling
- Line spacing
- Justification

TYPEFACES Figure 1-7 shows you some sample typefaces that come with First Publisher. The ones you choose for your publication are largely a matter of personal preference. Each typeface has a certain name; for instance, Swiss, Dutch, London, Elite, and Pica. You may recognize the last two, as they are popular typewriter styles.

Some typefaces contain extra lines and strokes called *serifs* at the ends and edges of each character. Most books, newspapers, and magazines use a serif 12-point font for the body of the text. When there is a lot of text to read, the text is more readable if a serif typeface is used. A typeface without the extra lines and strokes (called *sans serif*), such as the Swiss typeface, is clean-looking and is good for titles and centered headings on fliers.

Swiss - sans serif - 18 points
Swiss - sans serif - 24 points

Dutch - bold - serif - 12 points
Dutch - bold - serif - 24 points

𝕷𝖔𝖓𝖉𝖔𝖓 – 𝖘𝖊𝖗𝖎𝖋 – 18 𝖕𝖔𝖎𝖓𝖙𝖘

Elite – serif – 12 points

Pica – serif – 12 points

FIGURE 1-7.   Sample typefaces from First Publisher

TYPE SIZES   The size of a typeface character set is measured in *points*. Points measure the distance from the top of the tallest character (for instance, the capital letter *I*) to the bottom of the lowest descending character (such as the small *y*). A point is 1/72 of an inch. Therefore, in order to print 1-inch characters, you must find a typeface that has a 72-point type size. Some of the typefaces that come with First Publisher have several sizes. For instance, the Swiss typeface comes in both 18 and 24 points.

Every combination of typeface and size constitutes a different *font*. For instance, the Swiss 18-point characters make up one font while the Swiss 24-point characters are another font. This book will use the term "font" frequently to designate a specific typeface and size such as the "London 18-point font." Figure 1-7 shows seven font examples but only five typefaces.

≡*note*≡   Version 2 users should substitute Helvetica for the Swiss font mentioned here.

Starting with version 3.0, First Publisher can print *scalable fonts*. Scalable fonts are fonts that can be increased or decreased to any size needed. They do not take room on the disk for every size, but rather, you create the size you need at the time you need it. Chapter 7 describes the process of scaling fonts to fit your publishing needs.

If the selection of fonts and sizes is not enough for your publishing needs, you can order more from Software Publishing Corporation (SPC), the authors of First Publisher.

STYLING First Publisher's fonts can be *boldface, italicized,* or *normal.* Most typefaces can appear in any of these three styles. Figure 1-8 displays several examples. Each style, typeface, and size makes up a different font. The style you use is dictated by personal taste. Just as you should avoid combining too many typefaces on a page, you should not italicize and boldface too often throughout an entire publication. Reserve these styles for emphasis and highlighting of important points in your text.

Appendix B shows a sample of every font and style that comes with First Publisher version 3.0. These fonts are not all available at the same time, but they can be loaded into First Publisher as you need them. Chapter 3 describes the process of selecting the fonts your publication requires.

New York - Normal
New York - Bold
New York - Italicized

Chicago - Normal
Chicago - Bold
Chicago - Italicized

Elite - Normal
Elite - Bold
Elite - Italicized

=== **FIGURE 1-8.** Sample typeface styles from First Publisher

LINE SPACING   The spacing between each line of text is called the *leading* (which rhymes with "bedding"). Leading is measured in points just as fonts are. If you were to put underlines (also called *baselines*) under every line of text, as shown here:

This shows
proper leading   }◄─ Leading
from baseline
to baseline.

you would see that the leading is always measured from one underline to the next underline. Obviously, the leading should be larger than the font size.

Normally, a font's leading is one to two points more than the font size. However, the larger the font, the more leading is needed. Most of the time, you should not worry about a font's leading. First Publisher will adjust to make a proper leading size for the font you select. Figure 1-9 shows what can happen if you adjust the leading yourself. Some of these special adjustments may be needed for your specific text. Chapter 6 will demonstrate how you can change the leading if you need to do so.

JUSTIFICATION   One final aspect to consider when adding text to your published documents is the *justification* of the text. There are four justification styles to choose from: centered, left-justified, right-justified, and fully justified. As you can see from Figure 1-10, any justification can be applied to any font.

You may want to center text for headings, titles, and captions. Right justification may be useful for emphasis with an inserted graphic. Fully justified text is good for multiple-column newsletters with long blocks of text. Most of the rest of your text should remain left-justified (aligned at the left margin). First Publisher's default justification style is left-justified; you can change the default if you wish.

Working with Art

The placement, moving, copying, and cropping of art is the most enjoyable aspect of desktop publishing. When you first begin to learn First Publisher, you may want to look at several of the clip art sample files that come with

This is 12-point text printed
on several lines with the
standard 16-point leading.

This is 12-point text printed
on several lines with only
12-point leading.
(The same height as the font.)

This shows you what will happen
if you actually have a leading
that is smaller than the 12-point
font height.   This leading is 10
points.   First Publisher corrects
so lines do not run into previous ones.

This 12-point font has a 20-

point leading.   This is probably

too much for normal 12-point text.

FIGURE 1-9.   Leading is adjustable with First Publisher

your program. (As with added fonts, you can order more clip art from the Software Publishing Corporation.) Figure 1-11 shows you a small sample of some of the clip art files available for your system.

In First Publisher, you can manipulate art almost as easily as you manipulate text with your word processor. As you move the art, your text is not affected. This is an extremely important component of a desktop publishing program; moving the art around lets you see different possibilities for the final page makeup.

Importing Art

First Publisher can import art from other graphics programs just as it imports text. First Publisher recognizes art saved directly from within any of the following programs:

Logipaint   PC Paintbrush

Microsoft Paintbrush   Microsoft Windows Paint

Paintshow Plus   PC Paint Plus

Publisher's Paintbrush

First Publisher can also directly import art files saved with any of the following file extensions:

.ART   .MAC

.MSP   .PCX

.PIC   .TIF

 If you have a Macintosh and the MacPaint 1.5 software, you can transfer graphics files from there. You must, however, have the hardware capability to move these files to a PC-compatible disk format. Be sure to save the DOS file with an extension of .MAC.

Centered Swiss Type

These are left-justified lines of text.
Notice that each line hits the left column.

Right-justified lines of text.
Notice that each line hits the right column.

This text is typed in the full justification mode. When columns of text are fully justified, First Publisher ensures that both margins align evenly, just as the columns that appear in your newspaper do.

FIGURE 1-10. Four justifications are allowed in First Publisher

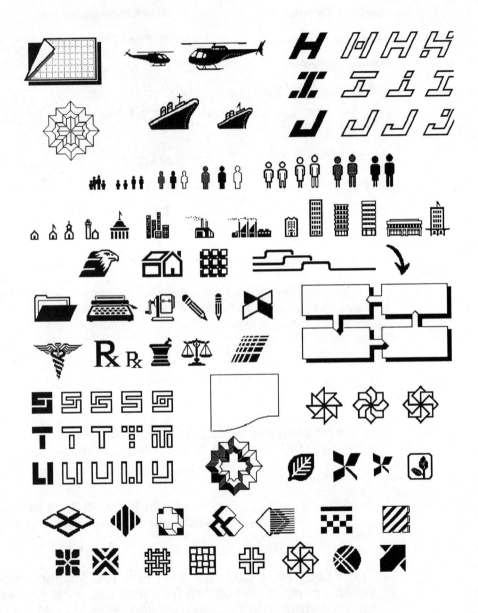

FIGURE 1-11. Many clip art files are available in First Publisher

If First Publisher's available clip art library is not complete enough for your art needs, or if your favorite graphics program is not among those listed above, you still have three more art options available:

- Drawing your own art from within First Publisher
- Capturing images from non-compatible graphics programs
- Scanning printed art from a hardcopy source

DRAWING WITHIN FIRST PUBLISHER   First Publisher offers several on-screen drawing tools that you can use to create your own art. In addition, these tools can be used to modify art you import from other sources. Once you create a drawing or modify art from another source, you can move, resize, duplicate, and rotate the art as easily as you can manipulate text. Figure 1-12 shows you one of the sample art images from First Publisher that has been modified and duplicated several ways.

The drawing tools include a pencil with four lead sizes (drawing widths) for line drawing, an eraser to correct any mistakes, a straight-line drawing tool for drawing straight lines of any length, a box-drawing tool to draw perfect boxes of any size, and a circle-drawing tool. You use each of these tools by selecting it on the screen with the keyboard or by pointing to the tool's symbol with the mouse.

CAPTURING OTHER ART   Your First Publisher package includes a program called SNAPSHOT that works with virtually any picture displayed on your monitor from any graphics program—even those not file-compatible with First Publisher. SNAPSHOT acts as a camera that sits in the background of your computer waiting to be activated. When you display a picture from any graphics program, you press a designated SNAPSHOT key to save a camera-like image to an art file. That file is taken through a second process, called SNAP2ART, that makes it fully compatible with First Publisher.

SCANNING PRINTED ART   As long as you have the proper scanning hardware, you can save art and graphics hardcopy (printed output) to a disk file to be read later by First Publisher. Scanning machines are becoming more popular and are part of the current desktop publishing boom. A *scanner* acts as a camera that takes pictures of your hardcopy and converts the pictures to a computer art file.

Any scanner that can scan at 300 DPI (dots per inch) and stores in one of the First Publisher art file formats (listed earlier) is compatible with First Publisher. For instance, the Hewlett-Packard ScanJet Desktop Scanner can be used for scanning with First Publisher.

NEW FEATURES OF VERSION 3.0

If you recently upgraded to version 3.0 of First Publisher, you might have noticed several new features. Although earlier versions of the program were very productive, version 3.0 adds many new features that extend its usefulness.

Version 3.0 adds the ability to select from 21 different page layouts from a *layout gallery*. Each layout describes the page format, fonts, number of columns, and placement of graphics. Before creating a publication, you can look through the layout gallery for the layout that most closely resembles

FIGURE 1-12. You can enlarge, rotate, and change an art image in several ways

your desired publication. First Publisher shows these layouts as thumbnail sketches that you can scroll through on the screen. One layout from the gallery is shown here:

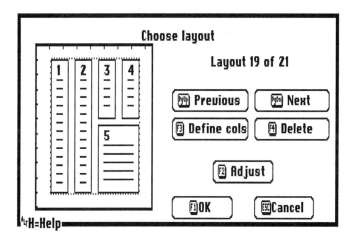

You can even add your own thumbnail layouts to the gallery if you do not see one that matches your needs.

First Publisher 3.0 goes the extra step in supplying high-resolution art and scalable font capabilities. With its collection of 155 standard clip art images, 20 of which are in a very high-resolution mode (300 DPI), you have enough supplied clip art images to work on many publications without having to create additional images. If you feel the need, you may purchase more clip art from SPC.

Sixteen high-resolution Bitstream fonts come with First Publisher 3.0. These are fonts you generate and add to First Publisher as you need them. You can request any of these 16 fonts in any point size (from 9 to 72 points). This saves you from having to have a different font for every style and size you will ever need on disk at the same time. Bitstream is a company that licenses these fonts to First Publisher's users. As you publish a wider variety of documents, you can add to the library of scalable fonts with other Bitstream fonts. Figure 1-13 shows a sample of Bitstream fonts that come with First Publisher.

Even experts in earlier versions of First Publisher will be pleased with the color VGA screens now supplied during the editing and creation of a publication. The color screens are more appealing to look at for extended publishing sessions. The built-in help capabilities have also been expanded to

Swiss 721+ Roman 10-point
Swiss 721+ Roman 12-point
Swiss 721+ Italic 10-point
Swiss 721+ Italic 12-point
Swiss 721+ Bold 10-point
Swiss 721+ Bold 12-point

Dutch 801+ Roman 10-point
Dutch 801+ Roman 12-point
Dutch 801+ Italic 10-point
Dutch 801+ Italic 12-point
Dutch 801+ Bold 10-point
Dutch 801+ Bold 12-point
Dutch 801+ Bold 24-point

FIGURE 1-13. Several Bitstream fonts supplied with First Publisher 3.0

include *context-sensitive* help. This gives you instant help on whatever command or menu option you are currently working with. An added circle- and oval-drawing tool is supplied to aid in drawing curves.

HARDWARE AND FIRST PUBLISHER

The basic hardware setup you will need to run First Publisher is shown in Figure 1-14. Although First Publisher works with virtually any IBM-compatible computer hardware, it will certainly work with the computer equipment from the following list:

- IBM PC, XT, AT, PS/2, and fully compatible computers with at least two floppy disk drives, or one floppy disk drive and a hard disk

- A minimum of 512K (approximately 512,000 characters) of internal RAM memory

- One of the following graphics adapters (or equivalents) and matching 80-column monitor:

IBM Color Graphics Adapter (CGA)
IBM Enhanced Graphics Adapter (EGA)
IBM VGA Graphics Adapter
Hercules Graphics Adapter

- Optionally, one of the following computer mice:

IBM PS/2 Mouse
Logitech Mouse
Microsoft Mouse
Mouse Systems' PC Mouse

- A PC-compatible dot-matrix, ink-jet, or laser printer

First Publisher and the Mouse

If you haven't got a computer mouse, don't despair. Unlike some other desktop publishers, First Publisher works with or without a mouse by taking full advantage of the keyboard. Through an intuitive use of the function keys

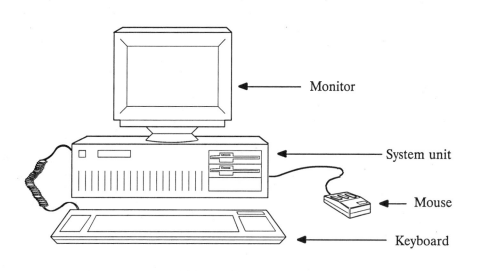

══════ **FIGURE 1-14.**   Standard hardware setup

(the keys labeled F1 through F10 on the left, or at the top, of your keyboard), First Publisher gives users without a mouse a viable interface to the program. Some tasks are even easier to perform from the keyboard than with the mouse.

There are several types of mice available. Two of the most popular computer mice are shown here.

The Microsoft mouse is shown on the left and the Mouse Systems mouse is on the right. First Publisher isn't picky about which mouse button you press. If you have a mouse with two or three buttons, you can press any of them when choosing and pointing.

 You must check the documentation that came with your mouse to see how to install the mouse and its corresponding software. The mouse software drivers must be loaded before starting First Publisher.

First Publisher and the Screen

The higher the resolution of your graphics card and monitor, the closer your screen will look to the final printed page. If you have a VGA adapter card and matching monitor, you will be able to see about two-thirds of a printed publication on the screen. If you have an EGA or Hercules adapter card with a matching monitor, you will be able to see one-half of a printed page on your monitor at any time. The *resolution* (the density of dots that make up characters and graphics on your screen) of these adapter cards lets you see more on your screen at one time, while displaying a sharper image than a regular CGA adapter and monitor.

Those with a CGA adapter and monitor will be able to view one-fourth of a publication's page on the screen at any time. The resolution of a CGA is not as high, and the text and art will not be as crisp as with the other adapter cards. Nevertheless, First Publisher works fine with a CGA monitor, and you will have no trouble producing quality publications with any of the adapters compatible with First Publisher.

Figure 1-15 shows a sample First Publisher screen produced on a CGA monitor. All of the screens in this book will be produced from a CGA screen. If you have a VGA, EGA, or Hercules graphics adapter, your screens will look slightly different. However, the same commands apply to all adapters, and the final printed page will be identical on all systems.

First Publisher and the Printer

As with graphics adapters and monitors, First Publisher's printed documents can vary in quality depending on the type of printer. If you have a dot-matrix printer, First Publisher's printed publication will look different from one printed on a laser printer. The higher cost of a laser printer adds the benefit of smooth-looking lines, curves, and text, as shown in Figure 1-16.

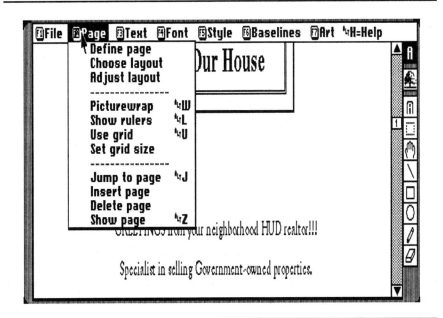

FIGURE 1-15.   A First Publisher screen as it appears on a CGA monitor

HUD/VA HOME SALES

GREETINGS from your neighborhood HUD realtor!!!

Specialist in selling Government-owned properties.

$50.00 DEPOSIT!

How about $50.00 deposit rent-to-own HUD? Nice homes in nice areas.

Did you know that non-veterans can purchase VA homes with nothing down for 7-1/2% Interest?

Call me for listings on homes available and information on qualifying.

Ask for CLIFF COOPER
622-1177

CONTINENTAL PROPERTIES, INC.
5436-E South Mingo
Tulsa, Oklahoma 74145

FIGURE 1-16. Laser printers offer better output at a much higher cost

Even with the same printer, First Publisher is capable of printing in various qualities. When you are ready to print your publication, First Publisher offers you three print resolutions: draft, standard, and smoothed. The difference involves both printing time and resolution. When creating publications, you will want to print the document throughout the editing stages so you can get an idea of how the final printed page will be laid out.

When you print your publication in the draft mode, First Publisher quickly prints your document, but prints only a rough draft and does not take the time to smooth out the curved lines in the art and text. The standard print mode looks better than the draft mode but takes more time to print. The smoothed mode takes the longest time to print, but produces the best quality of output possible with your printer and First Publisher.

 Use the smoothed mode only for your publication's final printing. Since you will print your publication often during the editing stages, the less time-consuming draft and standard modes are best to use.

STARTING FIRST PUBLISHER

If you have yet to install First Publisher on your computer, read Appendix A for instructions. Once you have installed the program, you can follow the section below that pertains to the disk drive configuration on your system.

Before installing First Publisher, make a backup of every disk that came with First Publisher. The operating system command DISKCOPY will make the backup. If you are unfamiliar with DISKCOPY, consult the reference manual that came with your operating system. Once you make the backups, place the original disks in a safe place and use the backups during the rest of the installation.

Start your computer system in the normal manner. Answer the date and time prompts if your computer does not have a built-in clock/calendar battery. You should start First Publisher from the DOS prompt, which is usually C> for hard disk systems and A> for floppy disk systems.

 Be sure the mouse driver program is resident in your computer's memory before starting First Publisher.

If You Have a Hard Disk

To start First Publisher on a hard disk system, you must change to the PUB subdirectory where you installed First Publisher to start the program. Follow these steps at the DOS C> prompt:

1. Type **CD\PUB**
2. Press ⟨ENTER⟩
3. Type **FP**
4. Press ⟨ENTER⟩

The First Publisher startup screen, shown in Figure 1-17, should appear on your system. As with all DOS commands, you can type using either upper-case or lowercase letters, or both.

Create a Batch File for Faster Startup

You may want to create a batch file to start the program. A *batch file* (a DOS file that contains a series of operating system commands) lets you execute First Publisher with one command rather than having to change

FIGURE 1-17. The First Publisher 3.0 startup screen

directories every time you begin the program. To create a batch file to replace the hard disk startup instructions above, follow these steps:

1. Make sure you are at the main directory by typing **CD**

2. Type **COPY CON FP.BAT**

3. Press the (**ENTER**) key

4. Type the following lines and press (**ENTER**) at the end of each line:

    CD\PUB
    FP
    CD

5. Press the (**F6**) key and then press (**ENTER**)

You can now start First Publisher by simply typing **FP** at the DOS prompt.

 If you installed First Publisher in a subdirectory other than PUB, substitute its name for "PUB" in the above examples.

If You Have a Floppy Disk

To start First Publisher on a floppy disk system, find the copy of the Program disk 1. Place it in drive A. If you are using a 5 1/4-inch disk drive, place the copy of the Fonts disk in drive B. Follow the steps below at the A> prompt:

1. Type **fp**

2. Press (**ENTER**)

As with all commands typed at the DOS prompt, you can type **fp** in either uppercase or lowercase letters, or both. After a brief pause, the opening screen, shown in Figure 1-17, will be displayed.

As soon as the opening screen appears, those with 5 1/4-inch disk drives should remove the Program disk from drive A and insert their own formatted data disk in drive A. The Fonts disk should always remain in drive B. If you are using 3 1/2-inch disk drives, you should put a formatted data disk in drive B when you start the program.

If You Have Problems

There may be several reasons why the opening screen does not appear. If you see the following message,

Sorry, cannot run First Publisher on a text display.

you do not have a graphics adapter card, or your graphics adapter's switches are set to text mode. If you are sure your card is compatible with the CGA, EGA, or the Hercules card, then make sure the switches on the board are set properly. You may also have to run the DOS MODE command to set your graphics card to 80-column graphics. Consult the DOS manual for details.

If you have a computer that has a lot of memory-resident programs (the popular *popup* programs, sometimes called *TSR* programs), you may not have enough computer memory left to run First Publisher. First Publisher knows when there is not enough memory to run and will display the following message.

Not enough available memory. Remove any memory-resident programs.

If you get this message, you need to free up some memory that has been grabbed by a memory-resident program.

The Publication Screen

After a brief pause, your opening screen will disappear and the publication screen, shown in Figure 1-18, will be displayed. (The mouse pointer will only appear on systems with a mouse.) This is the screen from which you will do almost all of your publishing. Chapter 2 describes this screen in detail and explains how to move around and select from the menus.

Stopping First Publisher

Any time you are ready to finish your First Publisher session, press (ALT-E). You will see this type of keystroke throughout this book. The (ALT) key is

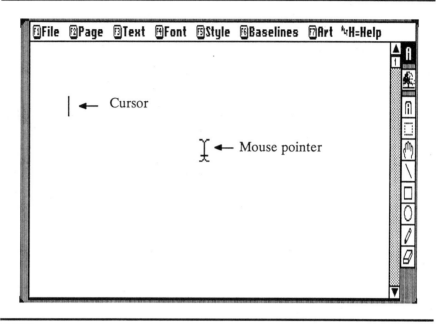

FIGURE 1-18. The publication screen with cursor and mouse
pointer

used the same way as the (**SHIFT**) keys are; press the (**ALT**) key, then press
the second letter (in this case (**E**)) while still pressing (**ALT**). Immediately
release both keys. You will be returned to DOS, where you can start another
program, or power-off your computer. As with any program, you should
always return to DOS before turning off your computer. This ensures that all
files are closed and properly saved.

 If you create or make changes to a document, and if you have not
saved that document's new changes, First Publisher will warn you that
you are about to exit the program without saving the most recent
changes. This gives you one last chance to save the work you did.

Summary

In this chapter you learned how to

- Plan publications before starting First Publisher. This gives you an idea of where you are heading and saves time when you eventually lay out text and graphics.
- Understand the differences between text typefaces, fonts, and styles
- Tell if your art files from programs other than First Publisher will work in First Publisher publications
- Start First Publisher on your computer system
- Exit the First Publisher environment and return to the DOS prompt

THE FIRST PUBLISHER ENVIRONMENT

The First Publisher Document Screen
Getting Help
The Wait Clock
The Elevator Bar
Side Tools
Customizing First Publisher

This chapter describes the environment of First Publisher. Once you understand the screen elements of the program, you can effectively use First Publisher to produce quality documents. Whether or not you have a mouse, you will soon be selecting commands from the helpful menu. First Publisher is one of the only desktop publishers on the market whose commands are intuitive. If you have never used First Publisher before, this chapter will give you a solid foundation for using the Document screen.

THE FIRST PUBLISHER DOCUMENT SCREEN

Figure 2-1 highlights important elements of the First Publisher Document screen. The large area in the center is called the *work area*. Your documents will appear here while you create or make changes to them. Using this screen will become second nature to you as you gain experience. The work area acts as a camera that "pans" the publication; since the entire publication will not appear on the screen all at once, you can *scroll* up and down the publication as you would pan a camera to get a glimpse of a large scene.

There are two cursors on the screen in Figure 2-1. The regular cursor (henceforth referred to as the "cursor") is the vertical line in the upper-left corner of the work area. The cursor shows where the next character you type

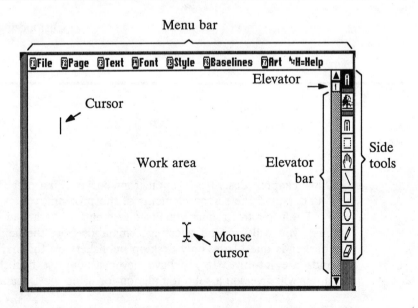

FIGURE 2-1. Looking at the Document screen

from the keyboard will appear. As you type characters, the cursor moves to the right one character at a time. Each character space the cursor moves is the size of the current font.

If you have a mouse, you will notice the mouse cursor in the middle of the screen. With the mouse cursor you can position characters and text, draw lines and boxes, and select from the menus. As you move the mouse on your desk, the mouse cursor moves in the direction of the mouse. Remember that keyboard users can perform every function that mouse users can perform. Some commands are more easily given with the mouse; others are more easily given from the keyboard.

 Both the cursor and the mouse cursor change shape as you use various functions of the program. For instance, the mouse cursor changes to an arrow when you move it over the menu bar. Later in this chapter, you will learn the various shapes both cursors assume.

The Menu Bar

An integral part of First Publisher is its menu system. The menu bar across the top of the screen logically subdivides all of the commands possible. A *menu* gives you a list of commands from which you can select at any time while in First Publisher. As with a menu in a restaurant, you can order the next command to be performed from the menu. Before you learn how to select commands, a brief review of the use of the mouse and keyboard is in order.

USING THE MOUSE As you move the mouse on your desk, the mouse cursor will move in the same direction. Position the mouse so its "tail" (the cord) points away from you. This is the upward pointer; to move the mouse cursor up the screen, move the mouse toward the tail. Feel free to experiment with moving the mouse cursor around the screen. You will not harm anything. As you use the mouse more and more, you will become quite accurate in pointing with it.

When you need to select an item with the mouse, click any of the mouse buttons; then release the button. A mouse symbol will appear in the upper-right corner of the screen as shown here:

Mouse symbol

Sometimes you will use the mouse to drag an object (such as a picture image) around the screen. For this, click a mouse button while the mouse pointer is over the object and *do not* release the button right away. While holding down the mouse button, move the mouse. This *drags* (moves) whatever element is under the mouse pointer. Once you position the element on the screen where you want it, release the mouse button. Chapter 4 describes this process in more detail.

USING THE KEYBOARD   As mentioned earlier, the keyboard can perform any function in First Publisher. The keyboard can even be used to act as a mouse. The (F10) key emulates the action performed by a click of one of the mouse buttons, and the arrow keys act as mouse movements. Any time you press (F10), the mouse symbol shown previously will appear. Whenever you are asked to click a mouse button but have no mouse, press the (F10) key on the keyboard.

If you press a key other than an arrow key when the mouse symbol is displayed, the mouse will disappear and you will be returned to the regular document session.

SELECTING FROM THE MENUS   First Publisher's menus are known as *pull-down* menus. The menu bar shows the categories of available menu options. When you select one of the menu bar's options by pointing with the mouse or by pressing the function key listed to the left of each menu bar option, that option expands to display all related commands. This list of commands is called a pull-down menu; when you select from the menu bar, you in effect pull down a list of further options. Figure 2-2 shows a screen with the Baselines pull-down menu shown. Notice that a new list of possible commands appears.

To pick one of the commands from a pull-down menu, either point to the command with the mouse pointer (which then changes to the shape of an arrow) and click a button, or press (UP ARROW) and (DOWN ARROW) to highlight any of the options and then press (ENTER). Here is what the Baselines pull-down menu looks like after (DOWN ARROW) is pressed three times:

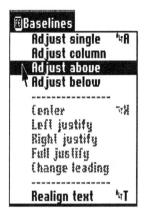

The pull-down menu command option Adjust above is highlighted. You can select this command now by pressing (**ENTER**) or by clicking a mouse button.

Not all options are available every time you pull down a menu; those that are not available are shown in light gray in the menu. For instance, the

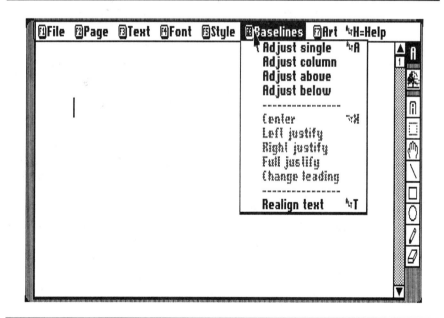

FIGURE 2-2.   The Baselines pull-down menu

options Center, Left justify, Right justify, Full justify, and Change leading were not available at the time Figure 2-2's Baselines menu was pulled down. However, if these commands are allowed at the time you pull down a menu, they will be in dark letters just as the rest of the commands are.

 Even mouse users will find that pressing a function key is usually faster than pointing the mouse to pull down a menu.

USING SPEED KEYS   Once you are familiar with the menu structure of First Publisher, you may want to use the *speed keys* to select from a menu. Speed keys are made up of an (ALT) keypress followed by another keypress, while the (ALT) key is still held down. Available speed keys are shown to the right of menu options. Mouse users will find that using the keyboard is faster than pointing for selecting a command that has an equivalent speed key. For instance, to select the Realign text option from the Baselines pull-down menu without using the speed key equivalent, you would

1. Point to the Baselines menu bar and click the mouse button. (You may also press (F6).)

2. Point to Realign text and click. (Keyboard users would press (DOWN ARROW) 12 times and then press (ENTER).)

The (ALT-T) to the right of the Realign text option indicates the speed key for this option. Rather than following the above steps, you could simply press (ALT-T) to select Realign text without having to pull down the Baselines menu. You will soon get familiar with the menus and their speed key equivalents.

 A speed key can combine (ALT) with either an uppercase or lowercase character. For instance, (ALT-T) and (ALT-t) are exactly the same, although (ALT-T) takes an extra (SHIFT) keypress unless the (CAPS LOCK) key has been pressed previously.

LEAVING A MENU   There are three ways to close a pull-down menu and return to the work area. You can do any of the following:

- Press the menu bar's corresponding function key again
- Press (ESC)
- Move the mouse cursor outside of the pull-down menu

Reviewing the Menus

Although First Publisher's pull-down menus are explained throughout the rest of the book, the menus and their speed key equivalents are introduced here. You may find it helpful to select the menu bar options as they are being discussed to familiarize yourself with opening and closing the pull-down menus.

Note to Version 2 Users Your pull-down menu options may be slightly different from those described below. Version 3.0 users also have a few more options.

FILE MENU Any time you need to save or retrieve something from the disk, select the File option from the menu bar. To load an already-written publication file, choose Get publication from the pull-down menu. Since you get publication files frequently, you will soon learn that (**ALT-G**) is the speed key for this command.

```
┌─────────────────────┐
│▛File                 │
├─────────────────────┤
│↑Get publication   ᴬ⌐G│
│ Save              ᴬ⌐S│
│ Print             ᴬ⌐P│
│ Delete file          │
│ ┄┄┄┄┄┄┄┄┄┄┄┄┄┄┄┄┄   │
│ Help topics          │
│ Customize            │
│ Status            ᴬ⌐I│
│ Customer info        │
│ ┄┄┄┄┄┄┄┄┄┄┄┄┄┄┄┄┄   │
│ Start over        ᴬ⌐Y│
│ Exit              ᴬ⌐E│
└─────────────────────┘
```

To save a publication, choose Save ((**ALT-S**)). Print ((**ALT-P**)) sends the current publication to the printer. Eventually, you may need to free disk space with the Delete file option.

Help topics offers on-line assistance for most of First Publisher. Customize is a new version 3.0 feature that lets you define screen colors, units of measure, margin defaults, and pathnames for saved publications. Status ((**ALT-I**)) displays a work area box as shown here:

```
PFS:First Publisher, Version 3.0
Filename:  NEW.PUB
Printer:  HP LaserJet series II/IID


Port:  LPT1:
Font:  Swiss 721+ 12 point Roman
Font leading:  13 points
Current page: 1 of 1
Characters visible: 3 Overflow: 0

            ⌐OK
ᴬₗₜH=Help
```

This gives you valuable information concerning the configuration of your First Publisher session.

Customer info is a new version 3.0 feature that gets you headed in the right direction when you want to know more about Software Publishing Corporation's customer support and assistance. It tells you where to get help on product updates, replacements, and customer service. All of this information is available from the Help topics option, and Customer info tells you how to access it.

If you want to start with a fresh work area, select Start over (ALT-Y) from the File pull-down menu. First Publisher erases the work area and resets the program back to its startup state.

As shown in Chapter 1, you can leave First Publisher any time by selecting Exit (ALT-E) from the File pull-down menu. This returns you to the starting DOS prompt. Be sure to save the current publication before leaving First Publisher. You should always leave First Publisher and return to the DOS prompt before turning off your computer.

PAGE MENU   The Page pull-down menu lets you refine the current page on the screen or display any other page on the screen. (First Publisher allows up to 99 pages within the same publication, although you can only edit one at a time.)

```
▣Page
  Define page
  Choose layout
  Adjust layout
  ........................
  Picturewrap      ᴬᴸᵂ
  Show rulers      ᴬᴸL
  Use grid         ᴬᴸU
  Set grid size
  ........................
  Jump to page     ᴬᴸJ
  Insert page
  Delete page
  Show page        ᴬᴸZ
```

Define page gives you the power to change the margins set on the current page. A new addition that almost eliminates the need for Define page is the Choose layout option directly below Define page. With Choose layout, version 3.0 users can select from a wide range of page layouts supplied with First Publisher. Adjust layout lets you change the column positioning as well as text within the columns in your publication.

Picturewrap (ALT-W) runs text around an art image as shown in Figure 2-3. Text that flows around an image is more visually appealing than text that stops above the image and starts again below it.

Show rulers (ALT-L) displays rulers down the left side and across the top of the screen. As you will see later, these rulers ensure that your text and art align properly on the page. You can also get an idea of how far down the page your text and art will appear when printed. The tick marks represent one-fourth of an inch on the final printed page.

Use grid (ALT-U) and Set grid size control the placement and size of the dot-matrix grid shown in Figure 2-4. When placing art images, the grid works in conjunction with the ruler line to help you position your art properly.

As mentioned earlier in this section, your publication can contain 99 pages. If you are working on one page and decide to change to another, select Jump to page (ALT-J) to move to another page in the current

FIGURE 2-3. Wrapping text around an image

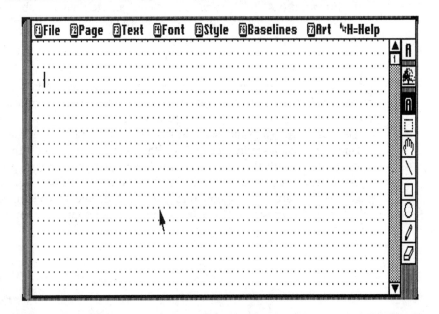

FIGURE 2-4. The alignment grid displayed in the work area

publication. First Publisher will prompt you for the page number. You can insert and delete between existing pages with the Insert page and Delete page options.

No matter which graphics adapter your system contains, your screen does not have the resolution to display an entire page of printed text. However, you can get a good preview of what the final printed page will look like when you select Show page (**ALT-Z**) from the Page pull-down menu. Figure 2-5 shows an example of a page that is previewed on the screen.

 Display your publication with Show page before printing it. You may notice something in the previewed thumbnail sketch that needs changing before the printing occurs. This saves you time, paper, and wear on your printer.

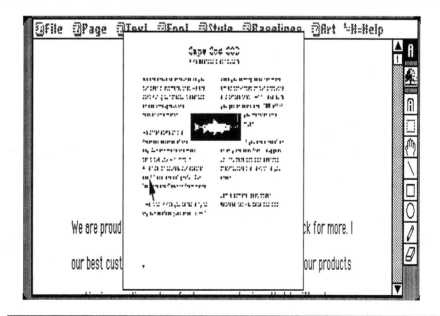

FIGURE 2-5. Looking at a page preview

TEXT MENU From the Text menu, you can Get text into your current publication and Save text from your current publication. The retrieved text can come from any of the popular word processors listed in Chapter 1.

Often you work with *blocks* of text. Blocks consist of text: a single character, a word, several words, or even a complete page of text. Once you mark a block of text (you'll learn how later), you can Cut the text from the current publication (**DEL** is the speed key for this command), Copy (**ALT-C**) the text to another area in your publication, and Paste (**ALT-V**) text that was previously cut. Cut text goes to a temporary work area called the *clipboard*. When you select Paste, all text on the clipboard is pasted back into the publication at the cursor's location.

FONT MENU The Font menu changes as you add and delete fonts in First Publisher. The Font menu shown here

is taken from a First Publisher session that contains several fonts. If you or someone else has already added fonts to your installation of First Publisher (described in detail in Chapter 3), you may have different fonts than those shown in this Font menu. When a font has a check mark beside it (as shown in the previous illustration), that font is the active font at the cursor. In other words, when you press a key, the character shown on the screen will appear in the font that is checked.

STYLE MENU   As with the Font menu, the Style menu changes depending on the fonts you currently have installed in your system. From the Style menu, you can choose a style of Bold, Italic, Normal, or Roman. If the font you select from the Font menu is not available in a certain style, that style will be listed in gray.

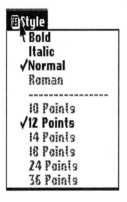

The Style menu is also where you select the point size for a selected font. As with styles, not all point sizes will be available for every selected font. As shown in the previous illustration, the larger point sizes are not available for the currently selected font; however, three of the four styles are available.

BASELINES MENU   Once you type or import text into your publication, you may want to change the line spacing. The Baselines menu lets you adjust text by displaying underlines (the *baselines*) below the text; when you move the lines, your text moves as well. The Baselines menu is also where you change the justification of your text. The Baselines menu will be discussed in later chapters.

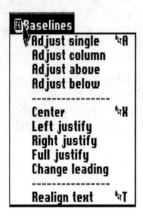

ART MENU   As with the Text menu, you need a way to manipulate art in your publication. The Art menu gives you the power to do this. With Get art and Save art, you can load and save art to and from the disk. You can use the clipboard to temporarily hold art with the options Cut (DEL), Copy (ALT-C), and Paste (ALT-V).

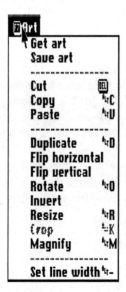

You have more options when working with art than with text. Once you select an art image, you can Duplicate (ALT-D) the art image anywhere on the current page, reverse it (a mirror image) with Flip horizontal, and turn the art image upside-down with Flip vertical. You can rotate the art clockwise by continuing to select Rotate (ALT-O) until the image is positioned the way you want. Invert takes a negative image of the art (the white becomes black and vice versa). Resize (ALT-R) shrinks or expands the image on standard art, and Crop (ALT-K) allows you to resize high-resolution art.

Magnify (ALT-M) gives you a close-up view of any image so that you can make detailed corrections to it. Figure 2-6 shows a graph that has been magnified. When you magnify an image, the image "zooms" inward so you can edit the art one *pixel* (or "picture element") at a time. As you make changes to the art (by adding and erasing individual pixels), the small picture in the upper-left corner changes to show you the overall effects from a distance.

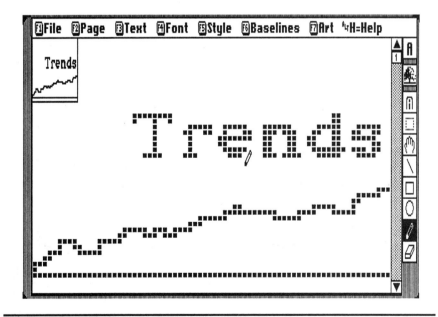

FIGURE 2-6. Magnifying an art image

Set line width (**ALT-HYPHEN**) is needed when you want to draw or erase a line that is a different thickness from the line width currently chosen. Bold lines can be drawn if you set a thick line width, and fine lines are drawn with the thin line width.

Note to Version 2 Users   You will be able to change the line width with the bottom four side tools described a little later.

Dialog Boxes

Often, First Publisher needs more information from you than just which command to perform next. Therefore, you may sometimes see a *dialog box*. Many times, dialog boxes appear when you select a menu choice. For instance, when you press **F2** to select the Page menu (or point to Page with the mouse pointer) and choose Define page from the pull-down menu, First Publisher needs to know exactly how you want the page defined. You will need to inform First Publisher of margin sizes, the number of columns, and so forth. The dialog box shown here

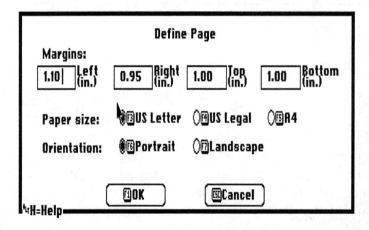

is displayed when you select Define page from the Page menu.

The following example shows how to answer dialog box prompts. Each prompt, such as Margins Left and Paper size, is called a *field*. If you want to keep a field's original value, you can do so by pressing the arrow keys, the mouse pointer, or (TAB). For instance, suppose you want to set all four of a publication's margins to 1 inch, the paper size to Legal, and the orientation to Landscape. You will do the following:

1. Press (F2), or click the mouse on Page in the menu bar. The Page menu will display.

2. Select Define page. The Define Page dialog box, shown earlier, will appear.

3. Type **1** at the Margins Left prompt. You do not need to type a decimal point and two zeroes. Notice that First Publisher's margins are set in inches (unless your copy has been changed at the Customize menu). The vertical bar (or dialog box cursor) next to the "1" you typed shows you which field is being prompted.

4. Press (RIGHT ARROW), (TAB), or (ENTER) and type **1** again at the Margins Right prompt. Repeat this procedure until a "1" is next to each margin option. The arrow keys and (TAB) take you between fields.

5. The remaining fields require either a function keypress or a mouse click over the appropriate response. There is no data entry required, only the selection between field options. Press (F4) to select US Legal paper size and (F7) to select Landscape orientation.

6. Press (F1) to indicate that the current dialog box's values are OK as shown at the bottom of the dialog box. Mouse users can point to OK and press a mouse button.

Depending on your printer, you may have a slightly different dialog box. If you make changes in the dialog box and then decide you do not want the changes to take effect, either press (ESC) or click the Cancel field with the mouse. Later chapters describe the Define Page dialog box in more detail. If you followed this example, select the Define Page dialog box again and change the fields back to their original values.

 The (SHIFT-TAB) key combination tabs backwards to previous fields for data entry within dialog boxes.

GETTING HELP

You can get help on most of First Publisher's features from the Help topics option of the Files menu, or press speed key (ALT-H) at any time to get context-sensitive help. When you ask for Help topics, First Publisher gives you an index of every subject you can get help on, as shown here:

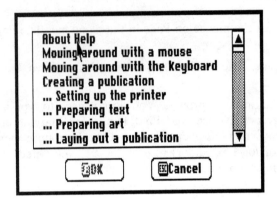

If you select context-sensitive help, First Publisher analyzes your current screen and gives you help on whatever you are doing at the time. If you are looking at the Baselines pull-down menu, (ALT-H) gives you help on that menu. If you are in the Define Page dialog box and press (ALT-H), First Publisher will describe those options.

The Help screens often take more room than will fit in the Help box, but you can scroll up or down as you would with a text file. When the Help screen is displayed, press (DOWN ARROW) to move the highlight down the help text a line at a time.

 Selecting (PGDN) and (PGUP) scrolls the highlight down and up seven topics at a time. This lets you move through the Help index faster.

When you select a topic, First Publisher displays help on the subject. For instance, suppose you want help on preparing art. Follow these steps to get help:

1. Press (F1) to display the File pull-down menu, or click the mouse pointer over File in the menu bar.

2. Select Help from the File pull-down menu.

3. Select Preparing art by clicking on it with the mouse or pointing to it and pressing (F10).

4. First Publisher displays a detailed helpful description on preparing art in your publications as shown here:

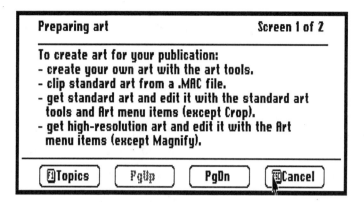

Since this Help consists of two screens, you may press `PGDN` and `PGUP` to see more Help.

5. When you are through with the Help screen, press `ESC` or click on Cancel to return to your publishing session exactly as it was before you asked for help.

 If you want to see the list of Help topics without returning to the publication screen to select Help topics again, press `F1` or click on Topics while reading any Help screen. The Help topics list will instantly return.

THE WAIT CLOCK

Even though First Publisher is quicker than many desktop publishing programs on the market, there are still times when a command takes a few seconds to finish. For instance, even the smallest publications take a while to load from disk into the computer's memory. Any time you select a command that First Publisher knows you will have to wait for, you will see the following *wait clock* displayed on the screen:

First Publisher displays the wait clock so you will know that something is happening, but that it will take a second or two to finish.

THE ELEVATOR BAR

A gray vertical bar goes down the length of the screen on the right side. This is called the *elevator bar*. On the elevator bar is a box called the *elevator*. The elevator bar and elevator are useful for two things:

- Scrolling up and down the current publication's page
- Showing you the relative position of the screen over the page

Version 3.0 users will find a horizontal elevator bar at the bottom of the screen if they change the page orientation to landscape mode. This allows left and right scrolling across a wide page. More information on landscape printing appears in Chapter 3.

Scrolling with the Elevator

Since your screen cannot display an entire page of the printed publication (only one-half of the publication if you have a VGA or EGA monitor and one-fourth if you have a CGA monitor), you need to have a way to scroll up and down the page. Moving the elevator along the elevator bar does just this. For example, Figure 2-7 shows part of a publication on the screen. At first, it may be unclear whether the screen is at the top or the bottom of the publication. You can tell by looking at the location of the elevator on the elevator bar. Since the elevator is at the bottom of the elevator bar, you know that the screen is showing the bottom of the publication. To scroll up so your screen displays the top of the publication, all you have to do is point to the top of the shaded elevator bar and click a mouse button. When you do, the elevator moves to the location of the click, and the screen shows the top of the document. Figure 2-8 shows the screen after this is done.

From this discussion, you can see that the elevator shows the *relative* position of the screen to the publication. If the elevator is in the middle of the elevator bar, your screen is showing you the middle portion of the publication. Keyboard users can scroll up and down the page of text by pressing (PGDN) and (PGUP). To scroll the screen in smaller increments, press (CTRL-PGDN) and (CTRL-PGUP).

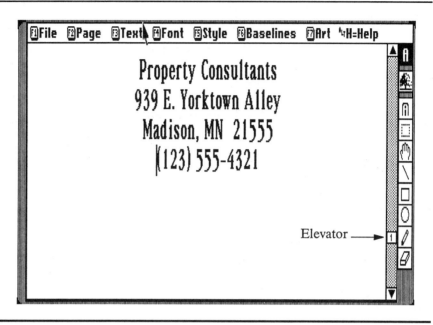

FIGURE 2-7.   Looking at the bottom of the document

FIGURE 2-8.   Looking at the top of the document

Elevators in Dialog Boxes

Some dialog boxes have a small elevator and elevator bar. For instance, if you select the File menu, and then choose Get publication, the following dialog box appears:

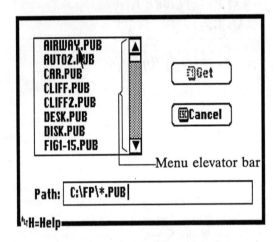

The dialog box shows a list of several files on the disk that you can choose from. This is helpful, because it means you do not have to remember all of your publication's filenames. If all of the files will not fit inside the dialog box, you can press `PGDN` and `PGUP` to scroll through the list of files or point to the elevator on the right side of the dialog box to scroll through the list as you would scroll up and down the screen with the main elevator bar.

 If you are using the keyboard to scroll, and the computer begins to beep several times in succession, you are holding down a scrolling key too long. The keyboard type-ahead buffer is warning you that it is full. Take your hands away from the keys until the beeping stops. First Publisher has now "caught up" with your keystrokes.

SIDE TOOLS

Chapter 1 mentioned that First Publisher offers several tools for text and art manipulation. They are on the far right side of the screen and are called the *side tools*. You will be using these side tools as if they were actual tools that you would pick up and use. The side tool currently in use is shown on the screen in reverse (a dark background with a light picture). When you first start First Publisher, the text tool is the tool in use. The following illustration shows the side tools and their names:

Text tool
High-resolution tool
Graphics text tool
Selection tool
Hand tool
Straight line tool
Box-drawing tool
Circle-drawing tool
Pencil tool
Eraser tool

When you change side tools, the mouse cursor changes shape. Different cursor shapes appear with certain tools.

Selecting a Side Tool

When you are ready to select a side tool, move the mouse pointer over the side tool you want to use and click a mouse button. The chosen side tool will be displayed in reverse and become available for use.

Keyboard users can select side tools by repeatedly pressing (**F9**). As you do so, each side tool down the list is chosen. When the side tool you need to use is shown in reverse, stop pressing (**F9**). That side tool is now in use. For instance, pressing (**F9**) four times selects the hand tool.

Since you will probably use the text tool most often, First Publisher offers a way to select it quickly; press (**SHIFT-F9**). No matter which side tool is in use, (**SHIFT-F9**) will select the text tool.

TOOLS AND LINE WIDTHS Some tools require that you choose a line width (the 1-point width through the 4-point width) as well as the side tool. For instance, when drawing lines, you can draw a line in a 1-, 2-, 3-, or

4-point width. Once you select the tool, select Set line width from the Art pull-down menu, or press the (**ALT-HYPHEN**) speed key. The following dialog box will then appear:

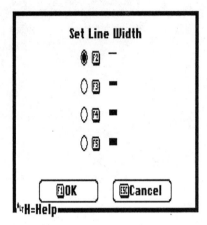

Either point the mouse at one of the circles next to a line width and press a mouse button, or press (**F2**), (**F3**), (**F4**), or (**F5**) to select the desired line width. Pressing (**F1**) accepts the line width choice and returns you to the publishing screen. The following side tools require you to set a line width:

- Pencil tool
- Straight line tool
- Box drawing tool

If you do not set a line width, First Publisher uses the 1-point width as a default setting.

Note to Version 2 Users The four line widths are available to you through the bottom four side tools. When you select a tool that requires a line width, point the mouse at one of the line widths and press a button, or press (**ALT-F9**) to cycle through each of the four line widths in succession.

CUSTOMIZING FIRST PUBLISHER

Selecting Customize from the File pull-down menu displays the Customize dialog box shown here:

```
┌──────────────────────────────────────────────────────────┐
│                         Customize                          │
│                                                            │
│  Color set:        ◉ ▣Blue    ○ ▣Grey    ○ ▣Black & White  │
│                                                            │
│  Units of measure:                                         │
│  Ruler and grid:   ◉ ▣inches      ○ ▣centimeters           │
│  Margins:          ◉ ▣inches      ○ ▣centimeters           │
│                                                            │
│                   ╭─────────────────╮                      │
│                   │ ▣Path defaults  │                      │
│                   ╰─────────────────╯                      │
│             ╭──────────╮      ╭──────────╮                 │
│             │  ▣OK     │      │ ▣Cancel  │                 │
│             ╰──────────╯      ╰──────────╯                 │
│ ▌H=Help═══════════════════════════════════════════════════│
└──────────────────────────────────────────────────────────┘
```

This is a new version 3.0 feature. Color set fields let some users choose a
different background screen color. CGA and monochrome users will always
stay in black and white mode regardless of the color chosen, since the
resolution does not support colors. EGA and VGA users, however, can
choose a different background color for their First Publisher editing sessions.

You have the choice of inches or centimeters as your units of measure.
Once you select one of these, all margin settings, ruler lines, and grid marks
will be spaced accordingly. First Publisher defaults to inches unless you
change the units of measure.

The Path defaults field lets you specify exactly where certain files are
located on the disk. If you are unfamiliar with pathnames and subdirectories,
read Appendix E for more information. When you select Path defaults, the
Default Drive & Path dialog box appears, as shown here:

```
┌──────────────────────────────────────────────────────────┐
│  Default drive & path              Extension:              │
│  Text files:                                               │
│   ┌───────────────────────────────┐     ┌──────────┐      │
│   │ C:\PUB\|                       │     │  .TXT    │      │
│   └───────────────────────────────┘     └──────────┘      │
│  Art files:                                                │
│   ┌───────────────────────────────┐     ┌──────────┐      │
│   │ C:\PUB\                        │     │  .ART    │      │
│   └───────────────────────────────┘     └──────────┘      │
│  Pub files:                                                │
│   ┌───────────────────────────────┐                       │
│   │ C:\PUB\                        │        .PUB           │
│   └───────────────────────────────┘                       │
│             ╭──────────╮      ╭──────────╮                 │
│             │  ▣OK     │      │ ▣Cancel  │                 │
│             ╰──────────╯      ╰──────────╯                 │
│ ▌H=Help═══════════════════════════════════════════════════│
└──────────────────────────────────────────────────────────┘
```

You can then specify exactly where all text files, art files, and publication files are to be stored. You also have the option of changing the default file extensions for text and art files. This is helpful if you routinely retrieve files from another program whose filename extension differs from First Publisher's defaults.

 You can override these default pathnames any time you save or retrieve within First Publisher if you are temporarily using another disk drive or subdirectory.

Summary

In this chapter you learned how to

- Understand the First Publisher screen
- Select from all of the pull-down menus at the top of the screen with the keyboard and mouse
- Work with dialog boxes to specify information and options needed when performing a menu command
- Use the speed keys to increase your productivity with First Publisher
- Get help on general topics as well as context-sensitive help that directly relates to whatever you happen to be working on when you ask for help
- Move around the First Publisher screen quickly with the elevator bar and elevator. You can scroll to the top or bottom of a publication very easily with a keyboard or mouse by utilizing the elevator bar. Its position also indicates the current position of the screen and printed page.
- Select from the various side tools which you will be using to create publications
- Customize your First Publisher environment (version 3.0 only) to change screen colors, units of measurement, and disk drive pathnames

YOUR PUBLICATION'S TEXT

Before diving into a discussion of First Publisher's graphics abilities, you should be familiar with its ability to manipulate text within a publication. After you understand the fundamentals of creating, moving, copying, and resizing text within a publication, you will be ready to add art and borders that give your publication a professional appearance.

This chapter describes how to use and change fonts and how to enter text into your publication. If you are producing documents with lots of text, you might find it more useful to use a word processor to create and edit the text. Once you finalize the text, import it into First Publisher to integrate the text with art and produce stunning publications.

PREPARING FOR YOUR TEXT

Before creating a new publication, make sure that First Publisher is started and the editing screen is blank. If you have been looking at another publication, or practicing with First Publisher, erase the publication on the screen with the following steps:

1. Select File from the pull-down menu by pressing (F1) or pointing to it and clicking a mouse button.

2. Select Start over from the menu. ((ALT-Y) is the speed key for version 3.0 users.)

3. If you have not saved the work you were editing, First Publisher will give you a chance to save with the prompt shown here.

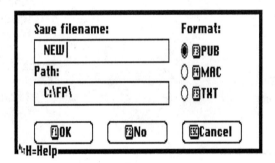

Save the file by typing its filename and pressing (F1). If you do not want to save the file, press (F2). By pressing (ESC), you can cancel the entire Start over operation.

The next few sections describe how to use the editing features of First Publisher to enter small sections of text into your publication. Later, you will see how to import larger sections of text from your word processor.

The Overlays

Whether typing text or creating art in First Publisher, you will always be typing on an *overlay*. Think of overlays as transparent sheets of paper. If you write on two of the sheets, and then lay one on top of the other, they will look like a single sheet. You also can change one without changing the other.

First Publisher has three overlays: a text overlay, a standard art overlay, and a high-resolution art overlay. Anything that you type with the text tool will be put onto the text overlay. All graphics that you import or draw will be placed on one of the art overlays. These overlays are always positioned on top of each other when you view the publication screen. This is how First Publisher keeps the text and art separated, even when it looks as though they are combined on a single sheet of paper on the screen.

To give you an idea of the overlay concept, Figure 3-1a shows you text on the text overlay, Figure 3-1b shows an art image on the standard art overlay, and Figure 3-1c shows what you see on the screen when both overlays are seen together, as they usually are. By combining the text and art overlays, First Publisher lets you see the integration of text and art while still allowing you to work with either part separately.

When you start with a blank publication, First Publisher displays the text overlay. The first side tool is the text tool that looks like a reverse-video *A* when active. If the text tool is not highlighted, you can point to it and click with the mouse or press (F9) until it is highlighted. When active, the text tool lets you type and edit text on the text overlay. There is no way you can type over art when the text tool is active. To work with art, you select one of the art tools.

The Clipboard

Chapter 2 briefly described the clipboard. Before seeing what you can do with First Publisher's text capabilities, it will be helpful to understand the clipboard further. The clipboard is a temporary holding area for up to 5,000 characters of text. This is equivalent to one full page of text. The clipboard is used for the block operations of First Publisher. These are the Copy, Delete, Insert, and Move commands. The block operations will be described later in this chapter.

 Unlike most word processors, First Publisher does not automatically send text to the next page when you fill up the previous one with text. You can only work with a single page of text at a time. If you attempt to put more than 5,000 characters on a single page, the clipboard can hold the excess characters until you place them on another page.

The text on the clipboard stays there until you overwrite the clipboard with new text or leave First Publisher. Loading another publication does not erase the clipboard's contents. This lets you copy text from one publication, load a second publication, and insert the clipped text from the first into the second.

a

The clipboard is a great place

to temporarily store what you

do not need. Later, you can go to

the clipboard and get it.

b

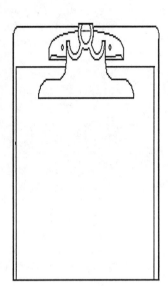

c

| ⊞File | ⊞Page | ⊞Text | ⊞Font | ⊞Style | ⊞Baselines | ⊞Art | ⁴ʰH=Help |

The clipboard is a great place

to temporarily store what you

do not need. Later, you can go to

the clipboard and get it.

FIGURE 3-1. Text on the text overlay (*a*), art on the art overlay (*b*), and both overlays displayed (*c*)

TYPING SAMPLE TEXT

To become familiar with the method of typing text into a First Publisher document, type the sample text provided here. In this example text, a seafood distributor is sending out an announcement of a current sale and publishing it with First Publisher. You will use this text for examples in the next few chapters.

When typing the sample, do not worry about fonts or typestyles. First Publisher always begins with text in the 12-point Swiss font in the roman style, unless you change to a different one. Later, you will change the heading's font, but for now, leave everything as it is. Do not worry if you make a mistake when typing. The next section describes how to correct text.

Press (ENTER) at the end of the heading. You should press (ENTER) after typing any block of text that ends before the right margin is reached. You will have to press (ENTER) a second time to leave a blank line between the heading and the body of the text.

For the body of the sample text, press (ENTER) twice to end each paragraph and leave a blank line. First Publisher will *word wrap* text if words go past the right margin. As you will see when typing the sample text, First Publisher sends the cursor down to the next line automatically at the end of each line. If a word is not finished by the time you get to the right margin, First Publisher will pull the entire word from the end of the previous line and put it on the next one, to keep the text within the right margin.

 If you hear beeps while typing, you may have to wait for First Publisher to catch up with your typing speed. This usually only occurs with slower computers.

Don't type two spaces after the period at the end of a sentence, as you usually would with word-processed text. First Publisher will be better able to format your text if you leave only a single space after periods.

```
[35 SPACEBARs]Cape Cod COD (ENTER)
[39 SPACEBARs]Great Seafood Distributors (ENTER)
(ENTER)
We are proud to announce to you, our best customers, that
we are continuing our discount seafood prices throughout
the rest of this month. (ENTER)
(ENTER)
We offer some of the freshest catches of the day. Our
lobsters are flown in from Maine. Our shrimp is the most
delicious you will find in America. Of course, our special
cod fillets are delightful. (ENTER)
(ENTER)
```

I want to invite you personally to try our seafood just
once. It will keep you coming back for more. I am so
convinced of our products and prices that I will make sure
you get an additional 15% off if you mention this
flyer. (ENTER)
(ENTER)
If you are a reseller of only the best fish, I suggest you
try Cape Cod COD Seafood Distributors the next time you
order. (ENTER)
(ENTER)
Jamie Somers, East Coast Representative (ENTER)

Figure 3-2 shows the text as it appears on the First Publisher screen. Once
you understand the concepts of baselines, covered in Chapter 6, you will see
a better way to center titles on a line.

═══ **FIGURE 3-2.** Sample text to type into First Publisher

MOVING THE CURSOR

If you make a mistake when typing, move your cursor back to the error by pressing ⬭UP ARROW⬭, ⬭DOWN ARROW⬭, ⬭LEFT ARROW⬭, or ⬭RIGHT ARROW⬭, or by pointing and clicking with the mouse. First Publisher will move the cursor, but will not destroy any text. The ⬭DEL⬭ key removes characters underneath the cursor and moves all other characters to the left to fill in the hole. Unlike ⬭LEFT ARROW⬭, ⬭BACKSPACE⬭ moves the cursor back one character, erasing characters to the left as it moves.

Do *not* press the ⬭INS⬭ key to toggle in and out of insert mode. This will not work. The ⬭INS⬭ key is used to insert a large block of blank text at the cursor's location. Figure 3-3 shows text before ⬭INS⬭ is pressed. Notice the location of the cursor. Figure 3-4 shows the result of pressing ⬭INS⬭ (do not do this with your sample text). Any time you have to insert a lot of text inside existing text, press ⬭INS⬭ to insert several blank lines first. This is faster than adding a space for every character typed.

The text overlay is always in the insert mode. If you type a character over another one, the text will "open up" to make room for the new character.

If you want to replace text, first delete the old text, then type in the new text.

There are many ways to move the cursor other than with the arrow keys. Mouse users can quickly move the cursor by pointing and clicking with the mouse. Although the mouse is faster than the arrow keys in many instances, there may be times when mouse users want to use the keyboard to position the cursor. The keyboard can, at times, more accurately place the cursor in certain locations, such as at the beginning or end of a line of text.

The basics of editing dictate that you master the cursor-movement commands, since the cursor directs the placement of the next character of text listed next. Table 3-1 reviews cursor-movement keystrokes and mouse movements. To try them, follow the practice steps.

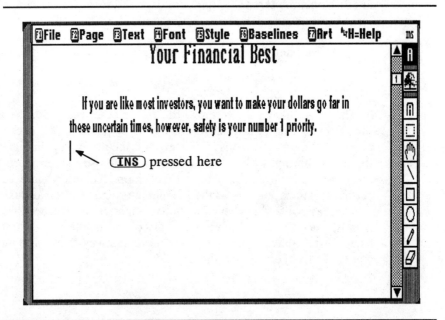

FIGURE 3-3. Before pressing (INS)

| 🗔File 🗔Page 🗔Text 🗔Font 🗔Style 🗔Baselines 🗔Art ↳H=Help |

Your Financial Best

If you are like most investors, you want to make your dollars go far in these uncertain times, however, safety is your number 1 priority.

At First Federal Financial, we can help you with all of your investment decisions. Please contact us when you are ready to start making your dollars work safely for you.

Cursor's location for insert

Sincerely,
Bruce G. Weber, Financial Advisor

| 🗔File 🗔Page 🗔Text 🗔Font 🗔Style 🗔Baselines 🗔Art ↳H=Help   ins |

Your Financial Best

If you are like most investors, you want to make your dollars go far in these uncertain times, however, safety is your number 1 priority.

(INS) pressed here

FIGURE 3-4. After pressing (INS)

Cursor-Movement Keys

Key	*Cursor Movement*
`LEFT ARROW`	Left one character
`RIGHT ARROW`	Right one character
`DOWN ARROW`	Down one line
`UP ARROW`	Up one line
`CTRL-LEFT ARROW`	Left one word
`CTRL-RIGHT ARROW`	Right one word
`PGDN`	Down a screen
`PGUP`	Up a screen
`CTRL-PGDN`	Down a portion of the screen
`CTRL-PGUP`	Up a portion of the screen
`HOME`	Beginning of current line
`END`	End of current line
`CTRL-HOME`	Beginning of current page
`CTRL-END`	End of current page
`CTRL-L`	Move to the left of the landscape screen
`CTRL-R`	Move to the right of the landscape screen
`CTRL-N`	Next column of a multiple-column publication
`CTRL-P`	Previous column of a multiple-column publication
`SHIFT- +`	Next page
`SHIFT-MINUS`	Previous page
`SHIFT-HOME`	Scroll landscape screen to the left
`SHIFT-END`	Scroll landscape screen to the right

Mouse Movements

Cursor Movement	*Action*
Next word	Point to first character of the next word and click a mouse button.

TABLE 3-1.   Cursor and Mouse Movement Commands

Mouse Movements

Cursor Movement	*Action*
Previous word	Point to first character of the previous word and click a mouse button.
Beginning of page	Point to the top of the elevator bar and click a mouse button.
Last line of current page	Point to the bottom of the elevator bar and click a mouse button.
Any column of a multiple-column page	Point to the column and click a mouse button.
Left of landscape screen	Click on left arrow of horizontal elevator bar.
Right of landscape screen	Click on right arrow of horizontal elevator bar.
End of current line	Point to the last character on the line and click a mouse button.
Beginning of current line	Point to the first character on the line and click a mouse button.
Another page	Point to Jump to page from the Page pull-down menu and type the page number.

TABLE 3-1. Cursor and Mouse Movement Commands (*continued*)

To practice with the keyboard:

1. Move the cursor to the start of the top line by holding the CTRL key, then pressing HOME (designated as CTRL-HOME in the rest of the book).

2. Move the cursor to the end of the bottom line by pressing CTRL-END.

3. Move the cursor to the beginning of the last line by pressing the HOME key.

4. Move back to the end of the line by pressing END. As you can see, HOME and END move the cursor to the beginning or end of the *current* line and CTRL-HOME and CTRL-END move you to the beginning of the first line and the end of the last line in the publication.

5. Move quickly from word to word by pressing (**CTRL-LEFT ARROW**) and (**CTRL-RIGHT ARROW**) several times.

6. This sample text may take less than a full screen of text, or more, depending on your specific graphics adapter. If you were working on a page that spanned more than a single screen, you would press (**PGDN**) and (**PGUP**) to scroll through the text. As described in Chapter 2, the elevator shows the relative position of the cursor within the document.

7. See the effects of scrolling a line at a time by pressing (**CTRL-PGDN**) and (**CTRL-PGUP**) several times.

8. Replace the first word in the second line of the title, "Great," with "Fine" by pressing the following sequence of keys: (**CTRL-HOME**), (**DOWN ARROW**), (**CTRL-RIGHT ARROW**), and (**DEL**) five times. Then type **Fine**. Figure 3-5 shows the screen at this point.

To practice with the mouse:

1. Move the mouse to the elevator bar, about halfway down, until it turns into a pointing arrow. Click the mouse button. The text will scroll downward.

2. Move the mouse cursor to any word in the document. After clicking the mouse button, the cursor will move to the letter that the mouse is pointing to within the word.

3. Point to the top of the elevator bar and click the mouse button to move the cursor to the top of the page.

4 Point to the bottom of the elevator bar and click the mouse button to move the cursor to the bottom of the page. You will see blank space, since there is no text at the bottom of the document.

5. Point to the upward-pointing or downward-pointing arrow at the top or bottom of the elevator bar. Clicking on one of these symbols moves the text up or down a notch.

6. Point to the *F* in "Fine" on the first word of the second line of text. Click the button to move the cursor to the beginning of the word. Press (**DEL**) four times, then type **Great** to replace the word. This is an example of using the mouse and keyboard in conjunction, as you will often do. Now change the text back to "Fine" as it was when you started practicing with the mouse. Figure 3-5 shows your screen at this point.

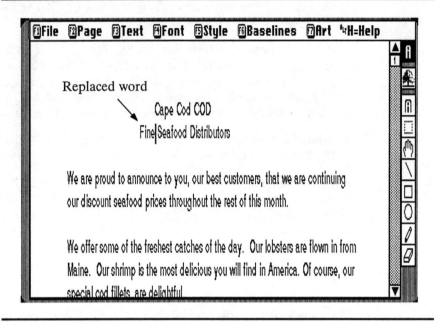

FIGURE 3-5.   Changing a word in the sample text

The rest of this book will assume that you will use either the mouse or keyboard, whichever best suits your needs. When instructed to move the cursor to a place on the screen, you can point with the mouse and click or use the keyboard.

BLOCK COMMANDS

When typing text, you are working with a single character at a time. However, there are many operations that work with blocks of text at a time. A block of text is made up of one or more characters of text. You are responsible for specifying a block of text (called *selecting*). Once you have selected a block of text, you can remove it, copy it or move it to another place in the current publication or another publication, or change the appearance of the block of text.

Selecting Text

To select a block of text, you must mark the starting and ending points of the block. You must always mark the block before performing one of the block-related commands. To gain experience in selecting a block of text, move a sentence in the sample text by following these steps:

1. Position the cursor at the beginning of the first occurrence of "Our" in the second paragraph of text.

2. You must press and hold the mouse button to mark the beginning of the block. If you don't have a mouse, you can simulate the press of a mouse button by pressing (**F10**). When you do, the mouse symbol appears in the upper-right corner.

3. Drag the mouse to the next line, or press (**DOWN ARROW**) to simulate moving the mouse. Drag the mouse, or press (**LEFT ARROW**) until only the sentence beginning with "Our" is highlighted. (Do not select space either before or after the sentence.) If you typed the text exactly as shown previously, the entire sentence will be highlighted as shown here.

We offer some of the freshest catches of the day. Our lobsters are flown in from Maine. Our shrimp is the most delicious you will find in America. Of course, our

4. Once the entire sentence is highlighted, release the mouse button or press (**F10**) again. The mouse symbol will disappear, and you can now perform a block operation on this selected text.

You can select as much as an entire page of text (up to 5,000 characters maximum).

To quickly select an entire page, you would follow these steps:

1. Move the cursor to the top of the page by pressing (**CTRL-HOME**).

2. Press (**F10**).

3. Press (**CTRL-END**) to move the cursor to the end of the page.

4. Press (**F10**) to finish the selection of the page. The entire page will then be highlighted.

ERASING SELECTED TEXT You can erase a block of selected text. To erase the selected block, press the (DEL) key. This is the speed key for selecting Cut from the Text pull-down menu. When you delete a block of text, the publication is "squeezed down" to fill in the hole left by the erased block. To practice erasing text, reselect the sentence from the previous section, and then press (DEL). The selected block of text will disappear and, once you delete the surrounding spaces, your screen will look like the one in Figure 3-6. You should delete the extra space before the word "Our."

The text is not really gone yet. Text goes to the clipboard whenever it is cut from your publication. This gives you a chance to change your mind if you want the text back. Also, after placing the block on the clipboard, you can insert the block into another location in your current publication or insert it into another publication.

 If there is text on the clipboard already, and you send more text to it, the original clipboard text will be replaced.

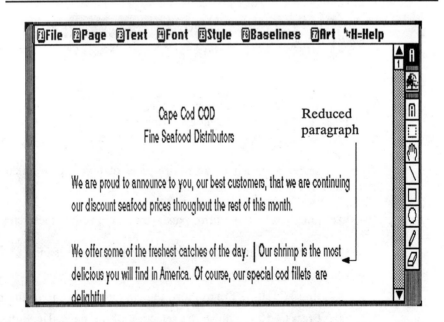

───── **FIGURE 3-6.** After cutting the selected sentence

PASTING CLIPBOARD TEXT You can perform a Move operation by deleting text to the clipboard as described above and then inserting the clipboard text at another location of the document. Inserting text from the clipboard is called *pasting*.

To see this work, move the current clipboard text (the sentence removed in the last example) to the end of the paragraph by following these steps:

1. Move the cursor to the end of the last line of the second paragraph, following the words "are delightful."

2. Press (**SPACEBAR**) to insert a space after the period.

3. Press (**ALT-V**) to insert the clipboard text at the cursor's location. This is the speed key for selecting Paste from the Text pull-down menu. Your screen should look like the one shown in Figure 3-7.

FIGURE 3-7.   After pasting the sentence back

COPYING TEXT   You may want to make a copy of the same block of text several times throughout your document. For instance, if you are creating a multiple-page publication that repeatedly cites your name and address, you can type it once and then copy it to the other locations instead of typing it again. In your sample publication, let's suppose that the author wants to copy the heading line ("Cape Cod COD") after her name, but still wants the heading left where it is. Follow these steps to do so:

1. Select the heading line as illustrated previously.

2. Press ⟨**ALT-C**⟩, the speed key for Copy from the Text pull-down menu, to copy the selected text to the clipboard.

3. Move the cursor to the end of the closing name and title.

4. Type a comma and press ⟨**SPACEBAR**⟩ after the title.

5. Press ⟨**ALT-V**⟩ to paste the clipboard text to the current position. Your screen should look like the one in Figure 3-8.

FIGURE 3-8.   After copying selected text

The Paste command does not remove the clipboard's contents. If you wanted to, you could insert the clipboard text several times in the same publication to perform several Copy operations.

 If you press ⟨**ALT-V**⟩ or select the Text pull-down menu, and the Paste command is gray, then the clipboard is empty and there is no text to paste.

CHANGING A FONT   You can change the font or typestyle of any block of selected text. Although you can choose a font before typing text, it is usually easier to concentrate on the text contents before worrying about the font selection, even for titles.

For instance, now that you have typed a title and text, you might want to separate the title from the rest of the document. You can do so easily. The following example changes the title font but does not change "Seafood Distributors" below the title.

1. Select the title, "Cape Cod COD," as shown here:

2. Press ⟨**F4**⟩ to display the Font pull-down menu. Swiss is the default font checked.
3. Select the New York option.
4. Press ⟨**ENTER**⟩. The selected text is now converted to the New York font.
5. Press ⟨**F5**⟩ to display the Style pull-down menu. 18 Points is highlighted, and that is the smallest point size available for the bold New York font. Select 24 Points. You will have to delete several spaces before the heading to center it now. The title on your screen should match the one shown here.

6. Press ⟨**F10**⟩ or click a mouse button to get rid of the highlighted text.

The text's font in the clipboard does not change. The original text appears in its original font since you have sent nothing else to it. Be sure to reselect the Swiss 12-point roman font so that future text will appear in its normal font.

Once you have had a chance to practice with the supplied fonts, Chapter 7 will show you how to add more fonts, including scalable Bitstream fonts.

EXPORTING SELECTED TEXT You can save selected text to an ASCII text file. The file will have no formatting or font information, but the characters will be saved. You can then use the exported ASCII file in another program, or in another publication. You have to select the text to be saved to the ASCII file even if it exists in the clipboard.

To save the text "Cape Cod COD" in its own file, follow these steps:

1. Select the title line again.

2. Press (F3) to display the Text pull-down menu.

3. Select Save text. There is no speed key for this option. First Publisher then displays the following filename prompt:

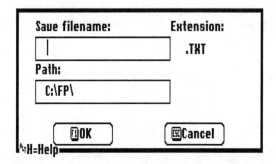

4. Type the filename (and path if needed); then press (F1) to save the file. Pressing (F2) or (ESC) cancels the command.

OVERFLOW TEXT

The sample text starts at the top of the page on the screen (page 1, as you can see from the elevator). If text takes more memory than a single page can hold (a total of 5,000 characters per page), First Publisher will beep to let you know when you have reached the end of the page. To continue the text onto another page, you must create a new page by selecting Jump to page from the Page pull-down menu. Inserting text in the middle of a page of existing text may also "push" some text past the 5,000-character limit. This section shows you how to handle overflow text.

All text that is pushed off of a page is sent to the overflow area. Each page has its own overflow area. The overflow area is not the same as the clipboard, and the clipboard block commands are not associated with the page overflow area. To see if text is in the overflow area, press ⌈**ALT-I**⌋ to select the Status screen from the File pull-down menu. If you press ⌈**ALT-I**⌋ after the example just entered, the following Status screen will appear:

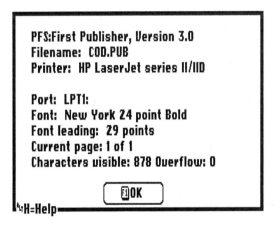

```
PFS:First Publisher, Version 3.0
Filename: COD.PUB
Printer: HP LaserJet series II/IID

Port: LPT1:
Font: New York 24 point Bold
Font leading: 29 points
Current page: 1 of 1
Characters visible: 878 Overflow: 0

            ⌈ ⊞OK ⌋

ᴬₒₕH=Help
```

The last line tells you that there is no text in the overflow area. The other statistics are also useful while creating a publication, and you might find it helpful to select Status often during an editing session. The text is taking up only a small portion of the 5,000-character limit (878 characters are on the current page in the Status screen just shown).

If you had text in the overflow area, you would have to do one of the following with it:

• Keep it there. The overflow text will never print, but it will always stay with the page it is associated with.

• Delete text on the page until the overflowed text "moves up" to the page. As you remove characters from the page, the same number of overflow characters will move to the end of the page.

• Move the overflow text to another page.

To move the overflow text to another page:

1. Press ⟨**ALT-J**⟩ to select Jump to page from the Page pull-down menu. You will see the Jump to Page screen shown here:

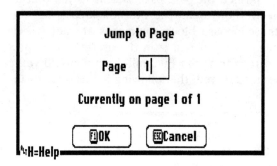

2. Type the page number to jump to.

3. Press ⟨**F1**⟩ to perform the jump. You can jump to a new page, or to one that you have edited before. The following screen will appear:

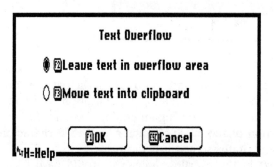

4. Press ⟨**F3**⟩ to move the overflow text to the clipboard. You will get this prompt any time you jump to a page from one that has overflow text. (If you want to leave the text in the overflow area, press ⟨**F2**⟩.)

5. Press ⟨**F1**⟩ to jump to the next page. If you want the clipboard text pasted to the new page, press ⟨**ALT-V**⟩. In later exercises involving longer publications, you will get a chance to work with overflow text.

SAVING THE PUBLICATION

After working on a publication, you will want to save it on a disk. You can then retrieve it for printing or editing. To save your publication, follow these steps:

1. Press ⌐ALT-S⌐ to select Save from the File pull-down menu. First Publisher will display the following Save filename screen:

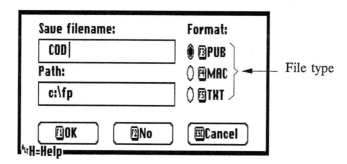

2. Type a filename for the publication. If you want to store the file in a directory path that is different from the one shown, press ⌐TAB⌐ and change the path. For now, type **JAMIE** as the filename. You can type the filename in uppercase or lowercase letters.

3. If you want to save the publication under a file format other than the First Publisher .PUB file, press ⌐F4⌐ or ⌐F5⌐ to select a .MAC or .TXT extension and file type.

 The .MAC file is an art image of the publication. Once it is saved as an art image, you cannot load the publication and perform text commands on it. However, you can manipulate the publication as if it were all art, as shown in the next chapter.

   The .TXT option will save the text in an ASCII file format. The font and style information cannot be saved. You can load the ASCII file into another program, or back into a First Publisher publication.

4. Press ⌐F1⌐ to save the file to the disk. (Pressing ⌐F2⌐ or ⌐ESC⌐ will cancel the command without saving the file.) Once saved, the filename will appear on the Status screen when you press the ⌐ALT-I⌐ speed key combination.

You should save your publication every 10 to 20 minutes. This will store valuable work safely away on the disk in case there is a power failure of any kind.

GETTING A PUBLICATION

Over time, you will create and work with many publications. Once saved, you can load a publication at another time for editing or printing. You can also load text files from other programs. To practice getting a publication from disk, reload the JAMIE.PUB publication you saved in the last section with the following steps:

1. Select Start over from the File pull-down menu. There is no speed key for this. If you get the Save filename screen, press (F2) to leave it, since you have already saved the file.

2. The screen will clear and "NEW" will appear in the upper-right corner of the screen for version 2 users. This is normally where the filename is displayed.

3. Press (ALT-G), the speed key for Get publication on the File pull-down menu. You will see a filename prompt like the one shown here:

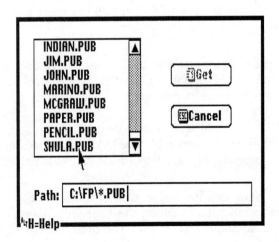

4. Type **JAMIE**, or press `PGDN` or `PGUP` to display JAMIE.PUB, and then select it. When you do, the "Please stand by" message will appear in the middle of the screen. After a brief pause, the publication will be loaded onto the screen.

Importing Another Text File

When you load a text file other than a First Publisher file onto your publication screen, you are *importing* a file. You can load the following word processor files directly:

PFS:First Choice 1, 2, 3	PFS:WRITE
Professional Write 1, 2	DCA/DisplayWrite
ASCII text files	Office Writer 6 and up
Microsoft Word 3, 4, 5	MultiMate 2 and up
Wang PC 2	WordPerfect 3, 4, 5
WordStar 3, 4, 5	

Depending on how the text was set up in the word processor, you may have to perform some minor editing on it once it is imported into First Publisher. Extra line feeds, carriage returns, and hyphens may need to be edited out of the publication's text. The following sections describe the process for importing files.

IMPORTING PROFESSIONAL WRITE 2 FILES Professional Write 2's fonts are fully compatible with First Publisher's fonts, as long as your MASTER.FNT file contains the same fonts as the Professional Write 2 fonts. If you are unfamiliar with the MASTER.FNT file, consult Chapter 7 to see how to add and list fonts in First Publisher's MASTER.FNT file.

Your Professional Write 2 document may use special fonts, but you do not have to import them; you are given the option of doing so. To import a Professional Write 2 document, you would follow these steps:

1. Start First Publisher if it is not already started.

2. Select Get text from the Text pull-down menu. There is no speed key for this. Type the Professional Write 2 filename to load, or select it from the list if it ends in the extension .TXT. Press `F1` to load the file.

3. You will be asked for the Professional Write 2 program pathname. First Publisher needs to be able to find the fonts used in the document. If you press (ESC) instead of typing a pathname, First Publisher will import the text file without respecting the special fonts used in the file.

4. Press (F1) to select OK to load the document and its fonts.

IMPORTING ASCII TEXT FILES With the ability to import an ASCII text file, you gain the ability to load files from many different programs. Almost every program on the market today will save a file in the ASCII text format. Make sure you save the file with the .TXT extension from within the other program before loading the file into First Publisher. If you need to import an ASCII text file, follow these steps:

1. Start First Publisher if it is not already started.

2. Select Get text from the Text pull-down menu. There is no speed key for this.

3. Select the file you want to load by typing the name or selecting it from the list.

4. Press (F1) to load the text file into your publication.

If a carriage return is pressed in the ASCII file, it will be converted to a space, and all remaining text will be wrapped to the next line. If two carriage returns appear together, a new paragraph and a blank line will be inserted into the imported text. If a carriage return is followed by a space, a new paragraph will be started, but a blank line will not be inserted.

IMPORTING OTHER FILES The procedure for importing text from formats other than First Publisher, Professional Write 2, or ASCII text files is similar to that described in the previous section. Follow the steps shown for ASCII text files to load files with other formats.

All of the boldfaced and italicized text in the following file formats will be retained and not converted into a normal style:

- Professional Write 1.0

- PFS:First Choice

- PFS:WRITE

Specifying Fonts in Non-Publication Files

Although Professional Write 2 is the only file format where First Publisher automatically recognizes character fonts and styles, you can specify First Publisher fonts within another word processor, even if that word processor has no special fonts. You use the *FONT* embedded text command to do this. (The abbreviated command is *f*.) For instance, suppose you typed the following paragraph using Microsoft Word:

```
*FONT New York 18 bold*Computers and You

*f Swiss 12 roman*Many people do not realize that they too
can learn how to use computers. When they finally sit down
to a good book on the subject, they see that it can be *f
Geneva 12 bold*fun*f Swiss 12 roman* to learn about them.
```

There are four embedded *FONT* commands in the above text. The *FONT* (or *f*) commands will not print, nor will they be imported into the First Publisher publication. However, First Publisher recognizes the commands and changes all text following the command—up until the start of the next command—to the font, size, and style specified. Figure 3-9 shows you the result of importing this text into First Publisher.

If you are very familiar with another word processor, you can create the text and specify the font information that First Publisher will use by typing these *FONT* commands. Make sure that you specify a font, size, and style that your First Publisher contains.

LANDSCAPE MODE

Some publications are wider than the standard 8 1/2-inch paper. First Publisher 3.0 supports the following paper sizes:

- 8 1/2 by 11 inches
- 8 1/2 by 14 inches
- 21 by 29.7 centimeters

Each of these page sizes can be specified on the Define Page screen. There are two orientations available for you to use, *portrait* and *landscape*. Portrait orientation prints the publication with the shortest edges making up the

FIGURE 3-9. After importing ASCII file with *FONT* commands

width. Landscape orientation prints the publication with the longest edges making up the width. These names are derived from the standard orientation of a portrait versus a landscape painting. Most publications will be printed in the portrait mode, although the supplied MAILER.PUB template is in landscape orientation (see Figure C-9 in Appendix C).

If you choose landscape orientation, you will see a second elevator bar across the bottom of the screen. Use it in the same way as you use the vertical elevator bar to scroll left and right across the page.

Note to Version 2 Users   Only portrait printing is available on version 2.

Summary

In this chapter you learned how to

- Add text to a publication using First Publisher's text overlay. Once on the text overlay, the text can be easily modified.

- Use the clipboard to hold blocks of selected text and overflow text that you can send to another page in the publication

- Move the cursor with the keyboard and mouse. First Publisher offers cursor movement between letters, words, columns, and pages of text.

- Save and retrieve publications to and from disk. You may also load files created in another program directly into First Publisher.

- Change fonts within your publication and specify fonts to be used by First Publisher in your word processor files

- Differentiate between portrait and landscape printing modes

YOUR
PUBLICATION'S ART

Art Files
Working with Art Images
Drawing Your Own Images
Combining Text and Art
High-Resolution Art
Importing Art

I f all you wanted to do was place text on the page, you would have little use for First Publisher. The power of First Publisher can be seen when you learn to manipulate art as easily as text. This chapter shows you the various ways art can be added to your publication. You will practice moving, resizing, copying, and deleting art.

First Publisher art tools allow you to incorporate freehand drawing, straight lines, circles, and boxes into your publications. Not only is freehand drawing useful for art, but also for signatures and borders. The First Publisher SNAPSHOT supplemental program described at the end of this chapter allows you to import art from sources other than First Publisher.

ART FILES

First Publisher works with two types of art files, .ART files and .MAC files. Files that end with the .ART extension contain a single picture and are either *standard art* (with resolution of 72 dots per inch) or *high-resolution art* (with resolution up to 300 dots per inch). Both resolutions look the same on the screen, but high-resolution art looks much better when printed. When you clip art from other sources, you will save this art as an .ART file. Art you save in an .ART file may or may not be in high-resolution mode, depending on the source you get the art from.

Note to Version 2 Users You do not have the capability to manipulate high-resolution images, but you can work with standard art in the same way that version 3.0 users do.

Files that end with the .MAC extension contain several pictures (called clip art). They are stored as standard art images. Many of your .ART files will be created from the .MAC files that come with your program's Sample Disk, from other First Publisher art disks you may purchase, and from your freehand drawing activities. Figure 4-1 shows an .ART file's contents, and

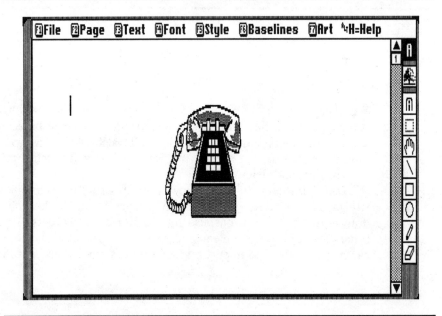

FIGURE 4-1. Sample .ART file image

Figure 4-2 shows a .MAC file. The .ART file was created from the .MAC file. .MAC files can be created with other drawing programs as well.

You have already seen the third type of file used with First Publisher, which is the .PUB file. This is your publication file that contains both art and text; it is the publication that you save to the disk. The table below summarizes the three file types and their retrieval commands:

Extension	Retrieval Command
.MAC, .ART	Select Get art from the Art menu
.PUB	Select Get publication from the File menu

This section gives you practice in loading a .MAC file into memory. You will then copy an individual art image from that file to an .ART file. There, you can paste the art image into the publication you created in the last chapter to see the effects of combining text and art.

FIGURE 4-2.   Sample .MAC file image

Loading a .MAC File

In this section, you'll take one of the sample .MAC files that come with your program disks and load that file into memory. Then you'll learn how to use many of the art tools to remove the extra art images that are not to be saved in the final .ART file.

To load a .MAC file, make sure that First Publisher is started and then get to a blank publication by selecting Start over from the File pull-down menu. Follow the steps below to load the .MAC file from disk to memory:

1. Display the Art pull-down menu by pointing and clicking with a mouse, or press F7.

2. Select Get art from the menu. First Publisher displays a list of files with the .ART extension. You must change the path to look for files ending in .MAC. To change the extension, press BACKSPACE three times and type **MAC**. Press ENTER to see a list of .MAC files.

Note to Version 2 Users You must select Get graphics from the File pull-down menu to retrieve .MAC files.

3. Scroll through the list with PGDN and the arrow keys—or scroll the elevator bar with the mouse—until you select LEISURE.MAC. LEISURE .MAC is one of the sample files that comes with First Publisher.

If you know the filename, you may save time by typing it instead of hunting through the list.

4. After pointing to LEISURE.MAC, press F10 and F1, or click with the mouse. First Publisher will warn you that the .MAC file may overwrite anything currently on the screen with the following dialog box:

The MAC file may overwrite any text or art on this page. Do you want to get the file?

OK   Cancel

FIGURE 4-3.   After loading the LEISURE.MAC file

Press (F1) to confirm that you want to load the file.

5. After a brief pause (the wait clock will be displayed), the hand placement symbol will appear on the screen. First Publisher needs to know exactly where you want the new .MAC file displayed.

6. Move the hand placement symbol to the upper-left corner of the screen and press (F10) twice, or click a mouse button. The LEISURE.MAC file will appear on the screen as shown in Figure 4-3.

7. Press (PGDN) until the fish and hook picture appears toward the right of the screen. It looks like this:

PULLING OUT AN ART IMAGE   To grab the fishing image from the .MAC file, you can either outline the image and save it to a file or delete all art around the image, and then save it to a file. It is easier to outline the image. This is known as selecting an art image, and the process involves the following steps:

1. You must select the dotted box (the fourth tool). Keyboard users simply press **ALT-F9** to back up one tool from the hand tool, which is currently active. This is the art box, and it is used to surround art images in your publication. When the art box is active, the cursor will change to an arrow.

2. Place the pointer just outside the upper-left corner of the fishing image. Press and hold the mouse button, or press **F10** once. This "anchors" one corner of the box that will eventually surround the art image.

3. While pressing the mouse button, move the mouse pointer down and right to cover the entire fishing image but none of the other images. Keyboard users can press the **DOWN ARROW** and **RIGHT ARROW** keys to extend the box down and enclose the entire fishing art image. Press **F10** or release the mouse button to let First Publisher know when the image is fully enclosed.

4. Select Save art from the Art pull-down menu. A Save Filename screen appears. For now, type **FISH** and press **F1** to save the file as FISH.ART. (The .ART extension will be added for you.)

   Keyboard users can move the pointing cursor quickly by pressing **SHIFT-LEFT ARROW** and **SHIFT-RIGHT ARROW**.

You might want to load and view every .MAC file that came with your First Publisher program. If you print each .MAC file (printing is discussed fully in Chapter 5), you will have a copy of every available image. You would waste too much disk space and time if you marked and saved each .MAC file image to its own .ART file. Nevertheless, by keeping each .MAC file printed for reference, you will be able to find an image easily when you need it.

After you save an image from a .MAC file, First Publisher will give you a chance to save the .MAC file again with the following dialog box.

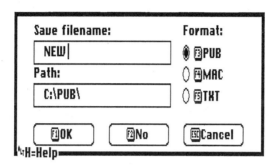

The default extension for this saved file is .PUB, because First Publisher tries to protect the original .MAC file. You can override this default extension by typing the filename with the .MAC extension. If you do so, however, you will lose the original .MAC file that was supplied with the First Publisher program.

  If you accidentally overwrite a .MAC file, you can reload it from the original program diskettes with the DOS COPY command.

WORKING WITH ART IMAGES

Before bringing the fishing image into the Cape Cod COD text that you created in Chapter 3, you should practice manipulating that image with the variety of art tools available. This section will describes how to copy, duplicate, move, erase, replace, resize, invert, and flip the art image. Follow these examples to get used to working with art. Once you have seen all that you can do with the image, you will combine it with the text file to create the final Cape Cod COD publication.

  The art clipped from .MAC files is standard art. With standard art (72 DPI) you can use all of the Art pull-down menu art-manipulation commands except Crop. A later section in this chapter discusses working with a high-resolution art image.

Loading the Art Image

To see all that you can do with art, load the fishing image into a blank publication screen. Follow these steps to load the fishing art image:

1. Select Start over from the File pull-down menu.

2. Display the Art pull-down menu by pressing (F7) or by moving the mouse pointer over Art on the top menu bar.

3. Select Get art from the Art menu. There is no speed key for this.

4. Type **FISH.ART** and press (ENTER). You will see the hand tool on the screen. This is the placement tool for the loaded art. The fishing image will be placed at the location of the hand tool. To move the tool, use the arrow keys or drag the hand by moving the mouse. Move the hand tool left and right to get an idea of its use. The hand is located at the upper-left corner of the still-invisible image that will be placed.

5. When the hand tool is placed where you want the art image to go, press and release the mouse button or press (F10) twice. The fishing image will be placed on the screen as shown in Figure 4-4.

Note to Version 2 Users   You should load .ART files from the Art pull-down menu unlike .MAC files, which are loaded from the File pull-down menu. The rest of the steps for placing the image are identical in versions 2 and 3.

Moving the Art Image

Moving a selected art image is one of the basic skills needed in desktop publishing. When you combine text and art, moving the art to achieve the best placement is very important. Any selected art image can be moved to another location on the screen. You can tell that an image is selected by the dotted box surrounding it. The hand tool can be used for image movement with these steps:

1. Make sure the hand tool is highlighted. If you have been doing the previous exercises, the hand tool is still active.

2. Move the hand tool so that it is within the dotted box of the selected image (if it is not already).

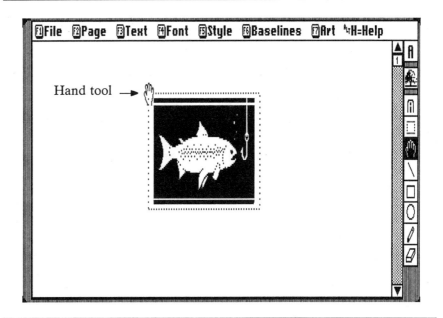

FIGURE 4-4.   After loading the fishing image

3. Press a mouse button and drag the mouse to the left and right. Keyboard users should press the (**F10**) key followed by the (**LEFT ARROW**) and (**RIGHT ARROW**). As you do, the dotted box follows the hand tool. Your screen will look something like the one in Figure 4-5, with the hand tool resting on the image.

4. To move and anchor the image within the moved dotted box, release the mouse button or press (**F10**) again.

You may also move an art image by first cutting the art and then pasting it (speed key (**ALT-V**)) in the new location. Cutting and pasting are discussed later in the chapter.

The Art Clipboard

You can store art images on the art clipboard as easily as you store text on the text clipboard. To copy and duplicate art, cut to and paste from the clipboard using the text operations learned in Chapter 3.

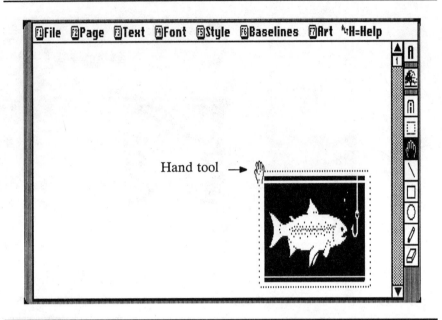

FIGURE 4-5. Moving the art image

COPYING, PASTING, AND DELETING IMAGES To send a selected image to the clipboard, first select Copy from the Art menu. If Copy is gray when the Art menu is displayed, you need to select an image. Press (**ALT-C**), the speed key for Copy, or select the Art menu and point and click on Copy.

Nothing seems to happen, but the image was placed on the Art clipboard. To see the result, select the hand tool and move *it* (not the image) to another place on the screen, away from the fishing image. Select the Paste command from the Art menu or press the (**ALT-V**) speed key; then press (**F10**) or click the mouse button. When you do, the fishing image will be copied from the clipboard to the location of the hand tool, as shown in Figure 4-6.

The clipboard is not erased when art is pasted back into text. Its contents remain there until you send another image to it or leave First Publisher. By keeping the art on the clipboard, First Publisher lets you copy the art image into more than one publication.

To remove an image from a publication, select Cut from the Art pull-down menu. (**DEL**) is the speed key for this. Whatever was previously on the art clipboard is replaced. To try cutting art, remove the second fishing image that you copied earlier by following these steps:

1. Select the second art image. Remember that the dotted box is used for this.

2. Press (**DEL**), or select Cut from the Art pull-down menu. The image will disappear and be sent to the clipboard.

 If you ever find that First Publisher cannot select an entire Art image, you have run out of room on the art clipboard. You can select the art in two pieces and manipulate it one half at a time.

DUPLICATING ART   First Publisher has a streamlined Copy and Paste operation called the *Duplicate* function. When you select Duplicate from the Art pull-down menu, a copy of the image is placed on the clipboard, and the hand tool automatically appears. You can easily place the image elsewhere (duplicating it) as many times as you like. The steps below will duplicate the fishing image several times.

1. Select the fishing image with the selection box tool.

2. Select Duplicate from the Art pull-down menu. (**ALT-D**) is the speed key for this.

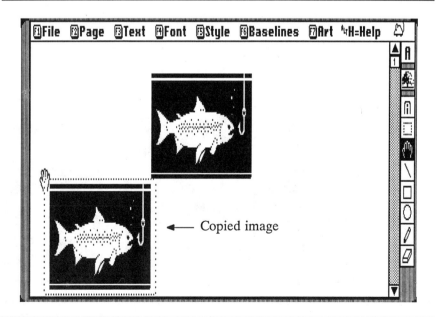

FIGURE 4-6.   After copying the selected art image

3. Move the mouse or press the arrow keys to move the hand tool where the duplicated image is to go.

4. Press (F10) twice or click a mouse button to place the duplicated image at the hand tool. Continue pressing (ALT-D) and (F10) to place the image in several places on the screen, as shown in Figure 4-7.

 The duplicate images you create can be selected and moved just as the original can.

Do not save the publication you have been working on in this section. These duplicated images are not needed.

Flipping, Rotating, and Inverting Art

You can change the orientation of a selected image by flipping it upside down or by reversing it to its mirror image. Images can be rotated 90 degrees at a time. You can also *invert* an image. The inversion process reverses the black and white, which makes the image look something like a photographic negative.

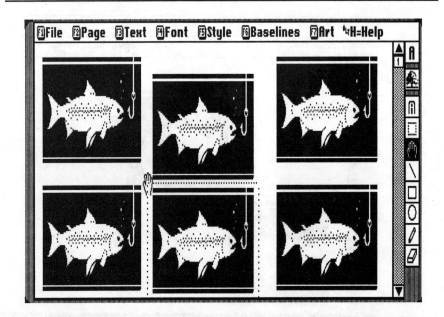

FIGURE 4-7. After duplicating the art image several times

FLIPPING ART IMAGES   To flip an image, select Start over from the File pull-down menu. Reload the FISH.ART file, as shown earlier in this chapter, by selecting Get art from the Art menu. Follow these steps to flip the fishing image to its mirror image:

1. Select the entire fishing image.

2. Select Flip horizontal from the Art pull-down menu. There is no speed key for this. The image will be reversed as shown here:

3. Select Flip horizontal again to return it to its original orientation.

   Flipping the image upside down is just as easy. Since the fishing image is already selected, you do not need to select it again. This time, select Flip vertical from the Art pull-down menu. No matter how much art is selected, the entire selection will always be turned upside down when you select Flip vertical. Select Flip vertical again to flip the image back to its original position before going on.

ROTATING ART IMAGES   You can rotate an image 90 degrees clockwise by selecting Rotate from the Art menu. The speed key for this is (**ALT-O**). Follow these steps to rotate the fishing image completely around:

1. Since the image is already selected, you do not have to select it again. Press (**ALT-O**) to rotate the image once clockwise. Notice that the image rotates 90 degrees. It will continue rotating 90 degrees every time you press (**ALT-O**).

2. Press (**ALT-O**) twice more. The image continues to rotate. Your screen will be similar to that of Figure 4-8. On some monitors, the image may appear to be stretched when it is rotated.

3. Put the image back as it was by rotating it back to its original orientation.

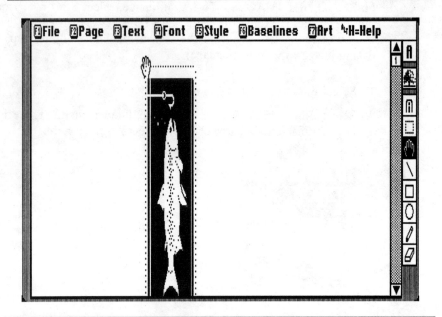

═══ **FIGURE 4-8.** The rotated art image

INVERTING ART IMAGES To reverse the black-and-white image to its negative form, select Invert from the Art pull-down menu. There is no speed key for this. All of the selected art will be inverted. The inverted fishing image looks like this:

To return the image to its original form, select Invert once more.

Resizing an Image

You can expand or shrink any selected art image. This gives you flexibility while working in First Publisher. To resize the fishing image, follow these steps:

1. Select the entire fishing image.

2. Press (**ALT-R**) to select Resize from the Art menu. First Publisher will display four *handles* on each of the four corners of the image as shown here:

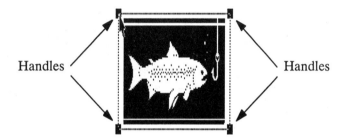

Handles   Handles

3. Move the mouse pointer to one of the four handles and either press and hold a mouse button or press (**F10**). The cursor can move in one of five directions; move left, right, up, down, or diagonally. As you do, you will see the handles move with the cursor. The dotted box changes to the new size of the image.

 You can simulate diagonal movement with a keyboard by pressing the four cursor movement keys to create a stair-stepping type of movement.

4. Let up on the button or press (**F10**) to see the fishing image redrawn to its new size.

5. Press (**ALT-R**) again to keep the image set at its new size. You could press (**ESC**) instead to return the image to its original state. As you can see from Figure 4-9, an image can be enlarged quite a bit.

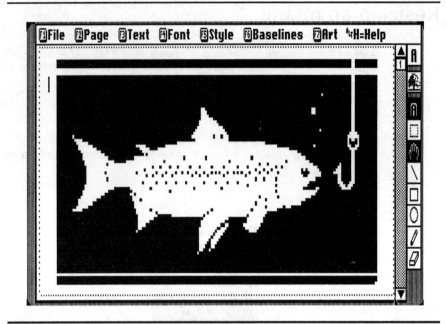

FIGURE 4-9. The expanded art image

DRAWING YOUR OWN IMAGES

The pencil tool is used for freehand drawing. When you select the pencil tool, shown just below the solid circle on the side tools, a pencil appears on the screen. You draw lines by moving the pencil. There are four line widths available. First Publisher helps you with a few standard drawing elements: straight lines, boxes, and circles.

Drawing with the Pencil

Drawing in the freehand style lets you create your own art images. You might want to draw your signature and put it into an .ART file for placement in later publications. Keep in mind that drawing with the pencil, whether or not you have a mouse, is tedious and takes practice.

To try freehand drawing, clear your current publication area (by selecting Start over from the File pull-down menu) and follow these steps:

1. Highlight the pencil tool. You will see the pencil in the center of the screen.

2. Move the pencil to its starting point with the mouse or with the arrow keys.

3. To draw, press and hold a mouse button. This places the pencil on the paper. Keyboard users should press (**F10**) once to do this.

4. Move the pencil with the mouse or with the arrow keys. The pencil is now touching the paper, and a line will follow as you move it. To pick up the pencil and move it without drawing, release the mouse button or press (**F10**) again. Continue drawing in this manner until the art is finished. Figure 4-10 shows an example freehand drawing that was produced with the pencil tool.

If you begin drawing when the pencil is over an existing line (the black part of an art image), a white line is drawn, in effect erasing the black line under the pencil. The next section shows an easier way to erase lines.

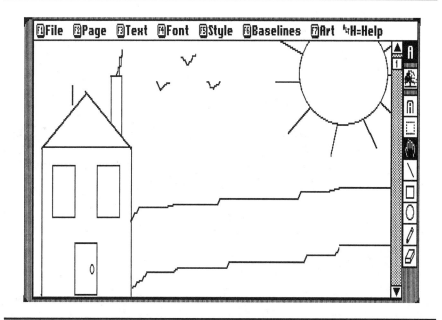

FIGURE 4-10. Sample freehand drawing

Mouse users may find it easier to cut corners and draw straight lines if they use keyboard commands for many of the drawing tasks.

CHANGING THE LINE THICKNESS   The lines you draw can be from one to four points wide. The four thickness selections appear when you select Set line width ((**ALT-HYPHEN**)) from the Art pull-down menu. The Set Line Width dialog box shown here will appear:

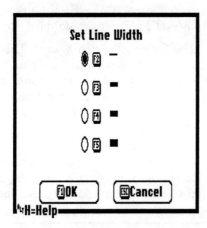

Note to Version 2 Users   After selecting the drawing pencil, you can change the thickness of the lines by either of the following methods:

- Point and click with the mouse over one of the line widths
- Press (**ALT-F9**)

   Each of these methods highlights the next line width. Changing the line width will not change the lines already on the screen. However, all new lines will be drawn with the new width. Figure 4-11 shows the preceding figure's art drawn with the thickest line width.

Erasing Art

You have learned how to erase using the Cut command. However, it is hard to touch up small portions of artwork by selecting and cutting. The eraser tool, the tool directly below the pencil, erases art on the art overlay. To erase lines, follow these steps:

1. Select the eraser tool. The eraser will appear on the screen.

2. Move the eraser over the area to be erased with the arrow keys or the mouse. The eraser will not erase as you move it.

3. To activate the eraser, press (**F10**) or press and hold a mouse button.

4. As you move the eraser across the screen, it will erase whatever art is underneath. You can always press (**F10**) or release the mouse button to move the eraser without erasing.

Drawing Straight Lines, Boxes, and Circles

The straight line tool draws a straight line between any two points you designate on the screen. The straight line tool is the diagonal line below the hand tool. Perfectly aligned boxes and rectangles are drawn with the box tool, the tool below the straight line tool. Boxes can be used to emphasize titles and important text. Circles and ovals are drawn with the circle tool below the box tool. Straight lines, boxes, and circles are drawn in whatever line thickness you have selected.

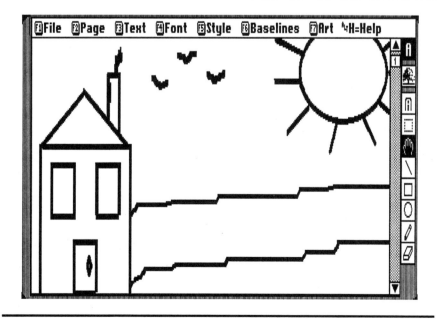

FIGURE 4-11. Using the 4-point drawing line width

To draw straight lines:

1. Select the straight line tool. You will see a cross on the screen.

2. Move the cross to the point where the straight line will begin.

3. Press and hold the mouse button, or press (F10) once to anchor the starting point of the straight line.

4. Move the cross with the mouse or arrow keys. As you do so, you will notice that a straight line follows the cross from the point where it was anchored. Figure 4-12 shows an anchored line being drawn.

5. The line will continue to follow the cross until you release the mouse button or press (F10). You can draw another line by repeating steps 2 through 5.

 Horizontal and vertical lines may print out with different widths even though the same line thickness is selected for both.

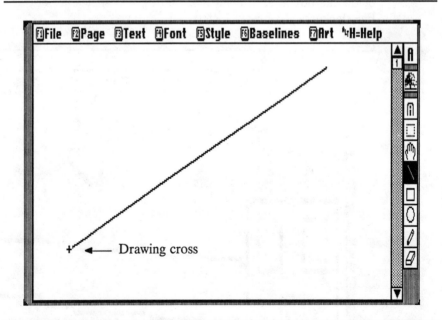

Drawing cross

FIGURE 4-12. Drawing a straight line

To draw boxes:

1. Select the box-drawing tool. You will see the cross on the screen.

2. Move the cross to the point where one of the four corners of the box is to begin.

3. Press and hold the mouse button or press (F10) once to anchor the starting point of the box.

4. Move the cross with the mouse or arrow keys. As you do, you will notice that the box follows the cross from the point at which it was anchored. The direction in which you move the cross dictates whether the box will be placed above, below, or to either side of the anchor point. An anchored box looks something like this:

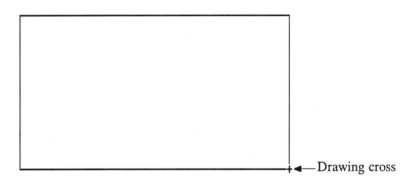
—Drawing cross

5. The box will continue to follow the cross until you release the mouse button or press (F10). You can draw another box by repeating steps 2 through 5.

To draw circles, follow the steps outlined above, only select the circle-drawing tool in step 1. The circle may not look perfect on the screen, but it will look better when printed.

 Do not add too many boxes, lines, and circles to your publication. Use them sparingly to accent titles and important text that is to stand out from the rest.

Editing Detailed Drawings

If you have been practicing freehand drawing, you have probably found out that erasing small portions of detailed images can be a very hard task. Luckily, First Publisher allows you to edit a close-up of your image and then view the entire image to see the results.

The fishing image you saved in its own .ART file has lots of dots along the side of the fish's body. If you wanted to erase them, you also might erase a part of the fish outline or one of its fins.

However, if you display a close-up view of the fishing image, the image grows to fill most of the screen. Use the Magnify option (**ALT-M**) from the Art pull-down menu to do this. You can then very easily and accurately edit the close-up view.

 Selecting the Magnify function will erase the art clipboard. Be sure to save the clipboard art, if you want it, before magnifying an image.

To edit the dots out of the fish's body, follow these steps:

1. Get the fish image from the FISH.ART file by selecting Get art from the Art pull-down menu.

2. Press **ALT-M** to select Magnify from the Art pull-down menu. You will see a magnifying glass like this on the screen:

3. Move the magnifying glass with the mouse or with the arrow keys, and click the mouse button. (Keyboard users will press **F10** twice.) First Publisher will display a magnified view of the art under the magnifying glass as shown in Figure 4-13. An editing pencil will appear with which you can edit the image. A smaller image of the magnified view appears in the upper-left corner so you can see the overall effects of changes made.

4. The list below summarizes the modifications you can make on the image:

Function	Procedure
Erase a dot	Place the pencil over the dot and click the mouse button (or **F10** twice).

Draw a dot   Position the pencil where you want the dot
                              and click the mouse button (or (F10) twice).

Erase multiple dots   Place the pencil over a dot you want to erase.
                              Press a mouse button and drag the mouse.
                              Keyboard users will press (F10)

                              followed by the arrow keys. Dots erase until
                              the mouse is released or (F10) is pressed
                              again.

Draw multiple dots   Position the pencil on the starting white
                              space, press a mouse button, and drag the
                              mouse. Keyboard users will press (F10)
                              once, then move the arrow keys. The drawing
                              stops when the mouse is released or (F10) is
                              pressed again.

Erase the dots in the body of the fish. As you do, you can see the overall
effect in the left corner's miniaturized image.

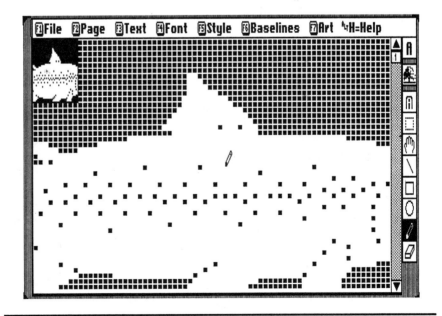

FIGURE 4-13. The magnified art image

5. Once all of the dots are erased, press (**ALT-M**) again to see the full view of the fishing image. The fish body is now clear, as shown here:

When in the magnified view, you cannot scroll the screen to see more of the image. First Publisher only magnifies one portion of the image at a time. To magnify another part of the image, you will have to move the magnifying glass and repeat the process.

Graphics Text

In Chapter 3, you saw several useful commands for manipulating text on the text overlay. Unfortunately, you cannot do things like inverting, resizing, and rotating on the text overlay.

There is, however, a way to place text on the art overlay. When you do, all of the art commands are available, but you lose the ability to use text commands (editing with (**DEL**) and (**BACKSPACE**), inserting the text between existing text, changing fonts and typestyles, and word-wrapping to succeeding lines). If you need inverted text for a banner, or rotated text for emphasis, you must type graphics text.

To type graphics text, make sure the graphics text tool is highlighted. This is the letter *A*, the second one of the side tools. Once the text tool is active, you can use the keyboard to "draw" any characters needed onto the art overlay. To practice with graphics art, perform the following steps:

1. Clear the publication work area by selecting Start over from the File pull-down menu. Do not be concerned about saving the current work you have been editing.

2. Select the graphics text tool.

3. Move the mouse cursor to the upper-center of the screen and click a button. Keyboard users can use the arrow keys and (**SHIFT-ARROW**) keys followed by (**F10**).

4. Press (**F4**) to display the Fonts pull-down menu. You cannot change the font or style of graphics characters after they are typed; therefore, you need to select the proper font before typing the character. Select the New York font.

5. Press (**F5**) to display the Style pull-down menu. Select Bold if it is not already selected, and press (**ENTER**). You then must press (**F5**) again to select a different point size. Select 24 points to increase the font size.

6. Type **Artful Text** and press (**ENTER**). From now on, the usual text-editing keys, such as (**BACKSPACE**) and (**DEL**), will not work on the text.

 The (**BACKSPACE**) key will work immediately after typing graphics text, as long as the cursor is still on the same line as the text. Once (**ENTER**) is pressed, (**BACKSPACE**) is inactive for graphics text.

7. Select the entire text with the art dotted box tool.

8. Press (**ALT-0**) twice to turn the graphics text upside down.

9. Select Invert from the Art pull-down menu. Since the graphics text is still selected, the entire image will be inverted, and will look similar to this:

Graphics text

 As you will see when you create fliers and newsletters in later chapters, you can save a graphics text heading with bordered banners (these make excellent letterheads) in an .ART file to place at the top of future publications.

COMBINING TEXT AND ART

Now that you have practiced manipulating both the text and standard art overlays separately, you are ready to combine the fishing art image and the Cape Cod COD text into a single publication. To get you started, follow these steps to load the text:

1. Select Start over from the File pull-down menu. If First Publisher displays a Save filename prompt, press (**F2**) to ignore the request.

2. Select Get publication from the File pull-down menu by pressing
   ALT-G.

3. Select the JAMIE.PUB file, or type **JAMIE.PUB** at the File List screen
   and press **ENTER**. After a brief pause, the text file will appear within
   the work area.

4. Make room for the fishing image by placing the cursor in the blank space
   before Cape Cod COD and pressing **ENTER** four times. Figure 4-14
   shows the screen at this point.

It is now time to load and place the fishing image. As soon as you get the
art, the art overlay will activate and the text will become gray to let you know
that it is not affected by the art manipulation. To see this:

1. Press **F7** to display the Art pull-down menu.

2. Select Get art from the menu.

3. Select the FISH.ART file or type **FISH.ART**. As soon as you do, the text
   will become gray and the hand tool will appear. Figure 4-15 shows the
   screen at this point.

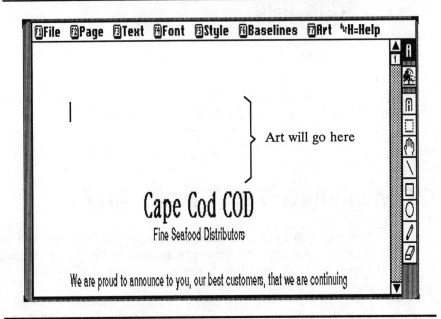

FIGURE 4-14. Before inserting the art image

4. Position the hand tool at the blank space before the first paragraph and press (**F10**) or click the mouse button to place the image. While in the standard art overlay, you can move the image until it is placed exactly where you want it.

5. To activate the text overlay and see the combined art and text, select the top text tool by clicking with the mouse or by pressing (**SHIFT-F9**). Figure 4-16 shows how the screen should look after you do so.

6. Save the publication by pressing (**ALT-S**) followed by (**F1**) to accept the default JAMIE filename. It will have the extension .PUB, as indicated by the format at the right of the Save Filename screen. You will see the message:

   The file "jamie.pub" already exists. Do you want to replace it?

   Answer with a press of (**F1**) for "yes" to replace the old publication with the new one you just created.

The next two chapters will use this file to illustrate other features of First Publisher. You might think that all of the art manipulation practice was a tedious build-up to this relatively simple publication. Keep in mind that text and art manipulation skills are vital; many of them will become second

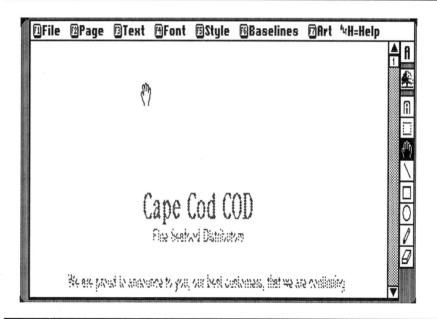

FIGURE 4-15. The text overlay is inactive

FIGURE 4-16. The final publication with text and art

nature as you create more involved publications. Once you learn about printing in Chapter 5 and layout skills in Chapter 6, you will be ready to start producing more advanced publications. The second part of this book devotes entire chapters to various types of advanced publications.

HIGH-RESOLUTION ART

First Publisher version 3 users will appreciate the high-resolution clip art that comes with First Publisher. High-resolution art prints up to 300 dots per inch, depending on the source of the art. If you import art into First Publisher (described in later sections of this chapter) at a resolution higher than 72 dots per inch, First Publisher will treat it as high-resolution art.

All high-resolution art is manipulated on the high-resolution art overlay. As with the text and standard art overlays, all placement and editing of high-resolution art will not affect the other two overlays.

The high-resolution art overlay is active when the high-resolution side tool is highlighted. This is the second side tool, which looks like a tree. All editing features of the Art pull-down menu except Magnify work with high-resolution art just as they do with standard art. You can only magnify art on the standard art overlay. There is an additional option on the Art pull-down menu, *Crop,* that does not work with standard art but does with high-resolution art images.

 You cannot draw lines, boxes, or circles, or erase high-resolution art with the side tools. You cannot create high-resolution art with First Publisher. You can only retrieve and crop high-resolution art from those images supplied with First Publisher or import other graphics.

Getting High-Resolution Art

To practice working with high-resolution art, load the BABY.ART file, one of the 20 high-resolution images supplied with First Publisher.

1. Select Start over from the File pull-down menu to clear your current work area.

2. Select Get art from the Art pull-down menu.

3. Type **BABY.ART** and press (ENTER) to load the image from disk. First Publisher acknowledges that the image is high-resolution art by displaying the following message while loading the image:

    Please stand by. Getting High-resolution art. . .

4. After a pause, the hand symbol will appear and you can place the baby image by pressing (F10) or clicking the mouse. The following baby image will appear on the screen:

Art you save from the .MAC clip art files supplied with First Publisher is always stored as standard art at 72 dots per inch.

SPECIFYING THE RESOLUTION OF ART If you get art that was imported or scanned from a source other than First Publisher, you will see the following resolution dialog box:

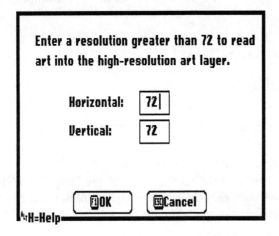

Art images with a filename extension other than .ART or .MAC will produce this dialog box when retrieved. Since First Publisher has never worked with the file, it needs to know the horizontal and vertical resolution (the number of dots per inch) that the image was first saved in.

If you want the art treated as standard art, type **72** for both horizontal and vertical resolution. Any number lower than 72 brings the art into First Publisher at a lower resolution and larger size than it was created in. If you type a number larger than 72, First Publisher will treat it as a high-resolution art image. Once you save the image to an .ART file, First Publisher will not need to know the resolution again.

Try to specify the same horizontal and vertical resolution that the image was created with. You may have to check the program that created the graphic image, or check the scanner manual used to scan the art. Later sections in this chapter describe getting art from sources other than First Publisher.

CROPPING HIGH-RESOLUTION ART Although you can't use the eraser tool to remove sections of high-resolution art, you can trim around the sides of high-resolution art by selecting Crop from the Art pull-down menu. (**ALT-K**) is the speed key for Crop. Cropping lets you slice off sides of a high-resolution art image so text can flow closer to the art, and allows you to use only portions of a high-resolution art image if you wish. To crop the baby image:

1. Press (**ALT-K**) to select Crop from the Art pull-down menu. Four handles will appear, one at each corner of the selected image.
2. Move the pointer to one of the corners and click the mouse button or press (**F10**).
3. Move the corner you selected away from the image to add white space or into the figure to trim off white space. Release the mouse button or press (**F10**) to end the cropping. When you do, the image will be cropped. Here is an example of a cropped baby image.

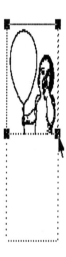

4. If you want to change your mind, you can press (**ESC**) to return the image to its original size. Otherwise, press (**ALT-K**) again to okay the cropping.

First Publisher still remembers the original image after it is cropped. If you select Crop again and crop in the opposite direction, the original image will return. You can save the cropped high-resolution art image to an .ART file.

IMPORTING ART

First Publisher comes with a rich assortment of .ART and .MAC files, and more are available from the Software Publishing Corporation. You can find a copy of these in Appendix C. If you have been using one of the following programs, you can import art files saved with them:

PC Paint Plus	PC Paintbrush
Microsoft Windows Paint (except version 2)	Logipaint
Publisher's Paintbrush	MacPaint (version 1.5)
Paintshow Plus	Microsoft Paintbrush

If you use a program other than one listed above, you can import art images as long as the filename extension is one of the following:

.ART .MAC .MSP .PCX .PIC .TIF

Use the Get art option of the Art pull-down menu to retrieve these files in the same way that you would get .ART files. Although you can load image files from these programs into First Publisher, you cannot save First Publisher artwork into images that these programs can directly read.

Importing with SNAPSHOT

First Publisher supplies a way to import art from program formats not listed above. By using two external programs called SNAPSHOT and SNAP2ART that come with First Publisher, you can capture other program screens into .ART files.

Here are the basic steps for creating .ART files from other program screens:

1. You first run SNAPSHOT from the DOS prompt.

2. Start the program whose screen you want to capture.

3. When the image you want to capture appears on the screen, you take a "snapshot" of it with the SNAPSHOT key combination (`SHIFT-PRTSC`).

Even though you are in another program, the SNAPSHOT program will activate.

4. After exiting to DOS, you run SNAP2ART to convert that captured image into an .ART file that you can retrieve from First Publisher.

STARTING SNAPSHOT   To prepare your system for capturing screens, you must load the SNAPSHOT program into memory from the DOS prompt. After doing this, your computer will function as though SNAPSHOT were not there. SNAPSHOT is hidden from view (called *resident in memory*) and will remain in the background until you request it.

To load the SNAPSHOT program:

1. At the DOS prompt, change to the First Publisher directory by typing **CD\PUB** and pressing (**ENTER**). If you stored First Publisher in a directory other than PUB, type that directory's name.

2. Type **snapshot** (in uppercase or lowercase letters) and press (**ENTER**). You should see the SNAPSHOT startup message shown here:

```
C:\PUB>snapshot
Snapshot program version 1.3
Copyright 1987, 1988 Software Publishing Corporation
Press [Shift-PrtSc] to take a snapshot.
Use SNAP2ART program to create .Art file from snapshot.
C:\PUB>
```

SNAPSHOT is now loaded and ready for use.

CAPTURING THE ART   First, start the program that will produce the graphic image you want to import into First Publisher. Even if you do not have another graphics program, you can still try SNAPSHOT by taking a picture of a First Publisher screen. All of the First Publisher screens are graphics-oriented and work nicely with SNAPSHOT.

Follow these steps:

1. Start First Publisher as usual.

2. When the publication screen is displayed, press (**SHIFT-PRTSC**). You should hear a beeping sound informing you that SNAPSHOT successfully took a picture. If instead of a beep you hear a low buzz for about a second, SNAPSHOT failed the screen capture. If you have a Hercules graphics card, see the Note below. Other than the special situation with

the Hercules card, SNAPSHOT can take pictures of IBM-compatible graphics screens only.

3. Exit First Publisher and return to the DOS prompt.

 If you have a Hercules card and the SNAPSHOT image does not get saved properly, start the SNAPSHOT program by typing **SNAPSHOT 1** at the DOS prompt, instead of **SNAPSHOT**.

CONVERTING THE PICTURE TO AN .ART FILE In the exercise in the last section, SNAPSHOT saved the screen in a graphics file. Since that type of file is not in a format compatible with .ART files, you must run the SNAP2ART program to convert the file to an art file. To do so:

1. Change to the First Publisher directory, if you need to, by typing **CD\PUB**.

2. Type **SNAP2ART** (in uppercase or lowercase characters) and press ENTER. You will see the saved screen, as shown in Figure 4-17, with a help banner across the middle.

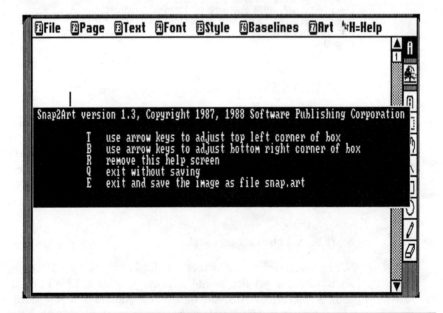

FIGURE 4-17. Getting ready to save the SNAP2ART image

3. Type **r** to get rid of the help banner.

4. Type **e** to convert the image to the .ART format and save the file. (If, at this point, you do not want to save the file, type **q** to leave the program.) You will see the following message at the DOS prompt:

   Wrote the snapshot file to snap.art.

You should now unload SNAPSHOT from memory before running First Publisher. To do so, type **snapshot u** at the DOS prompt and press ⌈ENTER⌉. This will free up the memory used by SNAPSHOT. Do the following to load the saved art image:

1. Start First Publisher.

2. At the blank publication screen, select Get art and load SNAP.ART—the name of the file you created with SNAP2ART.

3. After placing the art, your screen will be similar to that in Figure 4-18. There is a First Publisher screen inside of First Publisher! You can treat

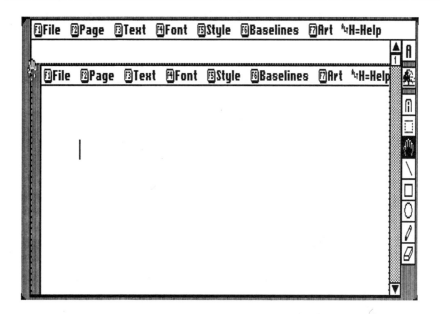

FIGURE 4-18.   After the placement of the SNAP2ART image

it like any other art. Figure 4-19 shows the art resized and placed in the middle of the work area.

If SNAP2ART finds a file with the name SNAP.ART, it will refuse to overwrite it. If you want to save more than one SNAP2ART file on disk, you must use a filename other than SNAP.ART. You can follow the SNAP2ART command with a filename to save the image in a file other than SNAP.ART. For instance, you would type **snap2art logo** to save the image in a file called LOGO.ART.

If the black-and-white images do not seem to be correct when the art is placed in your publication, you may have to invert the image. This is due to First Publisher's attempt to handle color screen captures properly.

If you get the message,

The video mode of the current snapshot is not supported by SNAP2ART

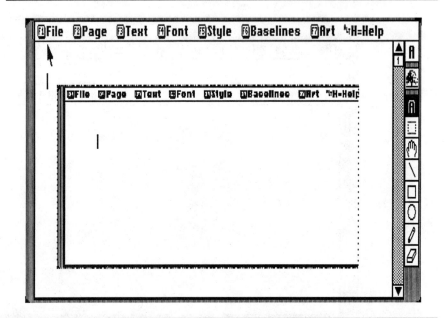

FIGURE 4-19. Resizing the SNAPSHOT art image

you must set the video mode to graphics by using the DOS MODE command. Consult your DOS reference manual for details.

 Files saved with SNAPSHOT will be in the standard art resolution, 72 dots per inch. You cannot create high-resolution art files with SNAPSHOT.

OTHER SNAP2ART OPTIONS   There are other tasks you can perform from the SNAP2ART screen, as listed in the help banner you get when you start the program. You can save a portion of the screen by cropping the picture.

When you start SNAP2ART and see the help banner, you can see that the T and B options adjust the top and bottom cropping of an image before saving it. For instance, suppose you only wanted to save the side tools from the First Publisher screen. You would use SNAPSHOT to take a picture of the entire screen. After loading SNAP2ART, you would crop that image down to include only the side tools, as shown below:

1. Once SNAP2ART is running and you see the help banner, type **r** to remove the help. You will see a flashing border around the image. This border fences what will eventually be saved.

2. Type **b** to start cropping off the bottom of the image. The B option controls the cropping of the bottom and right sides of the image. Press (UP ARROW) and (RIGHT ARROW) several times until the bottom of the border is just under the side tools, and the right border includes the side tools as well, as shown in Figure 4-20. The message below the lower-left corner of the border tells you that typing **?** will bring back the help banner.

3. Type **t** to begin cropping the top and left sides of the screen. Press (DOWN ARROW) and (RIGHT ARROW) until the side tools are completely enclosed in the flashing banner.

4. Type **e** to save the cropped image and exit SNAP2ART.

If you then loaded SNAP.ART into a publication, you would only see the side tools in the work area, not the entire Publication screen, as shown in Figure 4-21.

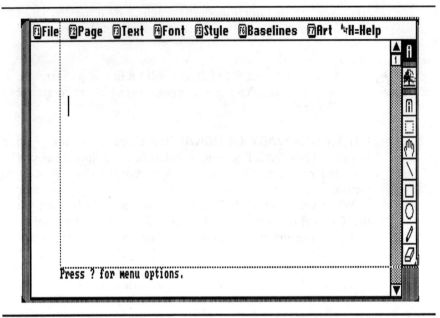

FIGURE 4-20. Cropping the SNAP2ART art image

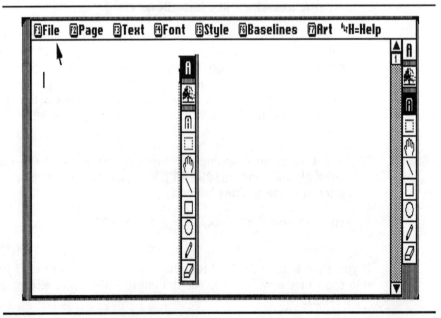

FIGURE 4-21. Bringing the cropped image into First Publisher

CHANGING THE SNAPSHOT ACTIVATE KEY   If you do not want to use the (SHIFT-PRTSC) key combination for the SNAPSHOT activation key (called the *hot key*), you can change it by following these steps:

1. Instead of typing **SNAPSHOT** at the DOS prompt, type **SNAPSHOT K** and press (ENTER). You are informing SNAPSHOT that you want to change the hot key. (Hercules users may have to type **SNAPSHOT K1**.)

2. Press the key you want to use when SNAPSHOT gives you this prompt:

    Please press the key you want to use as your hot key:

    Some choose to use an (ALT)-function key combination, such as (ALT-F1). Select a key that is not typically used by other programs.

After you change the hot key, SNAPSHOT will be resident. You can then take snapshots of screens with the new hot key combination. The hot key will stay the same unless you change it.

Importing Scanner Images

Any scanner that can produce graphic images for First Publisher-compatible file formats (listed earlier in the section called "Importing Art") can scan images for First Publisher. The art can be at a resolution as high as 300 dots per inch; however, you cannot edit art greater than 72 dots per inch within First Publisher. You must edit the image before scanning it to a First Publisher art file. You can scan printed art and then transfer that scanned image to your publication. Follow the instructions that came with your scanner for scanning and cropping the image you want.

After scanning the image, instruct the scanner software to convert your image to one of the file types compatible with First Publisher. Select Get art from the Art pull-down menu to load the file and convert it to an .ART file with Save art.

Note to Version 2 Users   You will have to treat scanned art as if it were a .MAC file. Select Get graphics from the File pull-down menu and convert the image to an .ART file with Save art.

Summary

In this chapter you learned how to

- Differentiate between standard art and high-resolution art files

- Save selected images from the various clip art files supplied with First Publisher

- Load art images into a publication and move, resize, copy, delete, and invert them

- Use the freehand drawing tools supplied with First Publisher, including the pencil and eraser, and the line-, box-, and circle-drawing tools

- Choose one of the four line widths available when freehand drawing

- Magnify standard art images to edit the art with a close-up view

- Type text using the graphics text tool so that you may apply all standard art editing tools to the text

- Get, load, edit, and crop high-resolution art images that print at a much higher resolution (up to 300 dots per inch) on the printer than standard art images

- Import art from other graphics programs whose file formats are consistent with those required by First Publisher

- Use the SNAPSHOT memory resident program supplied with First Publisher to capture art images from programs whose art files are not compatible with First Publisher's

PRINTING YOUR PUBLICATION

Previewing Your Publication
Printing Basics

Without the ability to print your publication, you would have little use for First Publisher. Fortunately, First Publisher supports many printers, including laser printers and dot-matrix printers. The final publication can be printed in a quick-speed draft mode or in a slower but higher-quality smoothed mode.

Since you cannot see the entire publication on your screen before you print, First Publisher offers a preview mode. With preview, you can see a thumbnail sketch showing you the overall appearance of the publication's margins and layouts. Preview is sometimes called the WYSIWYG ("What You See Is What You Get") feature of First Publisher.

If you want to send the printer output to a disk file to be printed later, you may do so. This works well for companies with several PCs and only a single laser printer. Each individual workstation PC can produce ready-to-print publications and take the disk files to the PC that is hooked to the printer.

PREVIEWING YOUR PUBLICATION

Figure 5-1 shows the top half of a publication, Figure 5-2 the bottom half. Both of these screens, like most screens in this book, are displayed from a CGA graphics card. VGA graphics adapter card users can see more of a publication at any one time. No matter which graphics card you have, you cannot see the entire publication on the screen.

Therefore, in order to see your publication in its final form, you must print it. There are three printing speeds, but even the fastest takes time and paper. Through the preview mode, you can get an idea of your publication's final appearance before printing.

 First Publisher versions 2.1 and below can only print to 8 1/2-by-11-inch paper in the portrait mode. Portrait mode prints the page 11 inches high and 8 1/2 inches wide.

Elevator at top

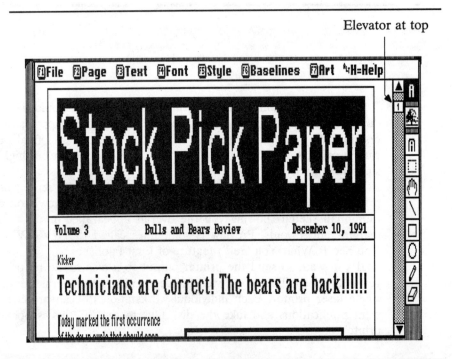

FIGURE 5-1.   Top half of a publication

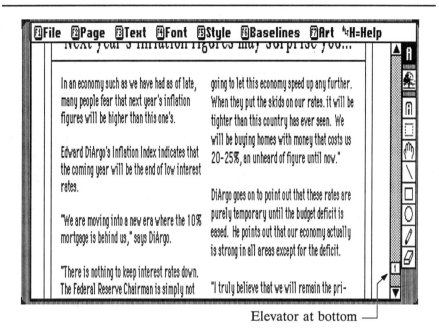

In an economy such as we have had as of late, many people fear that next year's inflation figures will be higher than this one's.

Edward DiArgo's Inflation Index indicates that the coming year will be the end of low interest rates.

"We are moving into a new era where the 10% mortgage is behind us," says DiArgo.

"There is nothing to keep interest rates down. The Federal Reserve Chairman is simply not

going to let this economy speed up any further. When they put the skids on our rates. it will be tighter than this country has ever seen. We will be buying homes with money that costs us 20-25%, an unheard of figure until now."

DiArgo goes on to point out that these rates are purely temporary until the budget deficit is eased. He points out that our economy actually is strong in all areas except for the deficit.

"I truly believe that we will remain the pri-

Elevator at bottom

FIGURE 5-2. Bottom half of a publication

Displaying the Preview

The speed key for previewing a document is (**ALT-Z**). This key combination selects the Show page option from the Page pull-down menu. Figure 5-3 shows the previous two figures together. As you can see, the text is not clear, but at least you can get an idea of what the final publication will look like before printing it. In the next sections, you will send JAMIE.PUB to the printer. Follow the steps below to preview the publication:

1. Load the publication by pressing (**ALT-G**) and selecting JAMIE.PUB.

2. After the publication is displayed, press (**ALT-Z**). You will see a preview of JAMIE.PUB like the one shown in Figure 5-4.

3. Press (**ALT-Z**) or (**ESC**) to return the screen to its normal display mode. Keep JAMIE.PUB loaded in memory for the next section.

FIGURE 5-3. Previewing the entire publication

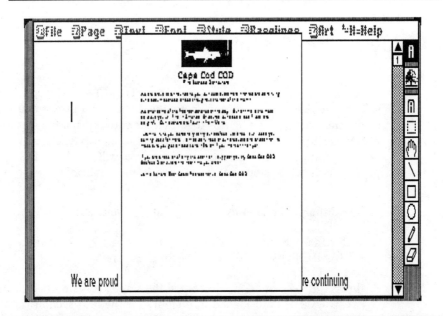

FIGURE 5-4. Previewing the sample publication

PRINTING BASICS

Make sure that you have selected a printer by completing all of the instructions in Appendix A, "Installing First Publisher." When selecting the printer, you also select the print scaling and the printer port, which become the program default printing selections. You can easily change the defaults when you print.

Printing Your Sample Publication

Before looking at the print options, print out your sample publication using all of the printing defaults. To print, follow these steps:

1. Press (**ALT-P**) to select Print from the File pull-down menu. You will see the Print options screen shown here:

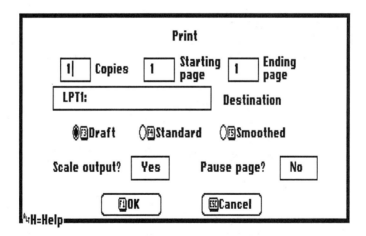

2. Make sure your printer is turned on, is on-line, and has paper. On some computers, your machine will freeze up if you print to a nonexistent or powered-off printer.

3. To print your publication, press (**F1**) to select OK from the Print options

screen. Your publication will then print. If you print in the smoothed mode, your output will be similar to that in Figure 5-5.

Changing the Print Options

There are eight options available from the Print options screen.

COPIES   By typing a number other than 1, you can print more than a single copy of your publication. If you need multiple copies, it may be faster to print one and copy it several times with a copy machine.

   If you have a laser printer, you will find that each copy after the first one prints rapidly.

PRINTING SELECTED PAGES   When you create multiple-page publications you can print the entire publication or only a portion of it. The pages to be printed are selected at the Starting page and Ending page prompts. The default for Starting page is 1, the first page of your publication. The default for Ending page is the last page number of your publication. Since JAMIE.PUB is only a single page, it starts and ends on page 1.

If you had a 20-page publication and only wanted to print pages 12 through 14, you would type a starting page number of **12** and an ending page number of **14**.

THE OUTPUT DESTINATION   Whatever port you selected when you installed First Publisher will be the default port after the Destination prompt. Usually this is LPT1: (also referred to as PRN: in DOS). The Status (ALT-I) screen will inform you of the default port. If you want to override the default printer port, type a new one, such as **LPT2:**.

   If you have two printers connected to your system, select the most-used one as your default printer when installing First Publisher. When you want to print to the other one, type the name of the second printer port at the Destination prompt. The next time you try to print in First Publisher, the default port will reappear.

If you have a serial printer, its port must be initialized from DOS with the MODE command. You may have to check your printer manual and the DOS reference manual for help with the MODE command.

Cape Cod COD
Fine Seafood Distributors

We are proud to announce to you, our best customers, that we are continuing our discount seafood prices throughout the rest of this month.

We offer some of the freshest catches of the day. Our shrimp is the most delicious you will find in America. Of course, our special cod fillets are delightful. Our lobsters are flown in from Maine.

I want to invite you personally to try our seafood just once. It will keep you coming back for more. I am so convinced of our products and prices that I will make sure you get an additional 15% off if you mention this flyer.

If you are a reseller of only the best fish, I suggest you try Cape Cod COD Seafood Distributors the next time you order.

Jamie Somers, East Coast Representative, Cape Cod COD

FIGURE 5-5. Output from printing JAMIE.PUB

You can also save a printed image to a disk file. The disk file is an exact image of the commands and characters sent to your printer. You cannot view the disk file on the screen; however, you can print the file later since it is a print file. The PRINT command will print the file.

Type the disk filename at the Destination prompt if you want to print to a file. For instance, the following Print options screen,

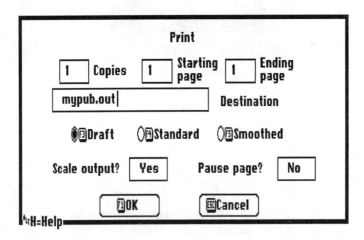

will send the publication to a file called MYPUB.OUT located in the PUB subdirectory on the disk drive C. You may send the file to the printer with the following PRINT command from the DOS prompt:

PRINT MYPUB.PUB

If you are unfamiliar with the DOS PRINT command, consult your operating system reference manual. You may find that only a smoothed publication will print properly.

If you work in a department with many computers, you can send the output to a floppy disk file, take that disk to another computer, and print it there. You *cannot* copy the First Publisher disks for use on more than one computer unless you are licensed to do so. However, you can print the document on other systems. This might be helpful if you have First Publisher at home and your office computer has a laser printer. You can output the publication to a disk file at home, and then print it at work, even if there is no First Publisher program at work.

When you create the disk file, be sure that First Publisher is set up to print to the final printer you will use. If First Publisher is set up to print to a dot-matrix printer and you send output to a disk file that will be printed on a laser printer, your output will be incorrect. (The format of the disk file will be in the printer's description language.)

 If you have several publications to print, print them to disk files. You then can use the PRINT command to queue them up for printing all at once. This frees up your computer for other uses during printing.

DRAFT, STANDARD, AND SMOOTHED MODES   The three separate print modes—draft, standard, and smoothed—each output the publication at different qualities and printing speeds. The draft mode (F3) prints quickly, but the quality is not as good as what you get with the other two modes. Use draft mode in the early stages of the publication, when you will not be concerned with printing in the highest quality possible, but may want to print the publication to see how it is laid out on the page. Figure 5-6 shows a publication output in draft mode.

The draft mode distorts small font sizes more than large ones. If you print a publication in smoothed mode (F5), the output will take longer, but the print resolution and clarity will be improved. Figure 5-7 shows an output of the same publication printed in smoothed mode.

The standard mode (F4) is an alternative to the smoothed mode. Sometimes smoothing affects the results of printing, and the standard mode gives better output. You will have to experiment to see how smoothing works on your machine.

If you use a laser printer (except an Apple LaserWriter or Apple Laser-Writer Plus) you will see the titles Draft, 150 DPI, and 300 DPI in place of Draft, Standard, and Smoothed. This more accurately describes the 150- and 300-dots-per-inch resolution available on these printers.

SCALING OUTPUT   The following printers do not use the scaled printing option:

- Apple LaserWriter

- Apple LaserWriter Plus

- Non-IBM compatible Okidata 92, 93, 182, 183, 192, 193, 292, 293, and 294

- Texas Instruments 855, 857

If you have one of these printers, you do not need to be concerned with scaled printing. However, if your First Publisher system is using a different printer, you have the option of printing scaled or unscaled images.

Stock Pick Paper

Things Could Look Better

Technicians are Correct! The Bears are Back!!!

Today marked the first occurrence of the down cycle that should span several years. The bears, primarily made up of stock technicians, have accurately predicted this fall in the financial markets. To the dismay of many investors, it looks as though the bears have taken the bull by the horns.

We are witnessing an increased move away from the financial markets toward the more stable cash positions. It is predicted that interest rates are going to sky-rocket; hence, the move to cash positions.

"I have been looking for this for some time now," says a vice president from a leading brokerage house. "I do not know if we have totally gone 100% cash, however, I do know that my firm has been thinking cash for around

Your city's lights may dim due to the economy

three months."

In another interview, Victor Young said that he does not believe the market has attained its highest peak. He believes that the majority is now right for the first time that any of us can remember. Mr. Young said he has

discussed these matters with Mr. Michael Stapp who had the following comments:

"Don't look at the past. The past does not ensure future sucess or failure."

Young believes that Stapp is going to the (see page 2)

Next Year's Inflation Figures Are Surprising

In an economy such as we have had as of late, many people fear that next year's inflation figures will be higher than this one's.

Edward DiArgo's inflation index indicates that the coming year will be the end of low interest rates.

"We are moving into a new era where the 10% mortgage is behind us," says DiArgo.

"There is nothing to keep interest rates down. The Federal Reserve Chairman is simply not

going to let this economy speed up any further. When they put the skids on our rates, it will be tighter than this country has ever seen. We will be buying homes with money that costs us 20-25%, an unheard of figure until now."

DiArgo goes on to point out that these rates are purely temporary until the budget deficit is eased. He points out that our economy actually is strong in all areas except for the deficit. When next month's rates are posted from the second quarter, you will find (see page 3)

FIGURE 5-6. Output from the draft mode

Stock Pick Paper

Things Could Look Better

Technicians are Correct! The Bears are Back!!!

Today marked the first occurrence of the down cycle that should span several years. The bears, primarily made up of stock technicians, have accurately predicted this fall in the financial markets. To the dismay of many investors, it looks as though the bears have taken the bull by the horns.

We are witnessing an increased move away from the financial markets toward the more stable cash positions. It is predicted that interest rates are going to sky-rocket; hence, the move to cash positions.

"I have been looking for this for some time now," says a vice president from a leading brokerage house. "I do not know if we have totally gone 100% cash, however, I do know that my firm has been thinking cash for around

Your city's lights may dim due to the economy

three months."

In another interview, Victor Young said that he does not believe the market has attained its highest peak. He believes that the majority is now right for the first time that any of us can remember. Mr.Young said he has

discussed these matters with Mr. Michael Stapp who had the following comments:

"Don't look at the past. The past does not ensure future success or failure."

Young believes that Stapp is going to the (see page 2)

Next Year's Inflation Figures Are Surprising

In an economy such as we have had as of late, many people fear that next year's inflation figures will be higher than this one's.

Edward DiArgo's inflation index indicates that the coming year will be the end of low interest rates.

"We are moving into a new era where the 10% mortgage is behind us," says DiArgo.

"There is nothing to keep interest rates down. The Federal Reserve Chairman is simply not

going to let this economy speed up any further. When they put the skids on our rates, it will be tighter than this country has ever seen. We will be buying homes with money that costs us 20-25%, an unheard of figure until now."

DiArgo goes on to point out that these rates are purely temporary until the budget deficit is eased. He points out that our economy actually is strong in all areas except for the deficit. When next month's rates are posted from the second quarter, you will find that all leading indicators are actually (see page 3)

FIGURE 5-7. Output from the smoothed mode

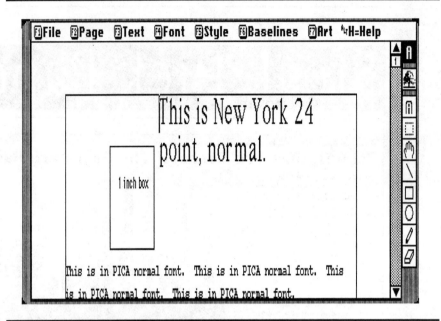

FIGURE 5-8. Looking at the TESTPRNT publication

You should check whether or not you want scaled printing before creating any publications. The difference between scaled and unscaled is small, but it could become critical if you are printing a lot of small text within your publication.

First Publisher includes a file called TESTPRNT.PUB that you can use to see if you should select scaled or unscaled mode. To test for scaling, perform the following steps:

1. Load TESTPRNT.PUB by pressing **ALT-G** and typing the filename. You should see the publication screen shown in Figure 5-8. (If you do not see this screen, insert the Art disk supplied with First Publisher in a floppy disk drive, and then type the drive name followed by **TESTPRNT .PUB**.)

2. Press **ALT-P** to select Print from the File pull-down menu.

3. Accept the default scaled output and press **F1** to print.

4. Repeat steps 2 and 3, only type **No** at the Scale output prompt if it was "Yes" before, or type **Yes** if it was "No."

Compare the results to the screen's appearance. When output is scaled, it sometimes matches the screen's appearance more closely than when it is not scaled. However, scaled printing takes more time to print.

PAUSE FOR NEW PAGE   If you feed individual sheets of paper to your printer as it prints, type **Yes** at the Pause page? prompt. For multiple-page publications, First Publisher will then pause at the end of each page, giving you a chance to insert a new piece of paper before the printing resumes. When you put each new sheet in, you must press (**F1**) to inform First Publisher that it should continue printing.

THE SCALED FONT DIALOG BOX   If you are printing with soft fonts or scaled fonts in standard or smoothed mode, First Publisher displays a Scaled font dialog box asking for the disk path that holds the soft font files, as shown here:

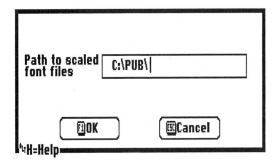

Usually this disk path is the PUB subdirectory, where First Publisher resides. Type the name of the path where the scaled fonts are located if it is not already displayed, and press (**F1**) to begin the printing.

Summary

In this chapter you learned how to

- Preview the printed publication on the screen before you print it, to save time and paper
- Choose among the many options available from the Print pull-down menu, such as number of copies, print quality, and printer destination
- Send a printed image of your publication to a disk to be printed on another computer or at a later time

chapter 6

THE PUBLICATION LAYOUT

Baselines
Adjusting the Sample Publication
Art Layout Help

N ow that you have mastered text and art placement, you can produce professional publications by learning the layout techniques available in First Publisher. This chapter walks you through the fine-tuning of publications by showing you some spacing concepts and multiple-column text layout tips.

The most important concept of the chapter involves using baselines to place text exactly where you want it to go. Baselines control multiple columns and spacing between lines of the text. With proper baseline usage, you can instruct First Publisher to automatically wrap text around a piece of art. Beginning with version 3.0, users will not have to specifically define all elements of the page such as the number of columns and their locations. Version 3.0 adds the capability of selecting from a predefined set of layouts.

Since this is a book from the "Made Easy" series, you will not get a lot of theory on baseline and layout usage. Rather, you will immediately walk through several hands-on examples that adjust the sample publication using available layout tools. The second part of this book takes what you learn here and expands on the concept of developing the layout as you create the publication.

BASELINES

Baselines are lines that your text rests upon. They are usually invisible, although you can display them when you want to work with them. Figure 6-1 shows you various baselines that are possible with First Publisher. (When creating multiple-column publications, you must first set the number of columns with the Page pull-down menu, as explained below.)

These baselines always exist, whether they are visible or not, on the text overlay. You can see the baselines for the sample JAMIE.PUB you created earlier by following these steps:

1. Load JAMIE.PUB, if you have not already done so, by pressing (ALT-G) to select Get publication from the File pull-down menu.

2. Press (F6) to display the Baselines pull-down menu. It looks like this:

3. Press (DOWN ARROW) to select Adjust single from the Baselines menu. You can press (ALT-A) to select Adjust single without using the menu. As soon as you do, your screen will look like Figure 6-2. Notice how the text slightly fades to highlight the baselines that appear. The baseline positioning has nothing to do with the art, only the text.

 Any graphics text in your publication will not fade, since all graphics text lies on the art overlay.

Selecting any of the first four Baselines options will cause the baselines to appear. Selecting any of them again will hide the baselines. For now, press (ALT-A) to hide the publication baselines on your screen.

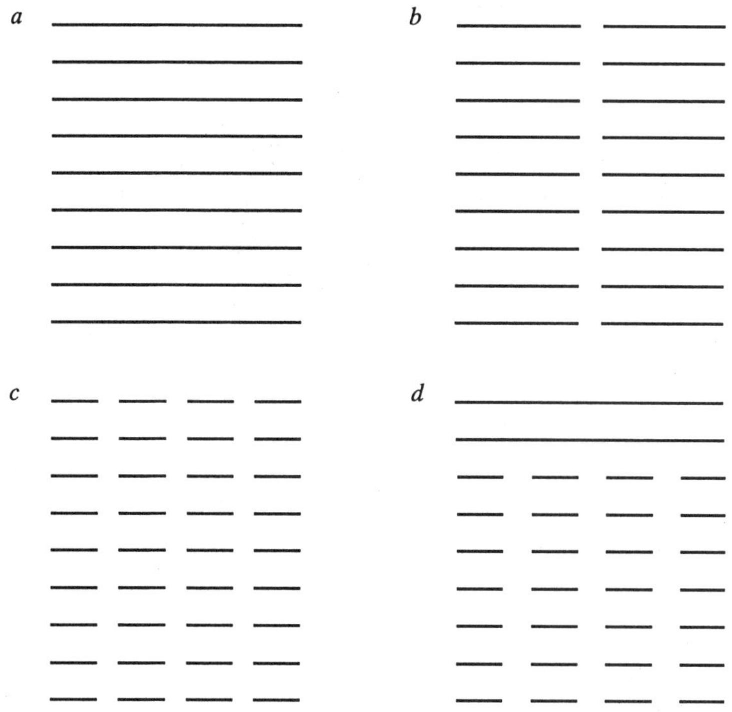

FIGURE 6-1. Examples of publications with single-column baselines (*a*), two-column baselines (*b*), four-column baselines (*c*), and varying multiple-column baselines (*d*)

You will use baselines to adjust the flow of text on the page. You can place art exactly where you want it; text, however, can only be placed where a baseline exists. Therefore, if you want a line of text placed slightly lower than it appears on the text overlay, you must lower the baseline that the line resides on. Baselines can also respect the placement of art so that the text automatically wraps around the art and does not overwrite it. Look at Table 6-1 to see a description of each of the Baselines pull-down menu choices.

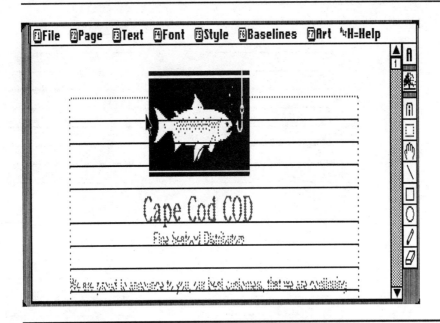

FIGURE 6-2. Displaying the sample publication's baselines

Defining the Page

Before delving into baselines any further, you should familiarize yourself with the Define Page screen from the Page pull-down menu. Version 3.0 users who press (F2) and select Define page will get the following screen:

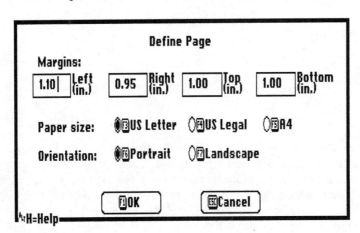

Option	Description
Adjust single (**ALT-A**)	Lets you adjust a single baseline without affecting others surrounding it.
Adjust column	Lets you adjust a column of baselines without affecting the other columns.
Adjust above	Lets you select a baseline with all other baselines above it. No other baselines in the publication will be affected.
Adjust below	Lets you select a baseline with all other baselines below it. No other baselines in the publication will be affected.
Center (**ALT-X**)	Centers selected baselines of text.
Left justify	Left-justifies a single baseline of text. This aligns the text against the left margin of the baseline.
Right justify	Right-justifies a single baseline of text. This aligns the text against the right margin of the baseline.
Full justify	Extends a single baseline of text from the far left of the baseline to the far right of the baseline.
Change leading	Lets you change the amount of space from one baseline to the next one.
Realign text (**ALT-T**)	Adjusts the text on the entire publication to fit the baselines.

TABLE 6-1. The Baselines Pull-Down Menu Options

The margin settings are the default settings for your printer and are given in inches. If you want the margin units of measure set to centimeters instead of inches, select Customize from the File pull-down menu and change this setting. The paper size is determined by the paper in your printer. Most publications will be created in the portrait mode. For very wide publications, use the landscape orientation. Chapter 3 describes paper size and orientation in more detail.

DEFINE PAGE WITH VERSION 2 The Define Page screen for version 2 users is a bit more complex than the one for version 3.0. More control of the page is allowed in version 2 than in the later version, although you cannot select from predefined layouts as you can in version 3.0. When version 2 users press (F2) and select Define page, they see the following dialog box:

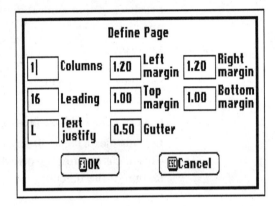

Table 6-2 describes each of the options from this screen. Figure 6-3 shows how each of the version 2 Define Page elements affects your publications.

 The margin settings you see are the *smallest* you should use. They are adjusted for the printer you selected when you installed First Publisher. If you want to adjust these settings, always increase their size (this decreases the width of your lines of text). Decreasing them could cause some of your publication to be cut off when printed.

ADJUSTING THE SAMPLE PUBLICATION

Now that you have been introduced to baselines and the Define Page screen, you are ready to see the power these tools give you. You created a publication

Option	Description
Columns	This number, from 1 to 4, dictates the number of columns in your publication.
Left margin	The number of inches from the left edge of the paper to the left margin of the publication.
Right margin	The number of inches between the right margin of the publication and the right edge of the paper.
Leading	The number of points (remember from Chapter 1 that one inch is 72 points high) from one baseline to the next one.
Top margin	The number of inches from the top margin of the publication to the top edge of the paper.
Bottom margin	The number of inches from the bottom margin of the publication to the bottom edge of the paper.
Text justify	Determines the type of justification (text alignment) that will be standard as you type text. You can override this for individual baselines. Type **L** for left-justification, **R** for right-justification, **J** for full-justification, and **C** to center text on the baselines. The standard setting is L.
Gutter	The measurement between columns.

TABLE 6-2.   The Version 2 Define Page Screen Options

called JAMIE.PUB in the last three chapters. This section shows you how to completely change the layout (or "look") of the publication.

This section is designed to get you working with baselines and layouts *after*

FIGURE 6-3. Placement of the Define Page elements

creating a sample publication. This will let you see how baselines and layouts directly influence the look of publications. Most of the time, however, you should decide on baselines and layouts *before* beginning the placement of text and art.

Before making any changes to JAMIE.PUB, you might want to make a copy of it so it remains intact. To do so, follow these steps.

1. Assuming you have JAMIE.PUB loaded from the previous example, press (ALT-S) to select Save publication from the File pull-down menu.

2. Type **JAMIE2** at the Save Filename prompt.

3. Press (F1) to save the file in a second file called JAMIE2.PUB. JAMIE .PUB will remain safely on the disk in its present form.

It will be easier to begin your hands-on work with baselines if you remove the art clipping of the fish. To delete the fishing image:

1. Highlight the dotted box called the selection tool.

2. Select the entire fishing image by pointing just above the upper-right corner of the image and pressing (F10) or a mouse button. Move the pointer below the lower-left corner of the image and press (F10) or a mouse button again.

3. Press (DEL), the speed key that cuts art images and sends them to the clipboard.

4. Highlight the text tool (the top side tool). The text will become clear again, since the text overlay is active.

5. Press (CTRL-HOME) to ensure that the cursor is placed at the top of the publication.

6. Press (DEL) four times to get rid of the blank space where the art image appeared. Your screen should look like the one in Figure 6-4.

The blank spaces centering the titles may cause confusion for First Publisher when you start using baselines. A little later in this chapter, you will let First Publisher center the text. For now, get rid of the spaces with these steps.

1. Press (CTRL-HOME), or point to the top of the elevator bar.

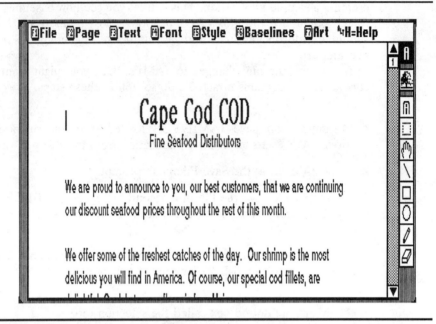

FIGURE 6-4. After deleting the art image

2. Press (DEL) until the title, "Cape Cod COD," moves to the far left margin.

3. Press (DOWN ARROW) to move the cursor to the beginning of the second line, "Fine Seafood Distributors," and press (DEL) until it also moves to the margin as shown here:

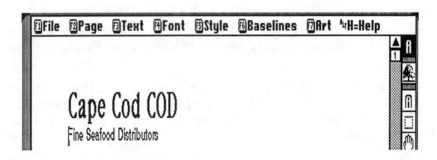

Creating Multiple Columns with Version 3

Most of the time, you will select a layout from the set of 21 predefined layouts supplied with First Publisher. Each of these predefined layouts is actually a thumbnail sketch of the baselines for the publication you want to create. Once you select the layout that most closely resembles the baselines you are looking for, you can fine-tune them by adjusting their locations or accept their default measurements and begin creating the publication. For now, you can select a predefined layout and make JAMIE2.PUB conform to that predefined layout.

 First Publisher gives you the ability to replace any of these 21 predefined layouts with your own.

LOOKING AT THE LAYOUTS To get an idea of the layout screen, press `F2` to display the Page pull-down menu. Select Choose layout and you will see the dialog box shown here:

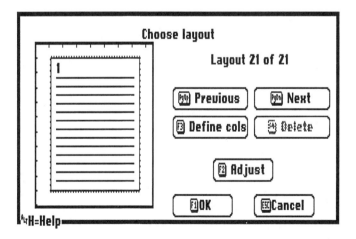

This is one of the 21 sample predefined layouts. To see others, press `PGDN` and `PGUP` to scroll through the list. When the layout has more than one column (as most of them do), the numbers inside the upper-right of each column tell you the order in which text will fill columns.

First Publisher always begins with a one-column assumption. If you have no need for multiple columns, you can use the default layout that First Publisher uses when you start the program. If you do not see a layout that will exactly suit your needs, you can modify any of them.

If you only want to increase or decrease the number of columns in the publication, you can press ⏎ F3 to display the following Define Columns dialog box.

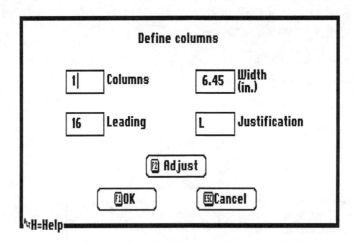

You can specify up to eight columns across the page, although three or four is usually the practical limit. The width specifies the width of *each* column. Make sure the number of columns multiplied by the column width does not exceed the page width (including enough room for the space between the columns, called the *gutter*). The leading measures distance from each baseline to the next and is usually correct as is. To justify text in each of the baselines, type **L** for left, **R** for right, and **J** for fully justified (left and right margins of text will be aligned with one another, similar to newspaper columns). Pressing F2 will make those adjustments to the layout you were viewing when you pressed F3 to go to the Define Page dialog box. Pressing F1 adjusts your current layout to the dialog box.

CHANGING THE SAMPLE BASELINES To change JAMIE2.PUB to a multiple-column newsletter, select Choose layout from the Page pull-down menu. Scroll through the list by pressing PGDN until Layout 2 appears, as shown here:

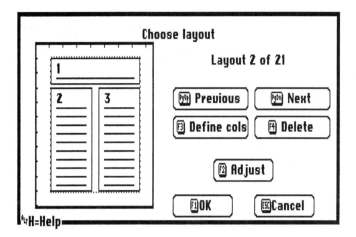

This is the form our publication will take—art and a title across the top of the page, and two columns of text flowing down below. The numbers on each of the layout's thumbnail sketches show that text will flow to column 3 as soon as it overflows column 2.

When you press (**F1**), First Publisher will split part of JAMIE2.PUB into two columns. You may not notice it at first, since the first few lines are extended across the page in one column. When you press (**PGDN**) once, you will see First Publisher's attempt to put the publication into two columns, as shown in Figure 6-5. The first few lines of text are not split, but then the newsletter is in multiple columns. You will have to fix the text to force all of the words beneath the title to move down to the multiple columns.

Move the cursor to the first word in the title, right before "Cape Cod COD." Press (**ENTER**) three times. This inserts three blank lines before the title, which is just enough to move the body of the letter down into the multiple columns where it belongs. Press (**PGDN**) followed by (**ALT-A**) to view the baselines underneath the letter, and you will see the multiple-column layout that you selected. When you center the titles and even out the two columns of text, the newsletter will be complete. This is discussed in a later section called "Centering the Titles."

Creating Multiple Columns with Version 2

Users of First Publisher version 2 must specify the number of columns of a multiple-column document from the Define page option of the Page pull-

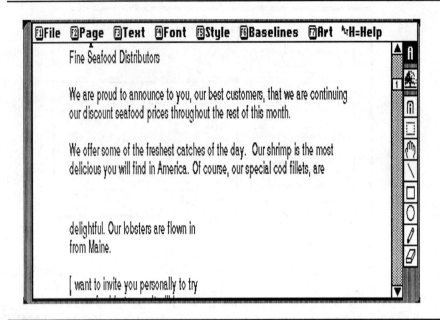

FIGURE 6-5. Forcing the lower publication into two columns

down menu. Version 3 users will be able to select from a set of predefined layouts, as discussed earlier in the chapter.

To give your letter more of a "newsletter" appearance, you will change JAMIE2.PUB into a two-column publication. Instead of a letterhead, you will center the two-line title over the two columns. First you must inform First Publisher that you want two columns with the Define Page screen. Follow these instructions:

1. Press (F2) to display the Page pull-down menu, or click over Page with the mouse.

2. Select Define page to display the Define Page screen.

3. Press **2** to change the number of columns. The rest of the options are okay as they are.

4. Press (F1) to activate the change. Your screen instantly takes on a two-column appearance, as shown in Figure 6-6.

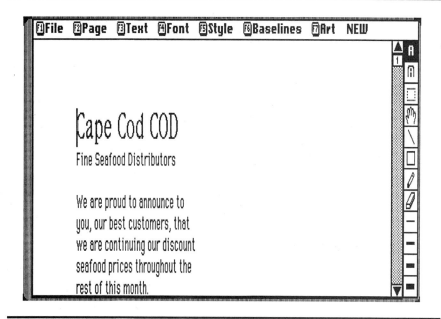

FIGURE 6-6. Placing the publication into two columns

After the page is set for multiple columns, you can manually improve its look. The first step is to put the two-line title in a single column that extends across the top of the page. To do this:

1. Press **F6** to display the Baselines pull-down menu.

2. Select Adjust column. You will see the two-column baselines appear. (You cannot edit text while the baselines are highlighted.)

In order to extend the top two baselines across the page, you need to move the second column down. To do this, follow these steps:

1. Since you just selected Adjust column, you can work with the entire second column at once. First, select it by moving the pointer to touch any baseline of the second column.

2. Click a mouse button or press **F10** twice. As you can see in Figure 6-7, three handles will appear on the baseline. Since you are adjusting a column, moving the top baseline will move all of the baselines in the column.

3. Move the mouse to the center handle.

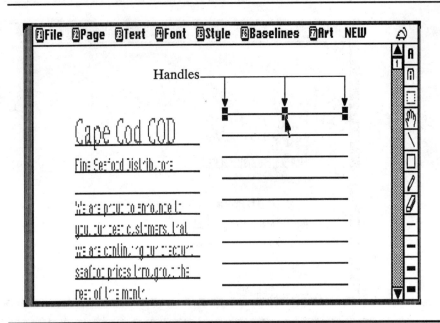

FIGURE 6-7. Displaying the baseline handles

4. Select the handle by pressing and holding a mouse button or by pressing ⟨F10⟩ once. This lets you drag the second column of baselines downward.

5. Press ⟨DOWN ARROW⟩ or move the mouse until the second column starts on the same line as the *fourth* baseline of the first column, then press ⟨F10⟩ or release the mouse. Figure 6-8 shows the result.

The top three baselines can now be extended across the page to make a single column for the titles. The rest of the text will remain in two columns, creating a newsletter appearance. To extend the top three baselines:

1. Select Adjust single from the Baselines pull-down menu by pressing ⟨ALT-A⟩. This will turn off the column baseline adjustment and allow you to adjust a single baseline.

2. Point to the first baseline of the first column and click the mouse button, or press ⟨F10⟩ twice. The handles of the first baseline will appear.

3. Point to the right handle. Press ⟨F10⟩ or click and hold a mouse button.

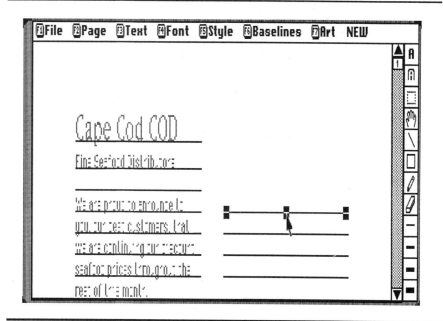

═══ **FIGURE 6-8.** Dropping the second column

4. Drag the baseline to the right side of the publication by moving the mouse or pressing the arrow keys. Extend the baseline until it is even with the second column's right margin as shown in Figure 6-9.

5. Press (**F10**) or release the mouse to anchor the baseline.

6. Repeat these steps for the next two baselines of the first column. Figure 6-10 shows the result of this.

Although the main text is still gray, the two titles disappeared completely. If First Publisher adjusted the text every time you adjusted a baseline, the program's operation would be too slow to be practical. Since the baselines are in the appropriate position, realign the text now by pressing (**ALT-T**). This selects Realign text from the Baselines pull-down menu. When you do, the text will appear on the baselines again.

Centering the Titles

Now it is time to put the finishing touches on the title. The title must be centered on the top two lines. Both versions of First Publisher accomplish

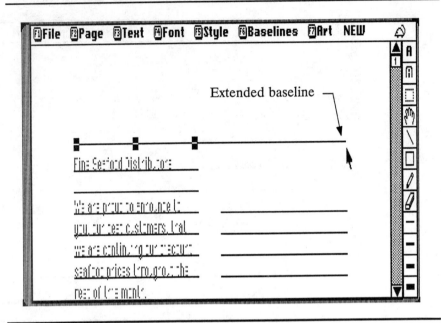

FIGURE 6-9. Extending the first title baseline

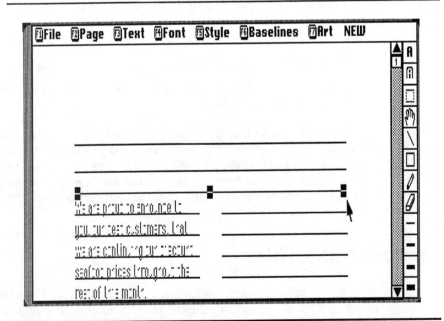

FIGURE 6-10. After extending the rest of the title lines

this the same way. You can manually insert spaces before the titles as you did when you first created the publication, but there is an easier, more accurate way. Follow these steps to center the title lines:

1. Display the baselines by pressing (**ALT-A**) to select Adjust single from the Baselines pull-down menu.

2. Select the title's baseline again by pointing to it and clicking the mouse button or by pressing (**F10**) twice. The handles will then appear.

3. Press (**ALT-X**). This selects Center from the Baselines pull-down menu. The title will center on the baseline.

4. Repeat the first two steps for the second title line.

5. Press (**ALT-A**) to turn off Adjust single and hide the baselines. The result is shown in Figure 6-11.

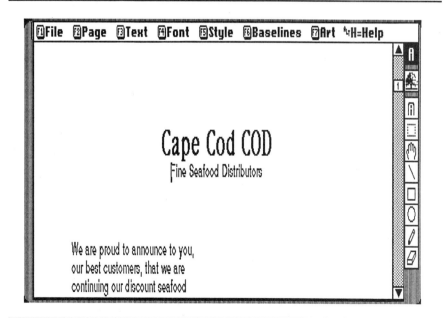

FIGURE 6-11.   The publication after centering the titles

FLOWING TEXT AND ART There are just a few steps to go before JAMIE.PUB turns into a newsletter. Many of these finishing touches vary with the type and style of your publication. Much of the end detailing takes patience and trial and error to get it "just right." Nevertheless, it is not difficult to create a finished newsletter with First Publisher's layout tools.

Follow the steps below to force the last half of the first column's text into the second column:

1. Position the cursor at the beginning of the second line in the third paragraph. This line starts with "our seafood just once . . ."

2. Press (ENTER) 24 times. This inserts several blank lines at the cursor's position. These lines will fill the bottom of the first column to push the last half of the text into the second column.

3. Press (CTRL-HOME) followed by (PGDN). Your screen will look like the one in Figure 6-12. There is still some more to be done to the text, but first you will place an art image in the publication.

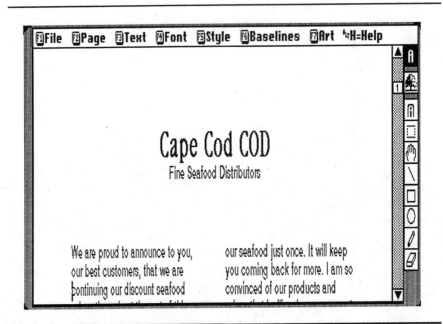

FIGURE 6-12. Pushing text into the second column

The placement of the extra blank lines was determined by trial and error. If you type an extra space or use a different font, you may have to adjust the number of (**ENTER**) keypresses you type. Try to arrange the (**ENTER**) keypresses to "even out" the two columns. When dividing a single column into more than one column of text, you may have to try several times before getting the division in the best location.

PICTUREWRAP   This publication will look better with the fishing image back on the page. With *picturewrap* you can place the image in the middle of the page and let the text surround the image.

Why use picturewrap? Figure 6-13 shows what can happen if you place art over text without picturewrap. Since the art and text are on two different overlays, the art covers up some of the text. To solve this problem manually would require tedious editing. Instead, use picturewrap.

1. Press (**ALT-W**) to turn on Picturewrap. If you press (**F2**) to see the Page pull-down menu, you will see a check mark next to "Picturewrap."

2. Press (**F7**) to display the Art pull-down menu.

FIGURE 6-13.   Without picturewrap, the art overwrites text

FIGURE 6-14. Getting ready to anchor the art image

3. Select Get art.

4. Type **FISH.ART** at the art image prompt.

5. Move the hand tool below the first paragraph in the first column. Place it below the word "month."

6. Press (F10) to see the box. Figure 6-14 shows how you should position it.

7. Press (F10) to place the image. All text should wrap around the art and flow smoothly around it.

8. Press (SHIFT-F9) to select the text tool. The publication's text will return to its regular mode. Figure 6-15 shows the publication at this point.

There is some minor editing left to do. The second column of text needs to be moved up one line, since the first column's text moved up to make room for the picture. This is easily accomplished by moving the cursor to the

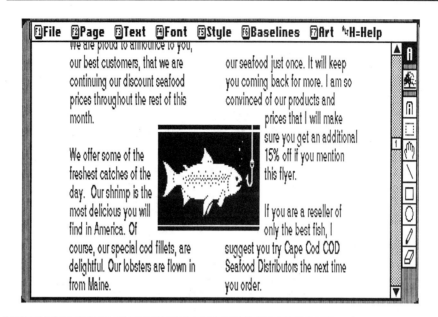

FIGURE 6-15. The two-column publication with art

blank line at the top of the second column and deleting the line. To get from column to column, remember the following two speed keys:

CTRL-N   Moves the cursor to the next column

CTRL-P   Moves the cursor to the previous column

Follow these steps to delete the extra blank line:

1. Press **DOWN ARROW** and **CTRL-N** to move the cursor to the second column. Make sure it rests just above the line that reads "our seafood just once."

2. Press **DEL** to delete the blank line. Your screen will look like the one in Figure 6-16.

There is a little more you can do. Press **ALT-Z** to preview the page and see how it will print. If this were to be printed on regular-sized paper, you would probably want to add text to fill out the page better, since the text only fills the top half of the page. You also might want to insert a border around the title, or lower the closing salutation by a line to even out the bottom of the publication.

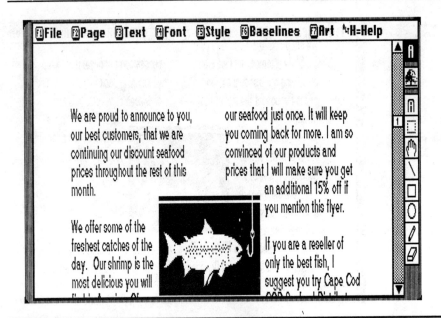

FIGURE 6-16. Finalizing the publication

The picturewrap feature works well, but sometimes you might want to fine-tune the positioning of the text or hyphenate words here and there to make the flow appear even smoother. By adjusting the baselines, you will be able to position the text so it looks more natural next to the art.

 Adjust single baselines to the right of a picturewrapped figure. This will get rid of the strict left-justification to the right of a figure and make the text flow better around the figure.

For now, leave the publication as it is. You should save it under the name of JAMIE2.PUB by pressing ‾ALT-S‾ and typing the filename. The next few sections will use JAMIE2.PUB for other layout exercises.

VERSION 2 LEADING AND GUTTER SIZES Version 2 users will find that leading (rhymes with "bedding") and gutter size can be modified. The leading is the space—measured in points—from one baseline to another, as shown here:

This shows
proper leading   } ← Leading
from baseline
to baseline.

First Publisher usually adjusts leading properly. However, if you are mixing several type sizes on the same page, you should make sure that the leading is set for the *smallest* font on the page. Set the leading from the Define Page screen according to the optimal values shown in the *First Publisher User's Guide* that comes with First Publisher.

The leading sizes range from 9 points to 72 points. Figure 6-17 shows JAMIE2.PUB with 25-point leading. (Do not change the leading on your sample publication.)

The gutter value indicates the size between columns in a publication (measured in inches). Usually the default setting is okay as is. If you ever want to increase or decrease the gutter size, type a new value at the Define Page screen.

 If you change the gutter size for a multiple-column publication, you might lose the centering of titles at the top of the page. If you do, you will have to center them again.

Finishing Up Layouts

Most of your layout work will be easier when you set up a layout *before* creating a publication. The next part of the book describes the creation of several different kinds of publications, and they all start with the appropriate layout. Usually, when developing a publication, you will follow these steps:

1. Display the Define Page screen of the Page pull-down menu to initialize columns, leading, gutter size, and margins on the page.

2. Change the baselines, if needed, to specify their proper placement for the publication.

FIGURE 6-17. Increasing the publication's leading size

3. Type or import the text into the publication. Since your baselines are already set up, this will be easy.

4. Create, import, and edit the graphic images from your clip art files or with freehand drawing. Make sure you use picturewrap if you want the text to flow around the art.

5. Save and print the publication.

 If you have a footnote to add to a publication, add it as graphics text. Baselines do not extend all the way down the page, but graphics text can be placed close to the bottom edge of the page.

ONE LAST BASELINE TIP As you will recall, when working with baselines of a multiple-column publication, First Publisher does not adjust the text and art every time you move a baseline. You must hide the baselines or realign the text to see the newly positioned text.

However, if you are working with text and need to add more text in the middle of a multiple-column publication, First Publisher adjusts the text *every time* you type a character. This can take up a lot of time. Follow one of these steps if you need to add text:

- Type the text in a word-processed file and import it at the point of the insertion. That way, all of the text will be realigned at one time.

- Place the cursor at the point of the insertion and press `INS`. First Publisher will temporarily erase all text below the cursor. You can add the new text at the cursor's position. When you press `INS` again, the hidden text will reappear after the new text. To illustrate this, Figure 6-18 shows a two-column publication before pressing `INS`, and Figure 6-19 shows the same publication after `INS` is pressed.

ART LAYOUT HELP

Picturewrap is not the only layout tool available for art. You can use rulers and grid lines to help with placement. Later chapters will describe how to use these tools in detail. The basics are explained here.

Grid Lines

When you were extending the top lines of the title, you wanted the lines to be even with the rest of the column's right margin. However, getting close to the right edge of the column is sometimes a guess. (Luckily, being close is sufficient in many instances.)

You can use the grid feature of First Publisher to help you position text, art, and baselines. The grid ensures that, in multiple-page publications, art and graphics text are placed uniformly on all of the pages. To see the grid in JAMIE2.PUB, follow these steps:

1. Load JAMIE2.PUB by pressing `ALT-G` and typing the filename.

2. Press `ALT-U` to select Use grid from the Page pull-down menu.

3. Press `F9` twice to select the graphics text tool. The grid lines will be displayed any time you work with the standard art overlay or use base-lines. Figure 6-20 shows the grid lines that appear on your screen after you press `PGDN`.

4. Press the `SHIFT` key and any of the arrow keys to see the cursor move from dot to dot on the grid.

You can change the space between the grid's dots to gain more accuracy in placement of graphics objects. The Set grid size option of the Page pull-down menu lets you set the grid size anywhere from 0.12 inch to 1 inch.

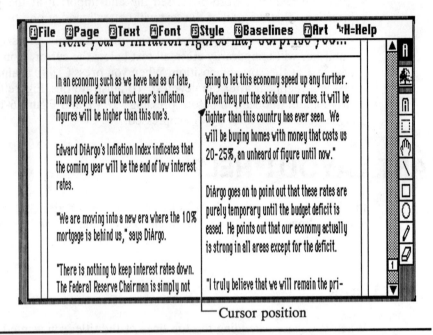

Cursor position

FIGURE 6-18. Before pressing INS

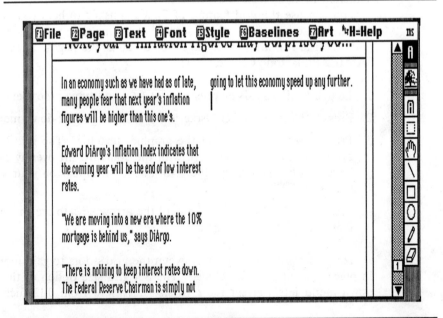

FIGURE 6-19. After pressing INS

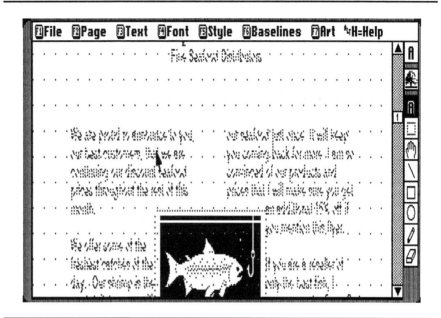

FIGURE 6-20. Displaying the grid lines

Figure 6-21 shows a screen with a grid size set to the smallest measurement of 0.12 inch. The Set Grid Size screen is shown here:

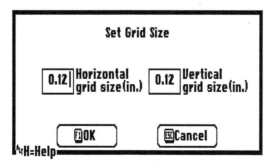

This screen lets you set a different horizontal grid spacing. You will find that grid lines make drawing straight lines and adjusting baselines much more accurate.

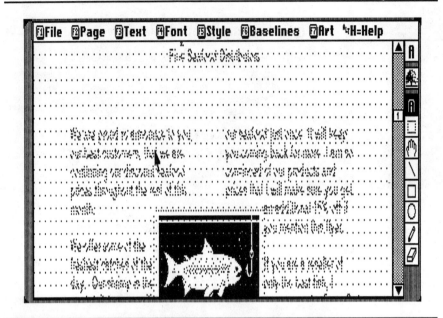

FIGURE 6-21. Decreasing the grid measurement for more accuracy

Rulers

You can add a video ruler to the publication screen by pressing **ALT-L** to select Show rulers from the Page pull-down menu. Figure 6-22 shows the rulers displayed for the JAMIE2.PUB publication. The ruler lines give you measurements in proportion to the printed page. Rulers can be displayed at all times on both the art and text overlays.

 You can display the rulers and grid at the same time.

Hairlines on the vertical and horizontal rulers show you exactly where the pointer is located at all times. As you move the pointer, the hairlines move as well. When you want to hide the ruler display, press **ALT-L** again.

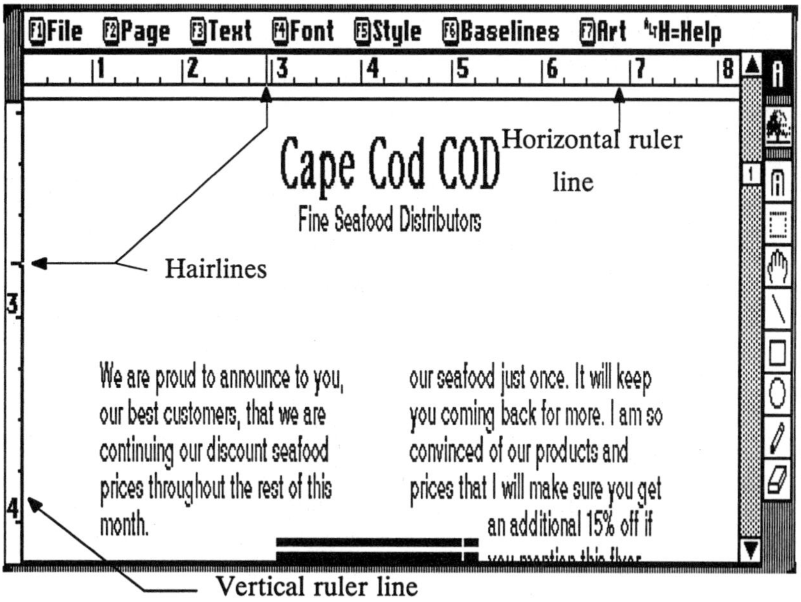

FIGURE 6-22. Hairlines on the vertical and horizontal rulers show you exactly where the pointer is located at all times

Summary

In this chapter you learned how to

- Display and use the baselines to place text on the page exactly where you want it. You saw how to change the text justification on baselines, as well as how to center text.

- Use the Define Page screen for versions 2 and 3. The Define page options are where you control the top, bottom, left, and right margins for the publication.

- Change a single-column publication to multiple columns. (Normally, you would define the publication as a multiple-column publication before adding text and art.)

- Select from the set of 21 predefined layouts supplied with version 3. With these layouts, you can control the number and placement of columns by selecting the look you want.

- Force text to wrap around art with the Picturewrap option from the Page pull-down menu. This keeps text separated from inserted art.

- Display grid lines and control their density to help with the placement of art and graphics text

- Use the horizontal and vertical rulers of First Publisher to see exactly where art and text will appear on the final page and to help you with their placement

ADVANCED FONT
SUPPORT

Font Files
Changing Fonts in Version 3
Changing Fonts in Version 2

N ow that you have mastered the fundamentals of First Publisher, you are
ready to take the program further by adding to your existing set of
fonts. First Publisher offers a wide range of support for fonts and, if your
printer is a laser, ink-jet, or other printer that has multiple-font capabilities,
you will need to know how to add, change, and remove fonts from the
default set of fonts first installed with the program.

This chapter covers working with the large library of fonts supplied with
First Publisher. You will learn more about the advanced laser printer support, including font cartridges and soft fonts. With version 3, First Publisher
supplied Bitstream scalable fonts that you can create and add as you need
them.

FONT FILES

The distribution disks that came with your First Publisher program contain
many fonts that you can use in your publications. However, not all of these

fonts are available at all times while working with First Publisher. Fonts take lots of computer memory, and your computer does not have enough memory to hold every font supplied with First Publisher during your publishing session. Therefore, you must select those fonts you want in your publication and move them into a file called *MASTER.FNT*. This is not difficult to do. Once you have used the program for a while, you will end up with a set of fonts in MASTER.FNT that you regularly use; you will only move other fonts into it for special publications. A later section in this chapter will describe how to move fonts into MASTER.FNT.

 First Publisher will *only* look in MASTER.FNT for fonts even though you will have several other font files on your disk.

There will be a point where you could have too many fonts in MASTER .FNT and you will have to remove a font before adding another. First Publisher can have a maximum of any of the following:

- 15 typefaces
- 16 styles or sizes
- 100 fonts

When any of these conditions are reached, you will have to remove a typeface, style, size, or font before adding another. Also, since large fonts take more memory than smaller ones, you may run out of memory *before* reaching one of the above limits. Any memory-resident programs will also take away from the available memory that you could be using for fonts. If you reach a limit, First Publisher will warn you with the error message "Not enough memory."

When you first installed First Publisher, the program's authors decided on a set of fonts for you by putting some into MASTER.FNT and leaving the rest in other files. If no changes have been made to your installed fonts, version 3 users will see the following list when they display the Font pull-down menu:

Version 2 users will see this Font menu:

Appendix B lists all of First Publisher's supplied fonts. Remember that a font is a specific typeface, size, and style. Therefore, Courier 12-point bold is a different font from Courier 10-point bold. This was explained more thoroughly in Chapter 1.

Sources of Fonts

There are several ways that you can use the fonts supplied in First Publisher's font files. Not all printers support all fonts, so it is important that you understand the abilities of your own printer and that you use only fonts that work with it. Fonts, like art, come in two different resolutions: *standard fonts* created at 72 DPI and *high-resolution fonts* created at the highest resolution your printer allows (up to 300 DPI). There are many more standard fonts supplied with First Publisher than high-resolution ones, but the print quality of high-resolution fonts is better.

 Text created with the graphics text tool will *always* be printed at the standard resolution, even if you type it with a high-resolution font.

INTERNAL, SCALED, CARTRIDGE, AND SOFT FONTS *Internal fonts* are fonts supplied with your printer; no additional hardware or software add-ons are needed. Dot-matrix printers usually support Pica and Elite internal fonts. Laser and ink-jet printers also come with internal fonts. For instance, the HP LaserJet series is supplied with the Courier font. All printers that work with First Publisher support at least one internal font.

Scaled fonts (sometimes called *scalable fonts*) are supplied by a company called *Bitstream*. Some Bitstream scaled fonts are included with First Publisher version 3. More are available. All dot-matrix and laser printers (except those that are PostScript-compatible) support scaled fonts. Not only do scaled fonts print at a higher resolution, but you create them at various point sizes within First Publisher as needed. Therefore, they do not take up disk space until you create them. The patterns of scalable fonts are supplied on disk; you use these patterns to specify the size of font you want when you need it.

Bitstream scalable fonts are displayed with a plus sign (+) following their names on the Font pull-down menu, such as Swiss 721+ and Dutch 801+.

Cartridge fonts are available for HP LaserJet and DeskJet printers. These are cartridges that plug into the printer's slots and, in effect, add more internal fonts to the printer. No special software or extra disk space is needed to print fonts from a font cartridge as long as it is a cartridge supported by First Publisher. These are the cartridges supported by First Publisher:

HP DeskJet Cartridges
A, D, E, F, G, H, J, P, Q

HP LaserJet Cartridges
B, F

If you have a font cartridge that combines several fonts, you can access only those fonts within the cartridge that are listed above.

Soft fonts reside in files on your disk, if you have them. None are supplied with First Publisher, but you can purchase them for both versions 2 and 3. Each soft font takes a different file on your disk; you can copy a soft font into MASTER.FNT and use it with First Publisher. First Publisher supports soft fonts for the HP LaserJet and DeskJet printers.

Although there is some terminology (and sometimes expense) that comes with adding these various font sources to your printer, doing so means that you can produce eye-catching publications with a diverse assortment of fonts.

.FNT and .FNB Files

The fonts supplied with First Publisher reside in files ending with the extensions .FNT and .FNB. One of these, MASTER.FNT, is the current source for fonts in your publications. Fonts from files other than MASTER .FNT (that end with .FNT and .FNB) can be added to MASTER.FNT when you need them.

Table 7-1 describes the types of fonts in files ending with the .FNT extension. Notice that many of them are specific to a printer; for instance, a font from the APLASER.FNT file will not work with an HP LaserJet. Table 7-2 lists the types of fonts in files ending with the .FNB extension. Each of these contain Bitstream scalable fonts. Any font from any of these files can be added to MASTER.FNT.

 If you want to use fonts exclusively from one of these files, you can rename that file on your working disk "MASTER.FNT" from DOS. You can also copy that file over MASTER.FNT with First Publisher, a procedure that will be described later in the chapter. (Do *not* change or rename the font files that came with your original distribution disks.)

CHANGING FONTS IN VERSION 3

When you want to modify a font file, you will use the Set up fonts option from the Font pull-down menu. You can add, change, or remove fonts from any .FNT file with the Set up fonts option, but you will primarily use it for modifying MASTER.FNT. Here is the Set Up Fonts menu:

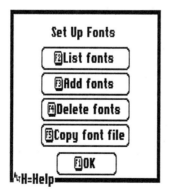

 First Publisher requires you to save your current publication before selecting Set up fonts from the Font pull-down menu.

.FNT Filename	Usage
APLASER.FNT	Fonts for PostScript, PostScript-compatible, and Apple LaserWriter printers.
DESKJET.FNT	Fonts for the HP DeskJet printers.
EXTRA1.FNT	Fonts in standard resolution for all printers.
EXTRA2.FNT	More fonts in standard resolution for all printers.
HPLASER.FNT	Fonts for the HP LaserJet printers.
MASTER.FNT	Fonts currently available to First Publisher (both standard and high-resolution fonts).

TABLE 7-1.   .FNT Font Files

.FNB Filename	Fonts
AMERIGOB.FNB	Amerigo Bold
AMERIGOR.FNB	Amerigo Roman
BROADWAY.FNB	Broadway
CLOISBLK.FNB	Cloister Black
DUTCHB.FNB	Dutch 801 Bold
DUTCHBI.FNB	Dutch 801 Bold Italic
DUTCHI.FNB	Dutch 801 Italic
DUTCHR.FNB	Dutch 801 Roman
GOUDYI.FNB	Goudy Old Style Italic
GOUDYR.FNB	Goudy Old Style Roman
SWISSB.FNB	Swiss 721 Bold
SWISSBI.FNB	Swiss 721 Bold Italic
SWISSI.FNB	Swiss 721 Italic
SWISSR.FNB	Swiss 721 Roman
ZURICHB.FNB	Zurich Black
ZURICHR.FNB	Zurich Roman

TABLE 7-2.   .FNB Font Files

Listing Fonts

The List fonts option (F2) will display the contents of any .FNT file. You must select which .FNT file you want to list. To see a list of fonts on the screen from MASTER.FNT, follow these steps:

1. Press F4 to display the Font pull-down menu.
2. Select the Set up fonts option.
3. Press F2 to select List fonts. A .FNT file listing, similar to the following, will appear on the screen:

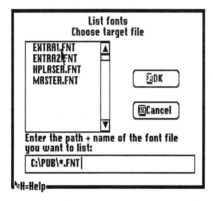

4. Select MASTER.FNT from the list. This is known as the *target file* that you want to list. You will see all fonts currently in the Font and Style menus, since they work directly from MASTER.FNT. An example of such a listing is shown here:

5. When you are done viewing the list, select OK. First Publisher gives you a chance to list fonts from another file. Choosing Cancel takes you back to the publication screen.

Adding Fonts

The Add fonts ((F3)) option from the Set Up Fonts menu lets you add fonts to MASTER.FNT or any other .FNT file. You can even create your own .FNT file from scratch by adding various fonts to it. You must copy the fonts to a target file, and then choose a *source file* to get the fonts from. The font is *not* removed from the source font file; it is only copied to the target file.

 Some people find it useful to have a different .FNT file for each type of publication they produce. For instance, you might create a NEWS.FNT file that contains a headline, byline, and body font for your newsletter, and a FLIER.FNT file that contains larger, fancier fonts for fliers.

To add a font to MASTER.FNT:

1. Press (F4) to select the Font pull-down menu.

2. Select Set up fonts.

3. Press (F3) to select Add fonts. A .FNT file listing will appear.

4. Select the target file that you want to add to. Point to it and press (F10) followed by (F1), or click the mouse button. If the target is named something other than MASTER.FNT, First Publisher will not automatically use the newly added font; you must rename the target .FNT file MASTER.FNT.

 To create a new .FNT file from scratch, type its name in the path box at the bottom of the Add Fonts dialog box.

5. A dialog box listing source files will be displayed, such as the one shown here. You now must select the source file from which a font will be copied.

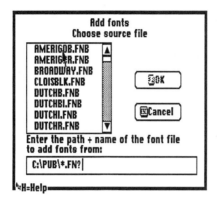

Depending on the type of source font, First Publisher will display one of three screens. The remaining steps differ as well. The next three sections describe the different steps for a .FNT file font, soft file font, or scalable font.

ADDING A .FNT FILE   This takes fewer steps than the other two font sources and will probably be the one you select most often. To add the New York 36-point bold font to your session of First Publisher (adding it to MASTER.FNT), you must copy it from EXTRA1.FNT as shown here.

1. At the Choose Source File screen, scroll down to select EXTRA1.FNT. When you select it, you will see a list of all the fonts in EXTRA1.FNT, as shown here:

2. Scroll to New York 36 bold at the bottom of the list. This is the font to copy to MASTER.FNT, the target file. You will see this message:

Please stand by. Adding font. . .

while First Publisher adds the 36-point New York bold font to MASTER.FNT.

3. You can continue adding fonts from EXTRA1.FNT by repeating step 2. When through, press (ESC) or click the mouse button over Cancel.

4. The Choose Source File dialog box will reappear. You may select another font file to copy from, or press (F1) to return to the publication screen.

ADDING SOFT FONTS   Soft font files hold a single soft font. You may use any soft font created by the Bitstream Fontware Installation Kit. The procedure for adding soft fonts is identical to that described in the last section for regular fonts, except that you must supply the name displayed in the Font pull-down menu (whereas the name is supplied automatically with other types of fonts). This name can be up to 15 characters long.

After selecting the soft font file you want to copy a font from, First Publisher will display a "Font name:" prompt and wait for you to type a name. Since soft font filenames are usually cryptic (for instance, GN110RPN.USP is the name of a soft font file), you may want to type something recognizable, such as Geneva Large, after the "Font name:" prompt. First Publisher will take a few moments to add the soft font. Once added, the name of the soft font will appear in the Font pull-down menu every time you select the menu.

ADDING SCALABLE FONTS   Two of the scalable fonts supplied with First Publisher, Dutch and Swiss, can be scaled to any point size between 9 and 70 points. The others, such as Goudy and Zurich, can only be scaled to certain sizes. First Publisher will only allow you to use the point sizes available for a given font.

At the Choose Source File screen, all fonts ending with .FNB are scalable Bitstream fonts. Once you select one, the appropriate Add Scaled Fonts screen will appear. For instance, to add the 36-point Broadway scaled font to MASTER.FNT, follow these steps:

1. Select BROADWAY.FNB from the font listing. When you do, you'll see the Add Scaled Fonts dialog box:

```
┌─────────────────────────────────────────────┐
│              Add scaled fonts                 │
│                                               │
│   Font name: ┌─────────────────────────────┐ │
│              │ Broadway                     │ │
│   Point size:├─────────────────────────────┤ │
│   (18,36)    │ I                            │ │
│              └─────────────────────────────┘ │
│   Style:        Regular                       │
│                                               │
│                                               │
│   Source filename:                            │
│   C:\PUB\BROADWAY.FNB                          │
│   Target filename:                            │
│   C:\PUB\MASTER.FNT                            │
│      ┌──────────┐      ┌───────────┐          │
│      │ [F1]Add  │      │ [ESC]Cancel│         │
│      └──────────┘      └───────────┘          │
│ [^]H=Help                                      │
└─────────────────────────────────────────────┘
```

2. You must select the point size desired. Notice that the Broadway font only comes in two sizes, 18 and 36. Type **36** after the "Point size:" prompt.

3. If you want a different name to appear in the listing of the Font pull-down menu, type the new name after the "Font name:" prompt.

4. Press (**F1**) to add the font to MASTER.FNT. First Publisher will display a message saying "Please stand by. Reading scaled font. . ." followed by "Please stand by. Making First Publisher font. . .", then "Please stand by. Adding font. . . ." It may take a while to add the scaled font to the list of current fonts in MASTER.FNT.

You can add other point sizes for the source font, or return to the publication screen. At any time during the process of adding fonts, if you change your mind and want to return to the publication screen, press (**ESC**) to cancel the operation.

Deleting Fonts

The Delete fonts ((**F4**)) option on the Set Up Fonts menu requires that you first select the target font file, then remove one or more fonts from it. If you find that you need to add a font to MASTER.FNT but have no room for it, you will have to remove one or more fonts *first*. For instance, to remove the Broadway 36-point font added earlier to MASTER.FNT, you should do the following:

1. Press ⊂F4⊃ at the Set Up Fonts menu to select Delete fonts. You will see the Delete Fonts screen. You must select a target file from which you will remove a font.

2. Select MASTER.FNT from the list. You will see a list of fonts from MASTER.FNT displayed on the screen.

3. Select Broadway + 36 Regular from the list. Remember that the plus sign (+) indicates that it is a Bitstream font.

4. First Publisher prompts you to confirm that you want to delete the font with this message:

    Delete "Broadway + 36 Regular"?

5. Press ⊂F1⊃ to confirm the deletion. The screen will display the following message:

    Please stand by. Deleting font. . .

After a pause, you will see another font listing showing all the fonts left in the file. You can select and delete another one, or select Cancel twice to return to the Set Up Fonts menu.

Copying Font Files

The Copy font file (⊂F5⊃) option from the Set Up Fonts menu lets you copy complete font files from one file to another. You cannot copy individual fonts with this option, only complete font files. The Copy font file option is similar to the DOS COPY command, but works only with font files.

The Copy font file option is a good way to make a backup of a font file before making drastic changes to it. If you are unhappy with later changes to the file, you will still have a copy of it in its original state. Also, if you have created several font files for specific purposes—for instance, a NEWS.FNT file for your newsletters—you can copy these files to MASTER.FNT to use the fonts. Before doing so, make sure you have a copy of MASTER.FNT, since the copy operation replaces all fonts in the target file.

To try Copy font file, make a backup of MASTER.FNT by following these steps:

1. Press ⊂F5⊃ to select Copy font from the Set Up Fonts menu.

2. First Publisher will ask for the source file to copy from. Select MASTER .FNT.

3. First Publisher will display the Copy Font File dialog box shown here:

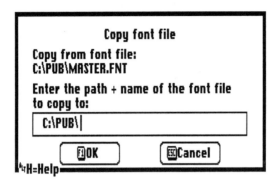

Type **MASTER2.FNT** and press ⬚F1⬚. First Publisher will begin making a
copy of MASTER.FNT and display the message:

Please stand by. Copying file. . .

Then it will return to the Set Up Fonts menu. There are now two
versions of the MASTER.FNT file on your disk: MASTER.FNT and
MASTER2.FNT.

CHANGING FONTS IN VERSION 2

You must run a program called FONTMOVE from the DOS prompt to
move fonts in and out of MASTER.FNT. Exit First Publisher (⬚ALT-E⬚) to
return to the DOS prompt. You must be in the First Publisher subdirectory
before running FONTMOVE. When you change to the First Publisher
subdirectory, type **FONTMOVE**. You should see the FONTMOVE Main
Menu shown in Figure 7-1.

Adding Fonts

Before adding fonts, you will probably find it useful to copy the additional
fonts to your hard disk. If you prefer, you can save disk space by keeping
them on floppy disks. To add fonts to the MASTER.FNT file, select the first
option, Move fonts, by pressing ⬚F1⬚. You will see the Move Fonts screen
shown in Figure 7-2. If you have fonts on a floppy disk, insert it into a disk
drive.

PFS:First Publisher Fontmove Program 2.01

Main Menu

F1 Move fonts

F2 Add HP LaserJet soft fonts

F3 Exit to DOS

Copyright (c) 1988 Software Publishing Corporation

FIGURE 7-1. The FONTMOVE Main Menu

Move fonts

F1 Help   F3 Show   F5 Create   F7 Erase
F2 Dir   F4 Destination   F6 Copy   Esc Quit

Waiting for command

DESTINATION file for COPY command

Commands:	Explanation:
F2-Dir	List the .FNT files
F3-Show	Show fonts in a .FNT file
	After Show command, select a font with Up and Down
	arrows, or PgUp and PgDn, and then choose one or
	more of the following commands:
F4-Destination	Set the destination .FNT file for Copy command
F5-Create	Create a new .FNT file
F6-Copy	Copy the selected font to the destination .FNT file
F7-Erase	Erase the selected font from the .FNT file
Esc-Quit	Return to the Main Menu

FIGURE 7-2. The FONTMOVE Move Fonts screen

You must display a directory listing of all font files. Font files compatible with First Publisher end with the file extension .FNT. When you press (**F2**) and type the disk drive (and optional path) of the fonts to move, you will get a directory of all .FNT files, as shown in Figure 7-3.

To select a file and display its available fonts, press (**F3**). You will be prompted with the "Show file" prompt. Type the name of a font file. For instance, if you type **EXTRA** (the .FNT extension is not necessary), you will see a list of all the fonts in this file, as shown in Figure 7-4. Press (**PGDN**) and (**PGUP**) to see other screens of fonts if the font file takes more than one screen.

To move a font from the selected font file to MASTER.FNT, you must select Destination by pressing (**F4**) and typing **MASTER**. (First Publisher only recognizes MASTER.FNT as its font file. If you have several font files, you can rename them to MASTER.FNT as needed with the DOS RENAME command.)

 If you are moving fonts to a file other than MASTER.FNT, and the file does not yet exist, you must first create it by pressing (**F5**) and typing a filename.

Highlight a font to move and press (**F6**) to copy it to the destination font file. Continue until you have copied all of the fonts needed.

Move fonts

| F1 Help | F3 Show | F5 Create | F7 Erase |
| F2 Dir | F4 Destination | F6 Copy | Esc Quit |

Waiting for command

DESTINATION file for COPY command

.FNT files in the current directory

| EXTRA.FNT | MASTER.FNT | SYSTEM.FNT | DESKJET.FNT |
| HPLASER.FNT | APLASER.FNT | | |

FIGURE 7-3. Looking at a listing of the font files

```
                                Move fonts

      F1 Help           F3 Show          F5 Create        F7 Erase
      F2 Dir            F4 Destination   F6 Copy          Esc Quit

   Waiting for command

   DESTINATION file for COPY command

   File shown below is: extra.fnt

   Font Name          Point     Style           Identification

   Athens              18       Normal          Athens
   Cairo               18       Normal          Cairo
   Chicago             12       Normal          Chicago
   Chicago             12       Bold            Chicago
   Chicago             12       Italic          Chicago
   London              18       Normal          London
   Los Angeles         12       Bold            Los Angeles
   Monaco              9        Normal          Monaco
   Monaco              9        Bold            Monaco
   Monaco              9        Italic          Monaco

        Use Up/Down arrows and PgUp, PgDn to highlight selected font
```

FIGURE 7-4.   A listing of all fonts in the selected font file

ERASING FONTS   You can erase fonts from MASTER.FNT (or other font files). If you do this, however, you *cannot* get the font back unless you have a copy of the font on another file (such as LASER.FNT or EXTRA.FNT). Therefore, only remove fonts when you have a backup of the font file.

 Always keep your original First Publisher disks safely stored away. Most of your font moves and deletions will be done with MASTER .FNT, and you will always have the original MASTER.FNT fonts on the distribution disks.

You will have to periodically remove fonts from MASTER.FNT to make room for new ones. To erase a font from the font file shown, highlight the font with the arrow keys and press (F7) to select Erase from the top of the screen.

When you leave the Move Fonts screen, press (ESC). You will be returned to the FONTMOVE Main Menu.

Adding Soft Fonts

You must know the exact filename of the soft font file you want to use with First Publisher. To add soft fonts:

1. Press ⟨F2⟩ to select Add HP LaserJet soft fonts from the Main Menu. You will see the screen shown in Figure 7-5.

2. Type the soft font filename after the "HP soft font filename:" prompt.

3. Press ⟨TAB⟩. Type the destination font file, such as **MASTER** (the .FNT extension is optional).

4. Type a 15-character description for this font. This description will appear with the other fonts in MASTER.FNT when you display the Font pull-down menu in First Publisher.

5. Press ⟨TAB⟩. You now must type the First Publisher pathname.

6. Press ⟨ENTER⟩ to send the soft fonts to the destination file.

7. Repeat steps 2 through 6 for each soft font you are adding.

Press ⟨ESC⟩ to return to the FONTMOVE Main Menu.

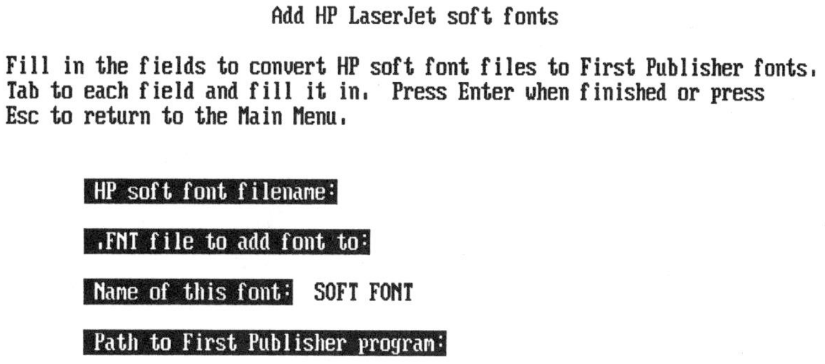

```
                      Add HP LaserJet soft fonts

      Fill in the fields to convert HP soft font files to First Publisher fonts.
      Tab to each field and fill it in. Press Enter when finished or press
      Esc to return to the Main Menu.


           HP soft font filename:

           .FNT file to add font to:

           Name of this font:  SOFT FONT

           Path to First Publisher program:
```

FIGURE 7-5.   Adding HP LaserJet fonts in FONTMOVE

Summary

In this chapter you learned how to

- Use the various fonts available with First Publisher, including the internal, cartridge, scalable, and soft fonts
- Use fonts designed for your specific printer
- Understand the difference between .FNT font files and .FNB scalable font files
- Move fonts to and from the MASTER.FNT file from the Set Up Fonts menu of version 3 and from the FONTMOVE program of version 2

APPLICATIONS FOR
FIRST PUBLISHER

I n the first section, you learned the fundamentals of desktop publishing
while seeing the environment, editing tools, and layout elements of the
First Publisher system. Each function and command for versions 2 and 3 of
First Publisher was described in the first seven chapters.

Part II will take you on a guided tour of several useful First Publisher
applications that use the commands you learned in Part I. Now that you have
tackled the basics, it is time to learn how to apply your knowledge.

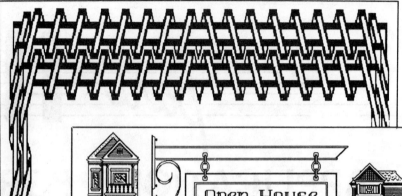

Open House

Th

to

ke

Fron
firs1
ball
over

Cont
our

The Teacher
Aug. 17, 1990 Vol.3, No. 8

School is Almost Here!

In less than a month, you are going to get a new group of 30 or so kids, all of whom are anxiously awaiting your professional teaching methods. Well, maybe they are not anxiously awaiting! Nevertheless, they are wondering how their new teacher is going to handle the class.

Your first week of school should be light. You want your children to know that you are not the ogre they have heard about (yes, word gets around, despite the fact that the word is often incorrect!) but that you are a kind and patient instructor who wants to help them learn. As you know, they can only learn when they WANT to learn. If nothing else, provide an atmosphere of understanding so they will feel comfortable in their new classroom.

When designing your bulletin boards, be sure to use lots of color. Drab, dull classrooms are fun neither for the students, nor for you. If (see page 2)

School Supplies are Ample for this Fiscal Year

Unlike the last five years, we have ample school supplies for the children throughout the entire school year of 1990-1991. You must, however, get your requests into your principal's office before the end of this month or you may lose out. We are donating all unused supplies to our bordering school districts since they are not as fortunate as we are. Due to their needs, we are wanting to give them those supplies as soon as we possibly can so they can get their year started too.

Be sure that your classrooms have plenty of the following supplies: pencils, pens, crayons, paper, staples, paper clips, rulers, chalk, bookcases, drawing pads, maps, erasers, and desks. We have made sure that each classroom has been repaired and is in top shape. You must also be (see page 3)

chapter **8**

RULER NOTATION
USED IN PART II

Horizontal and Vertical Placement

Before starting directly into the creation of applications with First Publisher, you should learn to use the special ruler line notation used throughout the rest of the book. This short chapter explains the ruler line notation. Since so many of the publications created in later chapters require exact placement of lines and art to match the figures in the book, the ruler line notation will ensure that your publications match those in the book.

HORIZONTAL AND VERTICAL PLACEMENT

Display the ruler lines on your screen by pressing (ALT-L). When you do, you will see the horizontal and vertical ruler lines shown in Figure 8-1. The ruler line will help position text, graphics, and baselines.

On each ruler line is a cross hair that indicates exactly where the cursor is located in a publication. The intersection of the cross hairs is the location of the cursor. When you are placing graphics text, or art, the cross hair tells you the position of the graphics cursor, hand placement tool, line- and box-drawing cross, pencil, and eraser.

Changing the Ruler Line Measurements

The measurement across the ruler line is in inches unless you change the program's default to centimeters. To change the measurement used on the ruler line to centimeters, follow these steps:

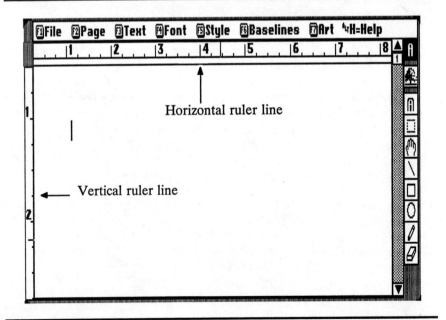

FIGURE 8-1. Looking at the horizontal and vertical ruler lines

1. Select Customize from the File pull-down menu.

2. Press (**F6**) to select the Centimeters option at the "Ruler and grid" prompt.

3. Press (**F1**) to accept the changes and return to the publication screen.

4. All subsequent ruler lines will appear in centimeters, as shown here:

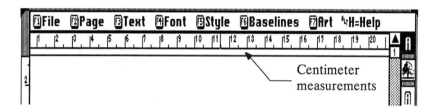

When you change the ruler line measurements, First Publisher will retain those measurements and use them in subsequent publishing sessions until you change them back. All ruler line measurements used in this book are set to inches.

Note to Version 2 Users   Your ruler line can only be set to inches.

Using the Notation

The notation in the rest of this book will use a horizontal measurement, designated by an *H* followed by a number, and a *V* followed by a number. In other words, if you see "H2.25, V1.25" in the book, you should position the pointer at the 2.25-inch position on the horizontal ruler and 1.25 inches down on the vertical ruler. Figure 8-2 shows a pointer located at the H2.25, V1.25 position.

   If more exact placement is needed (outside of the quarter-inch ruler marks), the ruler line measurement will be followed by an arrow keypress, such as "H2.25, V1.25, (**RIGHT ARROW**) three times, (**DOWN ARROW**) four times." To place your pointer here, position it at the quarter-inch measurements first ((**SHIFT-ARROW**) keypresses always take you to the nearest quarter-inch measurement), then press (**RIGHT ARROW**) three times and (**DOWN ARROW**) four times.

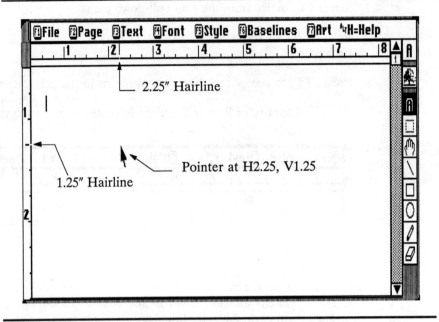

FIGURE 8-2. Exact placement of the pointer

Since the mouse is not exact enough for fine positioning, mouse users should use the arrow keys to get these exact placements. The mouse is, however, great for moving text and graphics over large areas; you can use the arrow keys to finalize the positioning. The arrow keys are also more helpful (and exact) for positioning the cross hairs on the ruler lines.

SINGLE- AND MULTIPLE-COLUMN NEWSLETTERS

Creating a Single-Column Newsletter
Creating a Multiple-Column Newsletter
One Final Tip for Version 2

This chapter walks you through designing newsletter baselines before adding text or graphics. You will find that creating the layout first makes the final editing easier.

The first half of this chapter describes the steps needed to produce a single-column newsletter. Then, a multiple-column newsletter is created so that you may learn the differences in design and layout.

While producing the second newsletter, you will see how supplied *template* publications give you predesigned layouts you can use for your own publications. You may not have as much flexibility with templates as you do with the newsletters you design from scratch; nevertheless, you can quickly create professional-looking newsletters by using the template files.

CREATING A SINGLE-COLUMN NEWSLETTER

Figure 9-1 shows a newsletter that you can create by following the steps described in the next few pages. You have already learned the steps needed to create this or any other publication. However, the detailed steps shown in this chapter help you put this knowledge together faster. You may want to customize this example with your own newsletter's text and art.

Grabbing the Needed Art

Before starting the sample publication, you will need the art images of the flag and the pen. The flag is located in the HOLIDAYS.MAC file, and the PERSONAL.MAC file holds the pen. You grabbed art from a .MAC file in Chapter 4, but this time will be a little different; this newsletter requires that you adjust the art before saving it. Follow the steps below to get the flag and pen:

1. Select the Get art option from the Art pull-down menu and load the HOLIDAYS.MAC file. Version 2 users will have to select Get graphics from the File pull-down menu.

2. Keep pressing (CTRL-PGDN) or point to the lower quarter of the elevator bar with the mouse to view the flag.

3. Since you have to fence the flag in a rectangle before capturing it (by using the selection tool), the surrounding art needs to be erased so that all four sides of the flag are clear. Select the eraser tool and erase the art around the flag. An example is shown in Figure 9-2.

4. Choose the selection tool and point above the upper-right corner of the flag. Press and hold a mouse button, or press (F10), to anchor the starting point. Drag the mouse down and to the left, or use the arrow keys, to enclose the entire flag. Press (F10) again to select the flag. Don't enclose any more of the white space around the flag than you have to, but be sure to include the entire flag.

5. Press (ALT-L) to display the ruler lines.

6. Press (ALT-R) to select Resize from the Art pull-down menu.

The Teacher

Aug. 17, 1990 Vol.3, No. 8

School is Almost Here!

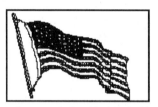

In less than a month, you are going to get a new group of 30 or so kids, all of whom are anxiously awaiting your professional teaching methods. Well, maybe they are not anxiously awaiting! Nevertheless, they are wondering how their new teacher is going to handle the class.

Your first week of school should be light. You want your children to know that you are not the ogre they have heard about (yes, word gets around, despite the fact that the word is often incorrect!) but that you are a kind and patient instructor who wants to help them learn. As you know, they can only learn when they WANT to learn. If nothing else, provide an atmosphere of understanding so they will feel comfortable in their new classroom.

When designing your bulletin boards, be sure to use lots of color. Drab, dull classrooms are fun neither for the students, nor for you. If (see page 2)

School Supplies are Ample for this Fiscal Year

Unlike the last five years, we have ample school supplies for the children throughout the entire school year of 1990-1991. You must, however, get your requests into your principal's office before the end of this month or you may lose out. We are donating all unused supplies to our bordering school districts since they are not as fortunate as we are. Due to their needs, we are wanting to give them those supplies as soon as we possibly can so they can get their year started too.

Be sure that your classrooms have plenty of the following supplies: pencils, pens, crayons, paper, staples, paper clips, rulers, chalk, bookcases, drawing pads, maps, erasers, and desks. We have made sure that each classroom has been repaired and is in top shape. You must also be (see page 3)

FIGURE 9-1.   A single-column newsletter

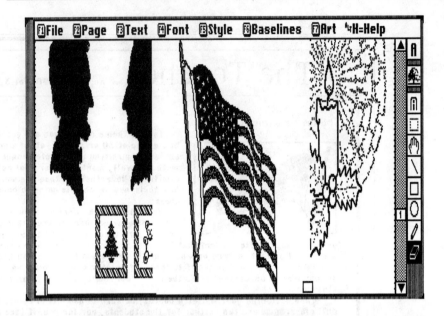

≡≡≡ **FIGURE 9-2.**   Clearing space around the flag art image

7. Resize the flag (refer to Chapter 4 for help if you need it) so that it is approximately 2 1/4 inches wide and 1 1/2 inches high. This will ensure that it fits in the newsletter box. Since the flag is not placed exactly on ruler quarter-inch marks, you will have to estimate. Figure 9-3 shows what your screen will look like.

8. Press (F7) to display the Art pull-down menu. Select Save art and type **FLAG** at the "Save filename" prompt.

Now you must get the pen. It is slightly easier to grab because of its placement in the PERSONAL.MAC file. Follow these steps:

1. Select Get art from the Art pull-down menu. Version 2 users will have to select Get graphics from the File pull-down menu.

2. Press (F2) to ignore the "Save filename" prompt.

3. Type **PERSONAL.MAC** to load the file.

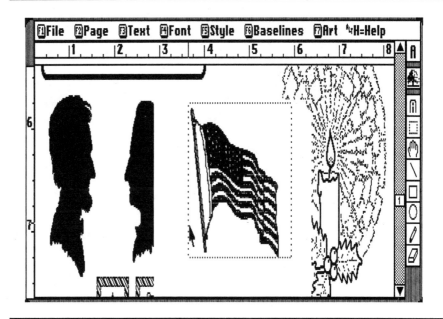

FIGURE 9-3.   After shrinking the art image

4. Scroll the screen downward until you see the pen. Erase the bottom half of the beer mug above the pen.

5. Select the pen with the selection tool. Do not select any more white space around the pen than you have to.

6. Press (**ALT-O**) (Rotate from the Art pull-down menu) three times to position the pen properly for the newsletter. Figure 9-4 shows your screen after this is done.

7. Save the pen under the name of PEN.ART by selecting Save art from the Art pull-down menu.

Now that you have the needed art files, it is time to start the publication. Select Start over ((**ALT-Y**)) from the File pull-down menu to clear the screen. Do not save the publication when prompted to do so.

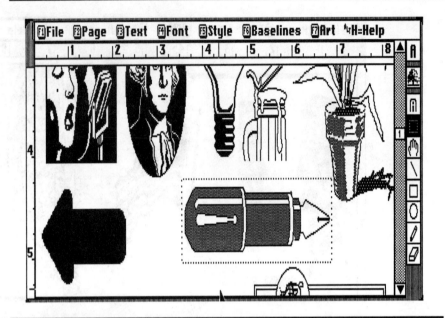

FIGURE 9-4. The rotated pen art image

Creating the Template

A template file is a file that contains baselines and unchanging art and text. For instance, in the newsletter that you are creating here, the title and placement of the art images will not change from issue to issue. The actual art, text, and headings may change, but their position on the page will not.

Once you get a good design for your newsletter, you will find it helpful to stick to it, or at least to two or three standard layouts. By doing this, you not only keep a familiar look for your readers, but you can also produce newsletters quickly without worrying about the layout each time.

The following sections will walk you through the newsletter's design and layout. Once completed, you will save the template file before adding the text and art.

INITIAL BASELINES Before starting the newsletter, adjust the baselines for the initial title and text. After there is a lot of art, the baselines are

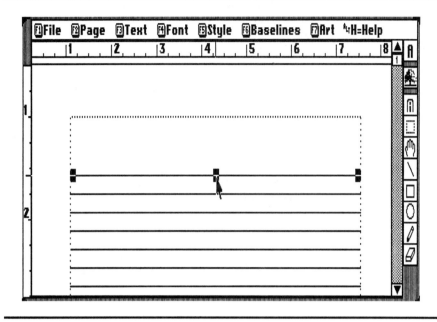

━━━━ **FIGURE 9-5.**   Pulling the baselines down the publication

harder to position. (If you need a review of baseline manipulation, refer to Chapter 6.) The following steps adjust the top baselines of the newsletter:

1. Press (**ALT-L**) to display the rulers.

2. Select Adjust column from the Baselines pull-down menu.

3. Select the top baseline (by pointing to it and pressing (**F10**)) and drag it down by the middle handle (which will eventually position the entire column of baselines) to V1.5. Press (**DOWN ARROW**) five times before releasing it by pressing (**F10**) again. Figure 9-5 shows your screen at this point. This is the date and issue number baseline.

4. Since this text will change, but the title will not, shorten the top baseline to hold only the date and issue information. Point to the left handle and drag it to H5.0.

You now must make room for the heading, "School is Almost Here!" The second baseline is not low enough for this heading, so pull it down by following these steps:

1. Select Adjust below from the Baselines pull-down menu since you want to adjust the second baseline and all baselines below it.

2. Select the second baseline by pointing to it and pressing **F10**.

3. Drop the baseline to V2.25. Press **F10** to move all the baselines down. Your screen will look like the one in Figure 9-6.

4. Press **F10** to anchor the baseline. Drag the left end of the second baseline to H1.0, V2.25 and press **RIGHT ARROW** four times.

5. Press **F10** to expand all of the baselines below the title.

OUTLINE AND TITLE BOX   You now will draw the lines to surround the newsletter and the box that will hold the title. Draw the outline by following these steps:

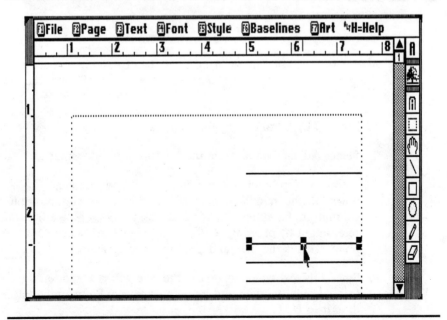

FIGURE 9-6. Making room for a heading

1. Select the box-drawing tool (above the circle).
2. Move the cross to H0.5, V0.75. Anchor the upper-left corner of the box by pressing (**F10**).
3. Press the arrow keys or drag the mouse until the lower-right corner of the box falls at H7.75, V10.25. Press (**F10**) to anchor the box.
4. Press (**CTRL-HOME**) to display the top of the newsletter. Your screen should look like the one in Figure 9-7.

Notice that there is a straight wide line drawn directly below the top of the outline in the final newsletter (see Figure 9-1). These types of lines help frame a publication. Use them sparingly to produce good effects. To draw the line:

1. Select the line-drawing tool (the slanted line).
2. Select the thickest line width. Version 3 users press (**ALT-HYPHEN**), while version 2 users press (**ALT-F9**).
3. Position the line-drawing cross to H0.5, V0.75. Press (**DOWN ARROW**) three times and (**RIGHT ARROW**) twice.
4. Press (**F10**) to anchor the line.

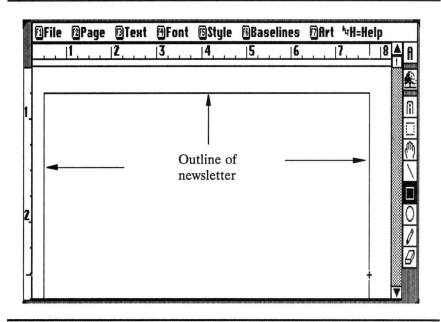

FIGURE 9-7.   Outlining the newsletter

5. Press (SHIFT-RIGHT ARROW) until the line extends all the way across the page to position H7.75. (The thick line will not appear until you anchor the end point.)

6. Press (LEFT ARROW) twice. Anchor the line with (F10). Your screen will look like this:

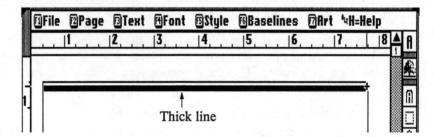

Thick line

 These instructions may seem tedious, but have patience. Remember that you only need to create templates once. From then on, the publication is much easier to produce. After this sample newsletter, the rest of the book uses many of First Publisher's predesigned templates.

Now follow these steps to draw the box that encloses the title.

1. Select the box-drawing tool.
2. Move the cross to H0.5, V1.0. Press (RIGHT ARROW) twice.
3. Select the thinnest line width.
4. Anchor the box by pressing (F10).
5. Drag the lower-right corner of the box to H7.75, V1.75, and press (LEFT ARROW) twice.
6. Press (F10) to anchor the box. Your screen will look like this:

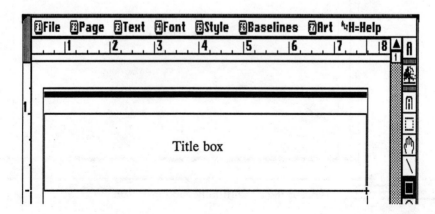

Title box

TYPING THE TITLE   The title lines are relatively easy. Remember, however, that the first baseline does *not* extend across the entire page; it is there
only for the date and issue numbers. Therefore, the title cannot be produced
with the text tool.

This is to your advantage. You will not be changing the title of the
publication (or if you do, it will be rare). By keeping the title in the art text
mode, you will not accidentally overwrite it when changing the date and issue
text. To type the title, follow these steps:

1. Select the graphics text tool.

2. Move the pointer to H1.5, V1.5. Press (**DOWN ARROW**) five times.

3. Press (**F10**) twice to move the cursor to the pointer location. This is
    where you will begin typing the title.

4. Press (**F4**) to change the font to New York.

5. Use the Style pull-down menu to change to the normal 36-point style.

6. Type **The Teacher**. This is graphics text, so be sure it is correct (press
    (**BACKSPACE**) if needed) before going further.

7. Press (**ALT-A**) to see the baselines. You are now able to get an idea of
    the newsletter's layout. Your screen should look similar to the one in
    Figure 9-8.

8. You will use the short top baseline next. Press (**ALT-A**) to get rid of the
    baselines temporarily.

     If your screen does not look exactly like the figures, do not be con-
cerned. By changing baselines or using the text- and art-editing tools,
you can modify your publication to match the figures as closely as
possible.

Now that the title is placed, it is time to type the date and issue number.
Even though you are still in the template-creation stage, go ahead and
completely type the date and issue number.

1. Press (**SHIFT-F9**) or point to the text tool. The cursor will move to the
    start of the top baseline.

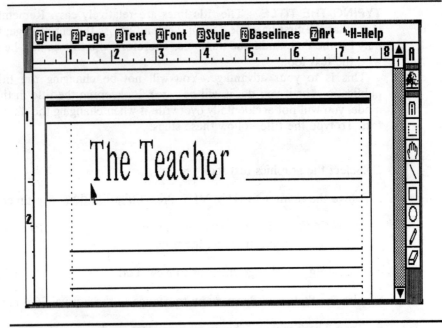

FIGURE 9-8. After typing the title

2. Press **F4** and change the font to Geneva.

3. Press **F5** and select Bold. Press **F5** again to select the 10-point size.

4. Type **Aug. 17, 1990 Vol. 3, No. 8**.

5. Press **ENTER** to move the cursor to the next baseline.

6. Press **ALT-A** again to see your publication and its baselines. It should look like this

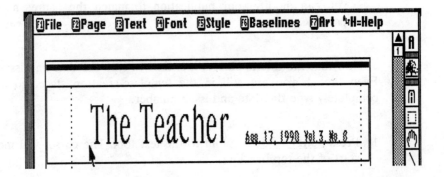

If your text is too high in the banner, adjust the single baseline to correct it.

ADDING THE VERTICAL LINE   Notice that the baselines in Figure 9-8 are not evenly placed within the outline of the publication. This is okay because you are going to put a vertical line in the empty space. This gives a downward feel to the page and enhances a single-column newsletter very well.

To add the line, follow these steps:

1. Select the line tool.

2. Select the widest line thickness.

3. Position the cross to H0.75, V2.0.

4. Press ⌐**F10**⌐ to anchor the line.

5. Press ⌐**SHIFT-DOWN ARROW**⌐, or carefully move the mouse downward, until the line is exactly at H0.75, V10.0.

6. Press ⌐**F10**⌐ again.

7. Press ⌐**CTRL-HOME**⌐ to see the top of the publication again. It will look like the one in Figure 9-9.

ADDING AN ART OUTLINE   The flag will go in a boxed outline positioned below the title. In future issues you can place other art inside the box where the flag will go now.

    If you do not use picturewrap, you may want to place art in boxes to separate it from the text.

To add the box to the publication, follow these steps:

1. Select the box-drawing tool.

2. Select the second line thickness.

3. Move the cross to H1.0, V2.5. Press ⌐**RIGHT ARROW**⌐ nine times.

4. Press ⌐**F10**⌐ to anchor the upper-left corner of the box.

5. Drag the lower-right corner of the box to H3.5, V4.0.

6. Press ⌐**F10**⌐ to finish the box.

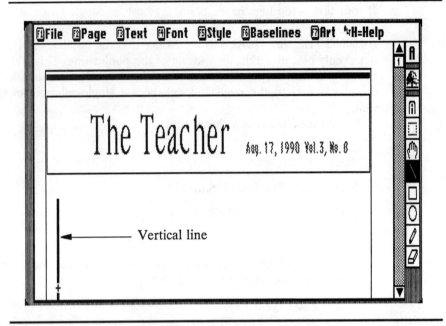

FIGURE 9-9. Adding the vertical line down the newsletter

On your monitor, the box may not look even. This is due to the increased or decreased resolution of some monitor graphics adapter cards. If you are unsure of the art dimensions, press **ALT-Z** to preview the page, or print a copy of it. Displaying the ruler lines (**ALT-L**) will help keep art and text in their proper perspective.

ADJUSTING THE BODY BASELINES The body of the text will start to the right of the flag image, and then span across the page below the flag. It is a relatively simple matter to adjust the baselines. Follow these steps:

1. Select Adjust below from the Baselines pull-down menu. You want to adjust the third baseline and all baselines that follow it.

2. Point to the third baseline (the one directly above the art box you just drew), and display its handles by pressing **F10**.

3. Point to the leftmost handle and drag the baseline to the right until the pointer is at H3.75, V2.5.

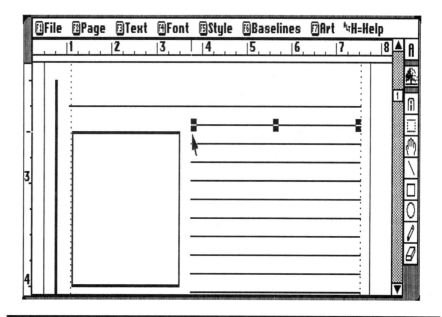

FIGURE 9-10.   Making room for the art outline

4. Press (**F10**) to adjust the rest of the baselines. Your screen should look like the one in Figure 9-10. (You may have to readjust the baselines to make them come out exactly like those in the the figure.)

Now you can extend the baselines below the art box back to the left margin. To do so

1. Select the eleventh baseline and display its handles. This is the line that falls well under the box just drawn.

2. Drag the leftmost handle to H1.0, V4.25. Press (**RIGHT ARROW**) nine times.

3. Press (**F10**) to anchor the baseline and adjust all those that fall below it. Your screen should look like the one in Figure 9-11.

DRAWING THE SECOND ART BOX   You are almost through with the template for this newsletter. It is time to draw the lower art outline, where the pen image will be placed for this issue. To do this, follow these steps:

1. Select the box-drawing tool.

2. Select the second line width.

3. Move the cross to H1.0, V5.5.

4. Press ⟨**RIGHT ARROW**⟩ nine times to align it with the text and the other art outline.

5. Press ⟨**F10**⟩ to anchor the upper-left corner of the box.

6. Drag the box to H7.5, V7.25.

7. Press ⟨**F10**⟩. The lower box will appear.

REPAIRING BASELINES   Notice that the baselines appear inside the box you just drew. You must move those baselines down below the box. Follow these steps:

1. Select Adjust below again from the Baselines pull-down menu.

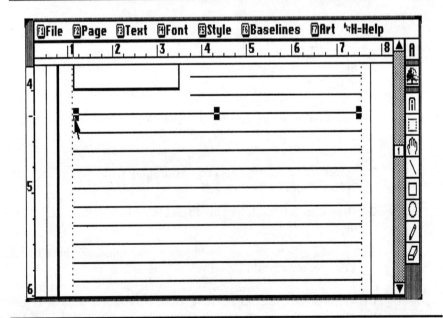

FIGURE 9-11.   Pulling the baselines back to the left margin

2. Select the highest baseline inside the box by displaying its handles.

3. Grab the middle handle and drag the baseline to V7.5.

4. Press **F10** to position the rest of the baselines.

Figure 9-12 shows your screen at this point. This is the complete template for the newsletter; save this file as NEWSLTR.PUB. From issue to issue, all you will have to do is load this template, fill in the appropriate text, and add the desired art images.

Finishing the Newsletter

Your newsletter needs a heading over each section of text. The headings for this publication are printed in Geneva 12-point bold type. Select the text tool and font style, move the cursor to the beginning of the second baseline, and type **School is Almost Here!.**

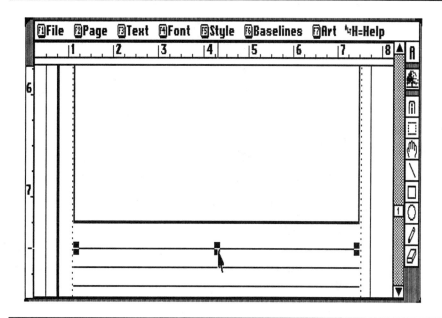

FIGURE 9-12. After adding the second art box

To finish the body of the newsletter, move the text cursor to the third baseline and type the following text in the Geneva 10-point bold font. Be sure to type only one space after each sentence before beginning the next one. To indent paragraphs, press (SPACEBAR) five times.

```
     In less than a month, you are going to get a new
group of 30 or so kids, all of whom are anxiously
awaiting your professional teaching methods. Well, maybe
they are not anxiously awaiting! Nevertheless, they are
wondering how their new teacher is going to handle the
class.
     Your first week of school should be light.  You
want your children to know that you are not the ogre
they have heard about (yes, word gets around, despite
the fact that the word is often incorrect!) but that you
are a kind and patient instructor who wants to help them
learn. As you know, they can only learn when they WANT
to learn. If nothing else, provide an atmosphere of
understanding so they will feel comfortable in their new
classroom.
     When designing your bulletin boards, be sure to use
lots of color. Drab, dull classrooms are fun neither for
the students, nor for you. If (see page 2)
```

The second heading is only slightly more complicated since it is centered on the baseline. To create this heading:

1. Move the cursor to the *second* baseline below the art outline.

2. Type **School Supplies are Ample for this Fiscal Year**, and then press (ENTER). (The Geneva 12-point bold type should still be selected; if it is not, select it before typing the heading.)

3. Press (ALT-A) to adjust a single baseline.

4. Select the baseline you just typed on.

5. Press (ALT-X) to center the text on this baseline.

Now move the cursor two lines below the second heading and type the following:

```
     Unlike the last five years, we have ample school
supplies for the children throughout the entire school
```

year of 1990-1991. You must, however, get your requests
into your principal's office before the end of this
month or you may lose out. We are donating all unused
supplies to our bordering school districts since they
are not as fortunate as we are. Due to their needs, we
are wanting to give them those supplies as soon as we
possibly can so they can get their year started too.

Be sure that your classrooms have plenty of the
following supplies: pencils, pens, crayons, paper,
staples, paper clips, rulers, chalk, bookcases, drawing
pads, maps, erasers, and desks. We have made sure that
each classroom has been repaired and is in top shape.
You must also be (see page 3)

Figure 9-13 shows your publication at this point. If your text does not fit the
space exactly as it does in the figure, you may have to end it early by typing
(see page 2) or **(see page 3)** sooner.

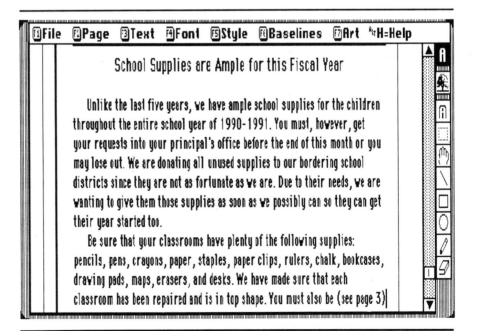

‗‗‗‗‗‗ **FIGURE 9-13.**   The text in the newsletter

GETTING THE ART   The two art images are the only things left to add. Since you already resized them to fit the art outlines, the placement will be easy. Follow these steps:

1. Select Get art from the Art pull-down menu.
2. Get the FLAG.ART file.
3. Move the hand tool until it rests over the outline for the flag.
4. Press ⟨F10⟩ or click a mouse button.
5. When the flag is centered inside the box, press ⟨F10⟩ again or release the mouse.

Repeat these steps for the PEN.ART file and place this image in the middle of the bottom box. Save your newsletter and print it out in the smoothed mode. It should look like the one shown in Figure 9-1.

Now take a rest. You deserve it.

CREATING A MULTIPLE-COLUMN NEWSLETTER

Now that you have seen the process for creating your own template files, most of the rest of the examples in this book work with First Publisher's supplied template files. If you can use any of these files, you will find that your publications are already professionally laid out for you.

Figure 9-14 shows the publication you will create using the NEWS.PUB template supplied with First Publisher. There are three columns in the top half and two columns in the bottom half of the publication. The titles span the entire width of the page.

Preparing for the Newsletter

Print a copy of NEWS.PUB so you can follow along. You will notice that there are some comments throughout the template, such as "First article, 1st column" and "Your own photo here." These comments are to help you place the art and text.

Stock Pick Paper

Things Could Look Better

Technicians are Correct! The Bears are Back!!!

Today marked the first occurrence of the down cycle that should span several years. The bears, primarily made up of stock technicians, have accurately predicted this fall in the financial markets. To the dismay of many investors, it looks as though the bears have taken the bull by the horns.

We are witnessing an increased move away from the financial markets toward the more stable cash positions. It is predicted that interest rates are going to sky-rocket; hence, the move to cash positions.

"I have been looking for this for some time now," says a vice president from a leading brokerage house. "I do not know if we have totally gone 100% cash, however, I do know that my firm has been thinking cash for around

Your city's lights may dim due to the economy

three months."

In another interview, Victor Young said that he does not believe the market has attained its highest peak. He believes that the majority is now right for the first time that any of us can remember. Mr. Young said he has

discussed these matters with Mr. Michael Stapp who had the following comments:

"Don't look at the past. The past does not ensure future success or failure."

Young believes that Stapp is going to the (see page 2)

Next Year's Inflation Figures Are Surprising

In an economy such as we have had as of late, many people fear that next year's inflation figures will be higher than this one's.

Edward DiArgo's inflation index indicates that the coming year will be the end of low interest rates.

"We are moving into a new era where the 10% mortgage is behind us," says DiArgo.

"There is nothing to keep interest rates down. The Federal Reserve Chairman is simply not

going to let this economy speed up any further. When they put the skids on our rates, it will be tighter than this country has ever seen. We will be buying homes with money that costs us 20-25%, an unheard of figure until now."

DiArgo goes on to point out that these rates are purely temporary until the budget deficit is eased. He points out that our economy actually is strong in all areas except for the deficit. When next month's rates are posted from the second quarter, you will find that all leading indicators are actually (see page 3)

FIGURE 9-14.   Sample multiple-column newsletter

All of the comments are placed on the template as graphics text, which makes it easy to erase them. Now that you have a printed copy of NEWS .PUB, select the eraser tool and erase the comments typed in the publication (such as "photo or art").

Save the publication as STOCK.PUB (do not overwrite NEWS.PUB, or you will lose the original template). Now you are ready to create the banner and art image in a separate art file to be brought into the newsletter later.

CREATING THE TITLE   Select Start over from the File pull-down menu. Your newsletter will be safely saved on disk under STOCK.PUB. Once you have a clear screen, you can create the "Stock Pick Paper" title. The title goes where the template "Banner" message appeared.

This title must be typed with graphics text so that you can invert the letters and get the light letters on a dark background. If you measure the template, you will see that a title of seven inches by one inch will fit nicely inside the banner area of the template. Follow these steps to produce the title:

1. Select the graphics text tool.

2. Press **F4** to display the Font pull-down menu.

3. Select the New York font if it is not still selected.

4. Press **F5** to display the Style pull-down menu.

5. Select 36 Points and the Normal style.

6. Type **Stock Pick Paper**. It does not matter where you place this on the blank screen, as you will save it to an art file in a moment.

7. Outline the graphics text with the selection tool. Be sure to include a small amount of white space on all four sides of the title.

8. Once you have outlined the title with the selection tool, choose Invert from the Art pull-down menu.

9. Press **ALT-L** to display the rulers.

You now must use the art-resizing skills you learned in Chapter 4 to resize the title to fit the banner area. Press **ALT-R** and resize the image to seven inches wide and one inch high. Use the ruler to guide you.

   You might find that moving the start of the image to an even quarter-inch mark will make the resizing easier.

Once resized, outline the image with the selection tool. Then save the art by selecting Save art from the Art pull-down menu and storing it under STITLE.

Getting the Art Image

Now you must get the city outline for the publication. Although the template says "Your own photo here," you can place any art in this space. The size of the space is 4 1/4 inches wide and 2 1/2 inches high. The art must be clipped from the PERSONAL.MAC graphics file and resized as follows:

1. Select Start over from the File pull-down menu. Do not save the publication when asked to do so (press **F2** at the prompt).

2. Select Get art from the Art pull-down menu. Version 2 users will have to select Get graphics from the File pull-down menu.

3. Load the PERSONAL.MAC clip art file that comes with First Publisher.

4. Outline the city image at the top of the file with the selection tool. Do not outline any more white space than you need in order to get all of the city.

5. Select Save art from the Art pull-down menu. Save the file as CITY .ART.

6. Select Start over (**ALT-Y**) from the File pull-down menu.

7. Select Get art and get the CITY.ART clip art. You now have a blank publication in which you can enlarge the city outline.

8. Resize the city to 4 1/4 inches wide and 2 1/2 inches tall. Do not worry about the surrounding art. The resized image will overwrite it.

9. Select Save art, and save the art image back under the filename of CITY.

10. Select Get publication from the File pull-down menu. Load the STOCK.PUB template. Do not save the PERSONAL publication when asked to do so.

Adding Text

It is now time to add text to STOCK.PUB. Press (ALT-A) to see the baselines where your text will appear. There are no baselines for the headings; you will have to add graphics text for these later.

To add the text, first press (ALT-A) to hide the baselines. Check the font to make sure Swiss 10-point normal type is selected. Select the text tool. If the cursor is not positioned at the start of the first column, move it there and type the following text. Be sure to type the hyphens where shown in the text since First Publisher does not hyphenate for you.

Today marked the first occur- rence of the down cycle
that should span several years. The bears, primarily
made up of stock technicians, have accurately predicted
this fall in the financial markets. To the dismay of
many investors, it looks as though the bears have taken
the bull by the horns.

We are witnessing an increased move away from the
financial markets toward the more stable cash positions.
It is predicted that interest rates are going to sky-
rocket; hence, the move to cash positions.

"I have been looking for this for some time now," says a
vice president from a leading brokerage house. "I do not
know if we have totally gone 100% cash, however, I do
know that my firm has been thinking cash for around
three months."

In another interview, Victor Young said that he does not
believe the market has attained its highest peak. He
believes that the majority is now right for the first
time that any of us can remember. Mr. Young said he has
discussed these matters with Mr. Michael Stapp who had
the following comments:

"Don't look at the past. The past does not ensure future
success or failure."

Young believes that Stapp is going to the (see page 2)

After you type the text, your screen will look like Figure 9-15. If the text does not fit as shown in the figure, you should check the spelling and hyphenation. Make sure the font style and size are set properly.

Move the cursor to the second half of the publication and type the following:

In an economy such as we have had as of late, many
people fear that next year's inflation figures will be
higher than this one's.

Edward DiArgo's inflation index indicates that the
coming year will be the end of low interest rates.

"We are moving into a new era where the 10% mortgage is
behind us," says DiArgo.

"There is nothing to keep interest rates down. The
Federal Reserve Chairman is simply not going to let this
economy speed up any further. When they put the skids on
our rates, it will be tighter than this country has ever
seen. We will be buying homes with money that costs us
20-25%, an unheard of figure until now."

DiArgo goes on to point out that these rates are purely
temporary until the budget deficit is eased. He points
out that our economy actually is strong in all areas
except for the deficit. When next month's rates are
posted from the second quarter, you will find that all
leading indicators are actually (see page 3)

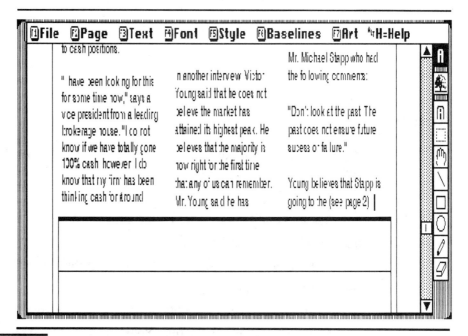

FIGURE 9-15. Adding the upper text

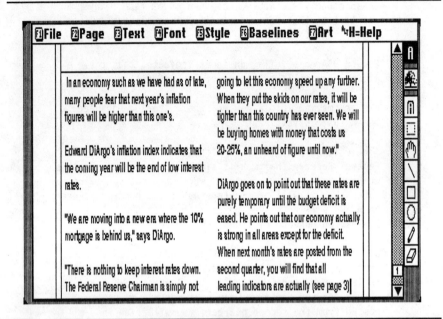

FIGURE 9-16. Adding the lower text

When you have finished typing, your screen will look like the one in Figure 9-16.

Adding the Title, Art, and Headings

Press `CTRL-HOME` to move to the top of the publication. The title is easy to place since you have already resized it to fit the banner space. To add the heading, follow these steps:

1. Select Get art from the Art pull-down menu.

2. Type **STITLE**, the filename of the title.

3. Move the hand pointer to the upper-left corner of the banner area.

4. Press `F10`. The title will appear.

5. Use the arrow keys to center the title inside the banner area.

6. Press `F10` again to anchor the title. Your screen will be similar to this:

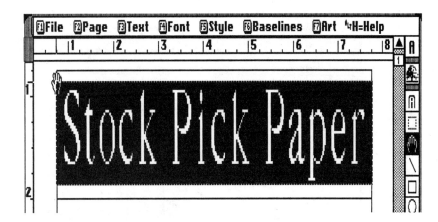

Repeat the above steps to add the city image from the art file saved as CITY.ART. Place it inside the outlined corners of the template file so it looks like the screen in Figure 9-17.

To add the headline, follow these steps:

1. Select the graphics text tool.

2. Select New York 18-point bold type.

3. Point to the template file at H0.75, V2.75, and press `UP ARROW` twice and `RIGHT ARROW` seven times.

4. Press `F10` to anchor the cursor.

5. Type **Technicians are Correct! The Bears are Back!!!**.

6. If you need to reposition the headline, select it and move it. Your screen should look like the one in Figure 9-18.

7. Add the "kicker" line of the template by pointing to H0.75, V2.25, followed by `DOWN ARROW` seven times and `RIGHT ARROW` six times.

8. Press `F10` to position the cursor.

9. Select Swiss 12-point roman type.

10. Type **Things Could Look Better** above the line.

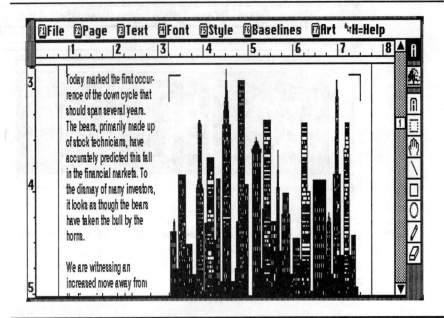

FIGURE 9-17. Placing the CITY.ART image

FIGURE 9-18. Typing the heading

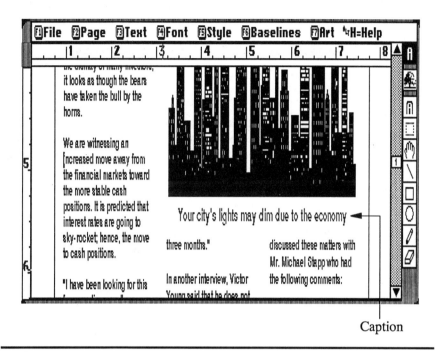

Caption

══ **FIGURE 9-19.**   The caption is added below the art

Now scroll downward to the city art image. You need to place a caption under the art. First change the font point size to 12; then follow these steps:

1. Point to H3.5, V5.5.
2. Press (**F10**) to anchor the cursor.
3. Type **Your city's lights may dim due to the economy.**
4. Clean up the newsletter by erasing the extra corner guides that enclose the art and captions. (You may have to magnify the screen with (**ALT-M**) to edit the fine points between text and art.) Once done, your screen will look like the one in Figure 9-19.

You are almost done. Type a centered heading above the second half of the text by following these steps:

1. Scroll down the screen and select the graphics text tool if it is not still selected.
2. Point to H1.25, V7.75.

3. Select New York 18-point bold (keep your headlines in a similar font).

4. Press (F10) to anchor the cursor.

5. Type **Next Year's Inflation Figures Are Surprising.**

6. Press (SHIFT-F9) to display the text. Your screen will look like the one in Figure 9-20.

You are now finished. Save your publication and print it out. Be proud of the job you did! Your publishing speed will improve as you create more publications. Even though a lot of work was required to produce this publication, it was much easier to do using the template file than it would have been to create it from scratch.

ONE FINAL TIP FOR VERSION 2

Version 2 of First Publisher comes with seven other newsletter template files you might want to load and print out for future use. These are available on

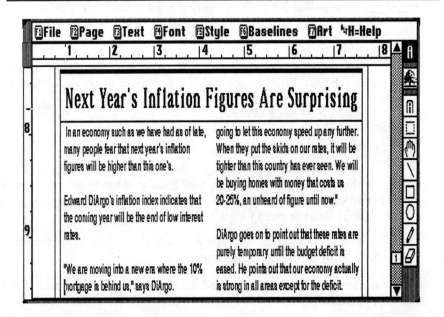

FIGURE 9-20. Centering the heading for the second section of text

Program Disk 2. Copy this to your hard disk, if you have not already done so, if you want to look at these templates.

The filenames of these templates are listed here:

1TOP2BOT.PUB

1TOP3BOT.PUB

2TOP1BOT.PUB

2TOP2BOT.PUB

2TOP3BOT.PUB

3TOP1BOT.PUB

3TOP2BOT.PUB

The first number of the filename is the number of columns in the upper half of the template. The second number is the bottom half's number of columns. For example, 2TOP3BOT.PUB has two columns above and three columns below.

Summary

In this chapter you saw how to create single- and multiple-column newsletters. You first created a template file that you can save for future newsletters, and then you

- Positioned the baselines for proper column placement
- Placed art and text on the newsletter within their borders
- Used the rich assortment of fonts within First Publisher to give your newsletter's headlines and titles a polished appearance

chapter **10**

ARTISTIC FLIERS

Creating a Flier
Adding a Coupon
Bordering the Entire Page

Fliers present special design considerations. They should be eye-catching images so that passers-by will stop to look at the advertisement. You need enough text to get your message across, but not *too* much—or no one will read it. A flier can consist of only text; if so, it must be laid out with a lot of white space. A general rule concerning text is

Less is better—keep it to the point.

In this chapter, you will create a flier. You learned most of the skills involved in earlier chapters.

Keep in mind that you want attention-getting fliers. Some interesting elements can be added to a flier, such as a coupon at the bottom to bring the reader into your place of business. You can also scan a drawing of your product and place it on the flier. Adding borders helps attract attention to the flier (borders are available from First Publisher's clip art).

CREATING A FLIER

Figure 10-1 shows the first flier you will create. It is relatively easy to produce since it fits nicely within the CIRCULAR.PUB template file available with First Publisher. Looking at the flier, you can see that it contains many important elements of good advertising:

- Lots of white space and little text. The reader always has time to read the entire flier.

- Attention-getting border placement. The *grabber* of the flier is "Your Dream Home!" Everybody wants a dream home, and the border makes these words jump out.

- Simple art that sticks to the main topic: houses. The "Open House" sign and adjacent houses at the top of the flier bring the reader's eyes downward.

- The company's name and address are included. Once you get your reader's attention, you want to tell the reader where to find you!

Preparing the Template

Select Get publication from the File pull-down menu and load CIRCULAR .PUB. Print it out to keep a copy of the original template while you make changes to it. Figure 10-2 shows CIRCULAR.PUB as it will print.

If you get the message "Cloister Black 36 isn't in MASTER. Okay to substitute Broadway 36?", press (F1) to accept and make the substitution. CIRCULAR.PUB was designed to use this font, found only in EXTRA1.FNT. Unless you have added Cloister 36 Black, First Publisher will ask if it is okay to substitute Broadway 36, which it is.

Take the time now to erase all of the words from the publication, but leave the positioning corners for art placement. You must use the eraser tool because all of the text ("Announcement," "House and trees," and so on) is graphics text. The CIRCULAR.PUB text is for reference only; obviously, not all of your fliers will be hotel-related.

Home Sales Realty
213 N. Main St.
Broken Arrow, KY 87123

Take advantage of our special rates!
From now until December 31st, we are offering a special 5%
first-year rate for home buyers. Sign up today for our special
balloon financing deals. No matter what your financial status
over the last few years has been, you can afford our homes.

Contact Bill or Gayle at the above address for more details on
our offerings. We hope you enjoy your happy home-buying!

FIGURE 10-1. Sample flier to create

Announcement

House and trees

Hotel name

Hotel address

Hotel description

FIGURE 10-2. Printout of the CIRCULAR.PUB template file

Save the file under a new name so you can modify it. The examples in this book assume you are saving the file as HOMESALE.PUB. First Publisher will supply the .PUB file extension when you select Save publication from the File pull-down menu.

As you might suspect, you should never save a template under its original filename if you have made changes to it. Keep the originals intact. If you have made backups of your original disks, as recommended in Appendix A, you can go back to those if you accidentally modify a template file.

GRABBING THE ART The first step in creating your sample flier is to get the clip art from the supplied .MAC files. The sign is stored in HOLIDAYS .MAC and the houses are located in PUBLICAT.MAC. Follow these steps to get the sign:

1. Clear your screen by pressing (**ALT-Y**) to select Start over from the File pull-down menu.

2. Select Get art from the Art pull-down menu. Version 2 users will need to select Get graphics from the File pull-down menu.

3. Type **HOLIDAYS.MAC** at the "Filename" prompt.

4. When the graphics file appears, scroll to the bottom of the page.

5. The "Open House" sign cannot be selected without erasing some of the surrounding art. Select the eraser tool and erase around the sign, as shown in Figure 10-3.

6. Choose the selection box again and select the sign.

If you are selecting the sign without a mouse, the (**SHIFT-ARROW**) keys will not take the pointer far enough down the page. You will have to use the arrow keys without the (**SHIFT**) key to get to the bottom of the sign.

7. Select Save art from the Art pull-down menu and type **HSIGN** at the "Save filename" prompt.

You now need the houses from the PUBLICAT.MAC file. Clip this art in a similar manner.

1. Select Start over from the File pull-down menu.

FIGURE 10-3. Making room to grab the sign

2. Select Get art from the Art pull-down menu. Press (F2) to ignore the "Save filename" prompt.

3. Type **PUBLICAT.MAC** for the graphics filename.

4. Scroll the screen down until the houses appear.

5. As with the sign, you will need to erase some of the lines from the clipboard that sits above the houses. Select the eraser tool and erase the bottom of the clipboard.

6. Choose the selection box tool and select both houses.

7. Select Save art from the Art pull-down menu.

8. Save the houses as HOUSES.

9. Select Get publication to load the HOMESALE.PUB file. Do not save the PUBLICAT file (press (F2) when prompted to do so).

PLACING THE TITLE BORDER You must move the border to the middle of the page for this flier. Follow these steps:

1. Press (ALT-L) to display the ruler lines.

2. Choose the selection box tool.

3. Select the entire border at the top of the page. Do not select any more white space than you have to.

4. Select the hand tool.

5. Press (**F10**) or click and hold the mouse. Drag the image until its bottom edge rests at the 6-inch line of the vertical ruler.

6. Press (**F10**) again or release the mouse.

The image should be centered within the middle corner marks, similar to Figure 10-4.

THE TOP ART   You must now load and position the art at the top of the flier. The houses pose a slight problem since you saved both of them together; they must be separated once placed on the flier. Load and position the houses by following these steps:

1. Scroll to the top of the document.

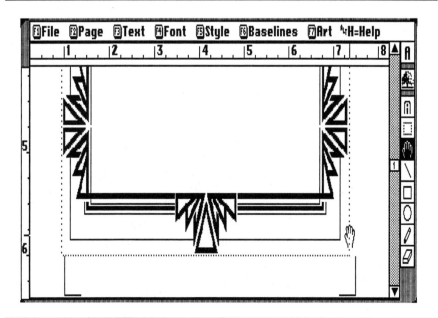

〓〓 **FIGURE 10-4.**   Centering the art image

2. Select Get art from the Art pull-down menu.

3. Type **HOUSES** at the "Filename" prompt.

4. Place the hand tool at the top of the page.

5. Press (**F10**) to display the houses. Move them as high as possible on the page, as shown in Figure 10-5.

 You should always look out for art that conflicts with the other art images. If you do not, you may have overlapping art that will have to be reloaded and repositioned.

To position the house art:

1. Select the first house.

2. Select the hand tool.

3. Press (**F10**) and move the house so it rests as close to V3.0 as possible and the top is placed at about H1.0.

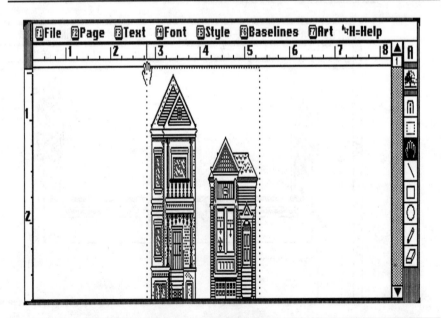

FIGURE 10-5. Placing the house art

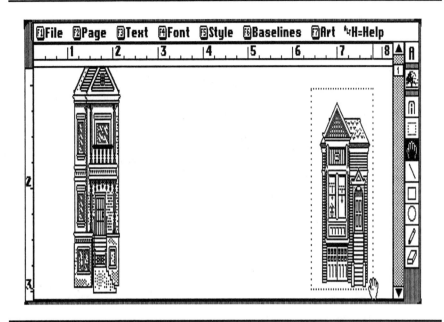

FIGURE 10-6. Moving the second house

4. Select the second house and move it so that it rests on V3.0 and the top of the house is at about H7.0.

Your screen will look similar to Figure 10-6.

Positioning the "Open House" sign is easy; simply get it (you saved it under HSIGN.ART) and place it evenly between the two houses. Make sure it rests approximately on the vertical 3.0 mark, too. Most fliers have a lot of room for positioning variances, but newsletters usually have precise columns of text. You can press (ALT-Z) to preview the flier as it stands. Figure 10-7 shows the previewed flier.

THE BANNER TEXT   Adding the banner text is straightforward. Since there are no baselines, you must type graphics text inside the banner. This also gives you the freedom to center the text by hand. To type the text:

1. Select the graphics text tool.

2. Select the New York 36-point normal font.

3. If you start the graphics text too high in the border, you will write over the top of the border. It is best to begin toward the bottom of the inside

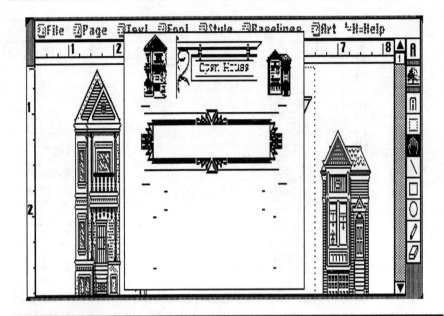

FIGURE 10-7. Previewing the flier

of the border, and then center the text by moving it after you have typed it. Therefore, position the pointer to H1.75, V5.25 and press **F10**.

4. Type **Your Dream Home!**.

5. Select the words with the selection box tool. Do not select any more of the surrounding white space than you have to. Center the text (leaving room for the lower line) within the sides of the border. Figure 10-8 shows the proper placement.

6. Select the New York 18-point bold font.

7. Repeat steps 4 and 5 to finish the bordered text with the "Can Be Yours!!!" line.

Erase the four corners around the bordered title. Leave the other corners for positioning the rest of the text.

THE FINAL TEXT   Type the name and address using the regular text tool. To add the name and address

1. Select the text tool.

FIGURE 10-8.   Positioning the banner text

2. Select the Geneva 12-point bold font.

3. Position the pointer so that it rests on the first full baseline in the corners for the name and address outline. This is approximately H3.0, V7.0.

4. Press (**F10**).

5. Type the following text:

   Home Sales Realty
   213 N. Main St.
   Broken Arrow, KY 87123

   Press (**ENTER**) at the end of each line. The graphics cursor will move to the next line at the same horizontal position as the beginning of the previous line. Continue pressing (**ENTER**) all the way down the page to add baselines for the rest of the text.

6. Choose Adjust above from the Baselines pull-down menu. Select the city and state baseline.

7. Press (**ALT-X**) to center all baselines above the city and state. This centers the name, address, and city lines.

8. Erase the four corners around the name and address. Your screen will look like the one in Figure 10-9.

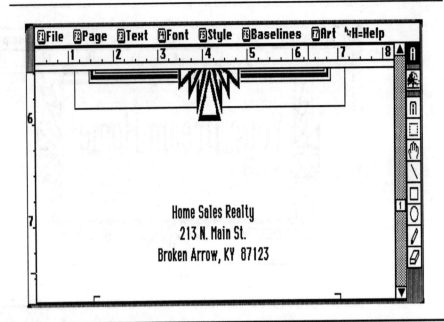

FIGURE 10-9. After typing the name and address

Scroll the screen so that the large text area is completely displayed. If you press ALT-A (to select Adjust single from the Baselines pull-down menu), you will see the baselines.

The heading of the text will be centered on the top baseline. To add the heading, follow these steps:

1. Select the top baseline by pointing to it and pressing F10 to display the handles.

2. Press ALT-X. This centers all of the baseline text. Although there is no text at this time, whatever text you type in the future will be centered.

3. Press ALT-A to hide the baselines. If the text tool is not selected, select it now. The cursor will be placed in the center of the hidden baseline.

4. Select the Geneva 12-point bold font.

5. Type the headline, **Take advantage of our special rates!** As you type, the text will automatically center because the baseline is set up for centering.

6. Press ENTER at the end of the heading.

The rest of the text is typed in the Geneva 12-point normal font. The cursor should be resting at the beginning of the second baseline. Type the following text:

```
From now until December 31st, we are offering a special 5% first-
year rate for home buyers. Sign up today for our special balloon
financing deals. No matter what your financial status over the
last few years has been, you can afford our homes.

Contact Bill or Gayle at the above address for more details on
our offerings. We hope you enjoy your happy home-buying!
```

If your spacing and typing were correct, your screen should look like the one in Figure 10-10. To finalize the flier, select the eraser tool and remove the corners around the text.

 If you want to add a footer or header near the edge of the flier (the "fine print" wording that is sometimes needed), you must add it as graphics text. The text tool and baselines cannot get as close to either end of the paper as the graphics tools can.

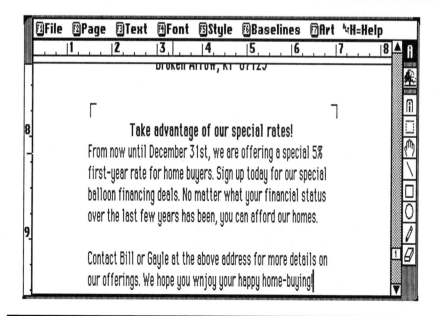

FIGURE 10-10. Looking at the text

This coupon entitles the bearer to:

10 - 35% Off!!!!

On all merchandise
from our overstock
sale item tables.

Hurry!
Sale ends on Thursday

FIGURE 10-11. A coupon created by First Publisher

ADDING A COUPON

Figure 10-11 shows a coupon. Coupons attract readers to fliers, so a coupon template might be handy to have. Creating this coupon is not difficult. Placing the vertical and horizontal dashes and scissors is easy to do with First Publisher. Since the details of coupons can vary greatly and you are working in such a small area, the placement, wording, and font sizes in the body of the coupon must be graphics art.

Once you save the coupon template, you can load it into a flier and individualize it. In the sections that follow, you'll learn how to create the coupon's template file.

Grabbing the Scissors Art

The first thing you need to do is clip the scissors from the file called PUBLICAT.MAC, supplied with First Publisher. To do so, follow these steps:

1. Select Start over from the File pull-down menu.

2. Select Get art from the Art pull-down menu. Version 2 users will have to select Get graphics from the File pull-down menu.

3. Type **PUBLICAT.MAC** when prompted for the filename. The clip art will appear with the scissors located at the top of the page.

4. Choose the selection box tool and select the scissors. Since surrounding art will not interfere, you do not need to erase any of it.

5. Select Save art from the Art pull-down menu. Save the art as SCISSORS .ART (First Publisher supplies the file extension).

6. Select Start over from the File pull-down menu to clear the screen again.

The Coupon Outline

Now you are ready to outline the body of the coupon. Since you are creating a template file that will be loaded and resized to suit the size of each flier, the dimensions of the coupon's outline are not critical. Create the dashed line by following these steps:

1. Press (**ALT-L**) to display the ruler lines.

2. Select the graphics tool.

3. Move the pointer to H1.0, V1.0 and press (**F10**) to anchor the graphics text cursor.

4. Select the New York 18-point bold font.

5. Press the minus sign 40 times. The last minus sign will fall under the 7.0 mark of the horizontal ruler line. Your screen will look like the one in Figure 10-12.

Since you want this dashed line to appear on all four sides, you must select

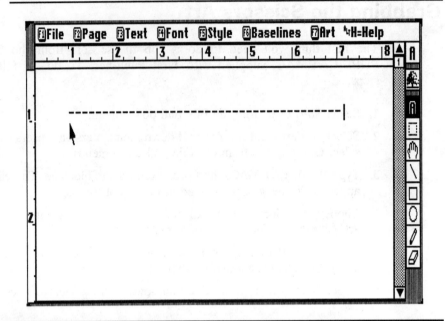

FIGURE 10-12.   After placing the top line of the coupon

the line and rotate it for the sides. You couldn't do this with normal text, but you can with the graphics text tool. To add the sides to the coupon:

1. Choose the selection box and select the dashed line. Do not select any more of the surrounding white space than you have to.

2. Press (**ALT-C**) to copy the line to the art clipboard. The line will remain on the screen.

3. Press (**ALT-V**) (to select Paste from the Art pull-down menu) and move the hand pointer underneath the start of the dashed line.

4. Press (**F10**) to see the pasted dashed line. At this point, your screen should look something like this:

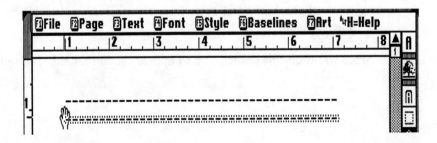

5. You must now flip the line. Press (**ALT-O**) to rotate the line down the left side of the coupon. You may have to move the line upward to position it closer to the top line.

6. You now need to add the other side. Since the dashed line is still on the art clipboard (you have sent nothing else to the clipboard, so the line is still there), press (**ALT-V**) to paste the line back on the screen.

7. Press (**F10**) to see the dashed line. Repeat step 5, except move the line to the right side of the coupon. Press (**F10**) to anchor it. (Mouse users can drag the line across; however, (**F10**) and the arrow keys may let you more accurately align it with the other side.) Your screen will be similar to that of Figure 10-13 after the line is placed.

8. Finish the coupon's outline by scrolling the screen downward until the bottom of the coupon is displayed. Since the dashed line is still on the art clipboard, press (**ALT-V**) to paste it at the bottom of the outline.

9. Press (**F10**) again and move the line to its proper place at the bottom of the coupon.

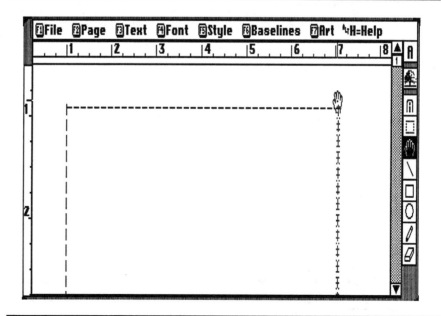

FIGURE 10-13. Positioning the right side

PLACING THE SCISSORS   You are working with a large coupon. Before shrinking it to a more manageable size, you need to add the scissors art image to the dashed line on the left. Follow these steps to add the scissors:

1. Scroll the screen to the top of the publication.

2. Select Get art from the Art pull-down menu.

3. Type **SCISSORS.ART** when prompted for the art filename.

4. Press (F10) to display the scissors outline box.

5. Move the scissors to the inside of the outline. Do not move them on top of the dashed line.

6. Press (ALT-0) to rotate the scissors to their proper orientation for the dashed line on the left.

7. The scissors are about twice the size they need to be. Press (ALT-R) to select Resize from the Art pull-down menu.

8. Point to the lower-left handle and press (F10), or click and hold the mouse button to grab it.

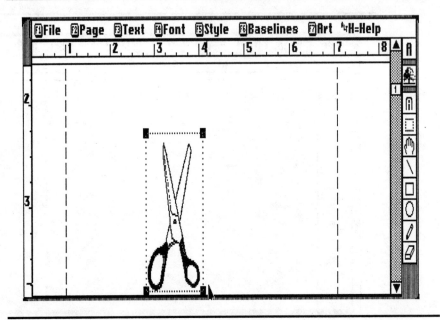

FIGURE 10-14.   Resizing the scissor's image

9. Move the bottom of the selection box upward until the selection box is about one-half its original size.

10. Press (**F10**) or release the mouse. Your screen should look something like the one in Figure 10-14.

Now, all you have to do is move the scissors to the left line and make one editing change. Since the scissors and the dashed line will overlap, you have to erase the dashed line where it passes through the scissors:

1. Select the hand tool.

2. Press (**F10**), or press and hold a mouse button, and drag the scissors to the dashed line. Make sure the dashed line falls between the blades of the scissors.

3. Press (**F10**) or release the mouse buton to anchor the scissors.

4. Select the pencil tool and move it to where the dashed line intercepts the scissors.

5. Press (**ALT-M**), then (**F10**), to magnify the area.

6. Erase the dashed line every place it overwrites the scissors art image. Figure 10-15 shows the magnified view after the dashed line is erased.

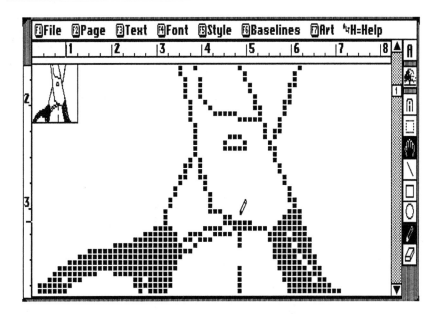

═══ **FIGURE 10-15.**   After erasing the dashed line through the scissors

7. Press (ALT-M) to return to the publication screen.

You must now shrink the coupon outline to make it more manageable. To do this, follow these steps:

1. Press (ALT-L) if your ruler lines are not displayed.
2. Select the entire dashed box of the coupon, including the scissors.
3. Press (ALT-R) to select Resize from the Art pull-down menu.
4. Grab the lower-right handle by pointing to it and pressing (F10), or by pressing and holding a mouse button.
5. Drag the art outline upwards until it is about 3.75 inches tall.
6. Press (F10) or release the mouse button.
7. Repeat these steps to shrink the horizontal dimension of the dashed line to approximately 3.75 inches. The dashed coupon will not look square, as seen in Figure 10-16, but you can see by the ruler lines that it is close. The coupon does not have to be a perfect square, as you will resize it for each flier you load it into.

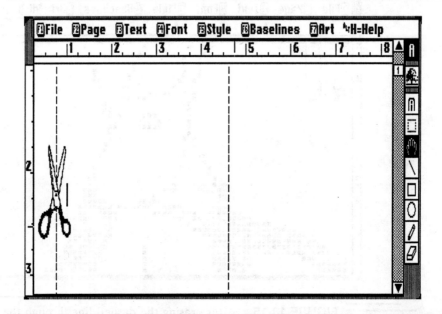

FIGURE 10-16. The coupon on the screen

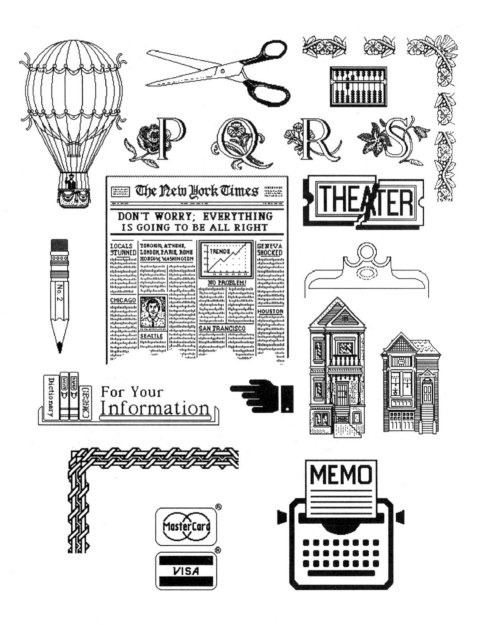

Figure 10-17. Printout of the PUBLICAT.MAC clip art file

FIGURE 10-18. A flier that uses an expanded border file

8. You can now save the coupon's template file by selecting it and choosing Save art from the Art pull-down menu.

 Always pull the coupon template into your flier and resize it before adding text. The flier's requirements dictate the size of the coupon, and your text will be easier to place once the coupon is at its final size. Remember to add the text as graphics text.

BORDERING THE ENTIRE PAGE

You can place a border around your entire flier. Borders that surround a newsletter distract from the text and make the page look much too "busy." However, a border around a flier that has little text sometimes enhances the page and gives the page an organized look.

The borders supplied with First Publisher are shown in Figure 10-17. The figure is a printout of the PUBLICAT.MAC clip art file. More borders are available from the Software Publishing Corporation in clip art files.

Creating a Border

You can use the same steps for creating a border that you used earlier in the chapter, in the section called "The Coupon Outline," to produce the outline for the coupon. As before, you must piece the border together, sometimes rotating the art to orient it properly.

There is an easier way to outline an entire page with the border that comes with CIRCULAR.PUB. It involves clearing away all but the border and resizing it to fit the entire page, as shown in Figure 10-18.

 When creating a flier that you want completely outlined in a border, place the border before placing the art and text. If you do not, you might find that the borders overwrite other art.

Summary

In this chapter you put your skills to work to create a flier by

- Preparing a template

- Getting and positioning art

- Centering text

- Adding a coupon

- Using borders

INVOICES AND ORDER FORMS

Creating an Invoice
Designing an Order Form

Most organizations use forms for ordering and invoicing. Many of these forms must be custom-designed. This chapter introduces you to building forms and invoices using First Publisher's line- and box-drawing tools.

To get started, you will use a predesigned template file supplied with First Publisher to create a simple invoice. Then you will create a more detailed order form from scratch.

CREATING AN INVOICE

Figure 11-1 shows a printout of an invoice you will create in this chapter. All of the text for the invoice is graphics text. When you create this invoice, you may want to add or remove detail lines to fit your own needs.

Note to Version 2 Users Use the INVOICE.PUB template, supplied with First Publisher, to speed up the invoice design process.

INVOICE No. [   ]

Super Soups, Inc.
1213 West Broadway
New York, NY 10021-1213
(212) 111-9203

Sold to			Shipped to		
Street & No			Street & No		
City	State	Zip	City	State	Zip

Customer's Order No.	Salesperson	Terms	F.O.B.	Date		

FIGURE 11-1. Sample invoice to create

Getting the Art

The soup bowl shown in the sample invoice is stored in LEISURE.MAC. You must clip the bowl and save it to an art file before bringing it into the invoice. To get the bowl, follow these steps:

1. Select Get art from the Art pull-down menu. Version 2 users will have to select Get graphics from the File pull-down menu.

2. Type **LEISURE.MAC** at the "Filename" prompt.

3. When the file is displayed, choose the selection box tool and select the soup art image. Do not get any more of the surrounding white space than you have to.

4. Save the bowl to an art file by selecting Save art from the Art pull-down menu and typing **BOWL** when prompted for a filename (First Publisher will add the .ART extension for you).

 You do not have to resize the bowl before saving it since it is smaller in the clip art file than it will be in its destination publication. You should resize a clip art image before saving it only if it is larger than its destination size.

Select Start over from the File pull-down menu to clear the screen for the invoice publication you will create. You now need to load the soup art image that you saved from LEISURE.MAC:

1. Press (ALT-L) to display the ruler lines.

2. Select Get art from the Art pull-down menu.

3. Type **BOWL** when prompted for the art image.

4. Move the hand over the outline in the upper-right corner of the screen.

5. Press (F10) to see the image. Position it as closely as possible to H5.5, V0.75. Figure 11-2 shows this placement.

6. Press (ALT-R) to resize the bowl, which is still selected. When the handles appear, grab the lower-right one and extend it to H7.75, V2.75, then press (UP ARROW) five times.

7. Press (F10) or release the mouse button to anchor the corner.

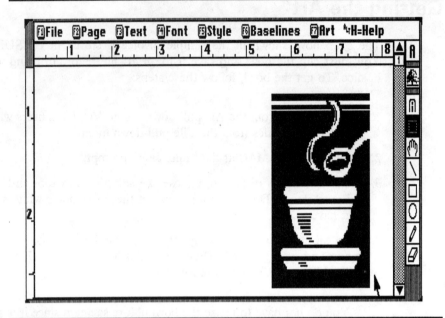

═══ **FIGURE 11-2.** Placing the soup bowl

The Invoice Number

To place the words "INVOICE No." and a box for the number, follow these steps:

1. Select the graphics text tool.
2. Select the 12-point Swiss bold font. Move the pointer to H1.0, V1.25 and press **F10** to position the graphics text cursor.
3. Type **INVOICE No.**.

Now place the box outline with the box-drawing tool.

1. Select the box-drawing tool.
2. Position the cross-hair cursor at H2.25, V1.0.
3. Select the second line thickness.
4. Press **F10**. Extend the lower-left corner of the box to H3.75, V1.25 by pressing the arrow keys or moving the mouse.

5. Press <kbd>F10</kbd> or release the mouse button to anchor the box. Figure 11-3 shows your screen at this point.

Adding the Company Name

Adding the company's name, address, and phone number is fairly straightforward. If you have additional fonts, you might want to type the name in a scripted font. Also, you may use your company logo (logos are discussed in the next chapter) instead of the art image, name, address, and phone number shown in the example invoice.

This book will stick to art and fonts that come with First Publisher. To add the name, address, and phone number, follow these steps:

1. Select the graphics text tool.
2. Select the 12-point Swiss bold font.
3. Move the pointer to H1.5, V1.75.

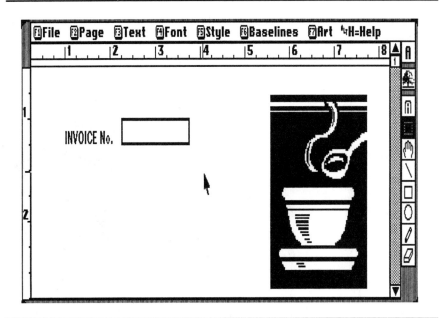

FIGURE 11-3. Drawing the box

4. Press (**F10**), or click a mouse button, to position the graphics text cursor at the pointer.

5. Type the following text:

```
Super Soups, Inc.
1213 West Broadway
New York, NY  10021-1213
(212) 111-9203
```

Press (**ENTER**) at the end of each line of text.

When typing graphics text, First Publisher knows to align each succeeding line with the one above it. Your screen will look like the one in Figure 11-4.

Adding the "Sold to" Box

The lines and boxes in the body of the invoice take a little time for exact adjustment when you are designing a new form. The placement of detail lines for this sample invoice was determined by trial and error. Notice that

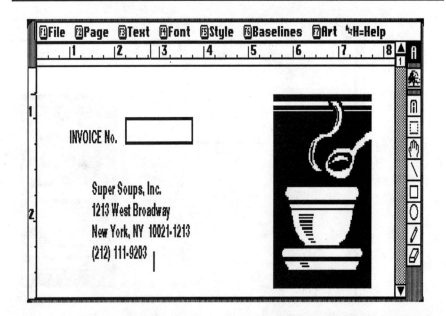

FIGURE 11-4. Typing the name and address text

the "Sold to" box is drawn in a thicker line width than the detail lines. This is to make the "Sold to" information stand out better. To add the outline of the "Sold to" box, follow these steps:

1. Select the box-drawing tool.

2. Select the second line thickness.

3. Position the cross-hair cursor to H0.75, V3.0, `RIGHT ARROW` eight times, `UP ARROW` seven times.

4. Anchor the box by pressing `F10` or by pressing and holding the mouse button.

5. Drag the lower-right corner of the box to H7.75, V4.0.

6. Press `F10` to anchor the box.

Now you must add the lines inside the box. Follow these steps:

1. Select the line-drawing tool.

2. Choose the thinnest line width.

3. Position the top of the line at H4.25, V3.0, `RIGHT ARROW` three times, `UP ARROW` seven times.

4. Press `F10`, or press and hold the mouse button, to anchor the top of the line.

5. Drag the line to V4.0, keeping the horizontal measurement even with the top of the line.

6. Press `F10` or release the mouse button. Figure 11-5 shows your screen at this point.

To add the horizontal lines in the boxes:

1. Select the line-drawing tool if it is not already selected.

2. Move the cursor to H0.75, V3.75, press `RIGHT ARROW` eight times, `UP ARROW` nine times.

3. Anchor the left side of the line by pressing `F10` or by pressing and holding the mouse button.

4. Drag the line to H7.75.

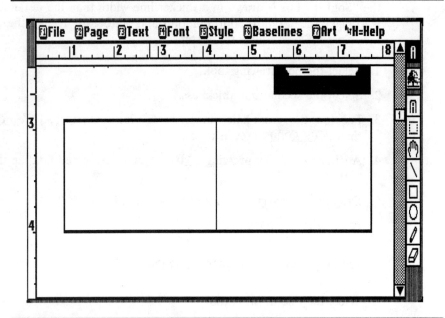

FIGURE 11-5. Separated information boxes

Repeat the previous steps to draw the second line in the "Sold to" box. Extend this line from H0.75, V3.25 across the box to the right side at H7.75 by pressing (**RIGHT ARROW**) eight times, (**DOWN ARROW**) once. Your screen will look similar to the one in Figure 11-6.

THE "SOLD TO" TEXT The text inside the "Sold to" boxes should be typed with the graphics text tool. Use the 10-point Swiss roman font. The following chart shows where to place the text.

Text	Location
Sold to	H1.0, V3.0, (**DOWN ARROW**) three times
Shipped to	H4.5, V3.0, (**LEFT ARROW**) three times, (**DOWN ARROW**) three times
Street & No	H1.0, V3.5, (**UP ARROW**) five times
Street & No	H4.5, V3.5, (**UP ARROW**) five times, (**LEFT ARROW**) three times
City	H1.0, V3.75, (**DOWN ARROW**) one time

State	H2.5, V3.75, (DOWN ARROW) one time
Zip	H3.5, V3.75, (DOWN ARROW) one time
City	H4.5, V3.75, (LEFT ARROW) three times, (DOWN ARROW) one time
State	H6.0, V3.75, (DOWN ARROW) one time
Zip	H7.0, V3.75, (DOWN ARROW) one time

This completes the "Sold to" boxes and text. The rest of the invoice is simpler.

The Body of the Invoice

The body of the invoice is made up of two parts: the "Customer's Order No." line and the blank detail lines (where the invoice information will be written in by hand when an order is placed).

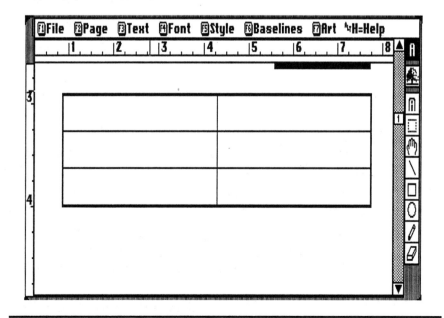

FIGURE 11-6. The added horizontal lines

To add the "Customer's Order No." line, follow these steps:

1. Select the box-drawing tool.

2. Anchor the upper-left corner of the box at H0.75, V4.0, (DOWN ARROW) two times, (RIGHT ARROW) eight times.

3. Extend the lower-right corner of the box to H7.75, V4.50, (UP ARROW) eight times.

4. Press (F10) or release the mouse button to anchor the lower-right corner of the box.

The text inside the "Customer's Order No." box should be typed in 10-point Swiss roman font with the graphics text tool. Place the text as specified in the following chart:

Text	Location
Customer's Order No.	H1.0, V4.25, (UP ARROW) five times
Salesperson	H2.75, V4.25, (UP ARROW) five times
Terms	H4.0, V4.25, (UP ARROW) five times
F.O.B.	H5.25, V4.25, (UP ARROW) five times
Date	H6.5, V4.25, (UP ARROW) five times

Draw the separating lines by following these steps:

1. Select the line-drawing tool.

2. Move the cross-hair cursor to H2.5, V4.0, (RIGHT ARROW) four times, (DOWN ARROW) twice.

3. Anchor the line and drag it down to the bottom of the box at V4.5, (UP ARROW) eight times.

4. Continue drawing lines from H3.75 to V4.5, (UP ARROW) eight times, from H4.75 to V4.5, (UP ARROW) eight times, and from H6.0 to V4.5, (UP ARROW) eight times. Figure 11-7 shows your screen at this point.

It is easiest to draw the detail lines of the invoice by drawing the top box and then duplicating it down the page with the Cut and Paste features of

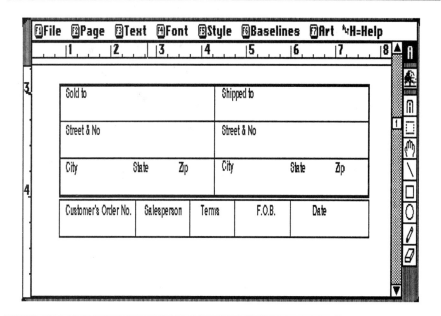

FIGURE 11-7. Text added to the information boxes

First Publisher. To draw the box, follow these steps:

1. Select the box-drawing tool.
2. Anchor the upper-left corner of the box at H0.75, V4.5, (**RIGHT ARROW**) eight times, (**UP ARROW**) eight times.
3. Extend the lower-right corner of the box to H7.75, V4.75, (**UP ARROW**) eight times.
4. Anchor the box.

Select the line-drawing tool and draw the separating lines from H2.0, V4.5, (**UP ARROW**) eight times to V4.75, (**UP ARROW**) eight times; from H5.0, V4.5, (**UP ARROW**) eight times to V4.75, (**UP ARROW**) eight times; from H6.25, V4.5, (**UP ARROW**) eight times to V4.75, (**UP ARROW**) eight times; from H6.75, V4.5, (**UP ARROW**) eight times to V4.75, (**UP ARROW**) eight times; and from H7.25, (**UP ARROW**) eight times to V4.75, (**UP ARROW**) eight times.

Your screen will look like the one in Figure 11-8. This is a lot of tedious line placement, especially when you first start drawing. However, you have probably found that the placement of these lines is sometimes easier with (**SHIFT-ARROW**) keypresses. In addition, you can "eyeball" many of these

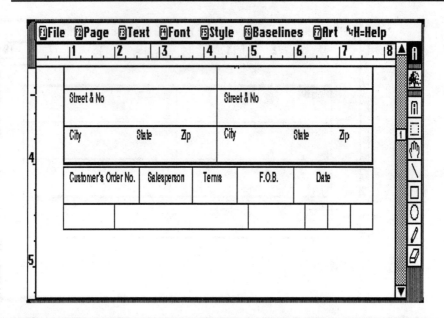

FIGURE 11-8. A detail line added to the invoice

line placements. Best of all, with the selection box tool and the Cut feature, it is always easy to adjust and change anything you draw.

 Use the Magnify feature (ALT-M) if a line seems off a bit and you need to erase part of it without erasing the surrounding publication.

All that is left for you to do is to duplicate the detail line boxes. The Copy and Paste features work best. Before starting this, however, save the publication as it is now. Any time you are going to do lots of Copy and Paste operations, save the publication first. Then you can retrieve the earlier version if you unintentionally copy over an existing line.

1. Select the last row of boxes (the detail box lines) with the selection tool. When you select it, place the selection box lines exactly over those in the box to copy.

2. Press ALT-C to select Copy from the Art pull-down menu.

3. Press ALT-V to select Paste from the Art pull-down menu.

4. Press F10 to see the dotted box where the copied box will be placed.

5. Move the box directly below the existing one. Make the top of the dotted outline overlap the line at the bottom of the invoice's detail line on the screen.

6. Press (F10) to place the box.

Continue copying the detail lines by pressing (ALT-V) (Paste) and (F10) repeatedly down the page. The detail line box is still in the clipboard, and you do not have to copy it again.

Duplicating lines such as these requires some patience to align them accurately. Mouse users may want to use the mouse to move the lines to a close position and then press the arrow keys to finalize the placement. The Magnify ((ALT-M)) feature works well for this clean-up.

DESIGNING AN ORDER FORM

Figure 11-9 shows an order form designed with First Publisher. The major difference between this form and the invoice is the lack of detail lines. This allows you more freedom in filling out the form. You can handwrite comments to go with the detail lines or type the detail without worrying about fitting the text into a small box.

 You can use First Publisher to create and design all of your forms and invoices. However, the program was not designed to be used as a word processor to fill out the forms.

The Design

Before creating the order form, set up baselines to help you center the headings and place the text that appears on the order form. Be sure to put some thought into your order form design. You want to keep the order form from being cramped, and you want to leave enough space for all of the information that the form will eventually hold.

If you just created the invoice in the last sections, you may find that you need to reset the baselines. Select Start over from the File pull-down menu now. Then press (ALT-A) to display the baselines. You may not see the baselines you expect.

If you ever display the baselines on a blank publication and find no baselines, or baselines from a former publication that you no longer want, display the Page pull-down menu and select Choose layout. Choose layout

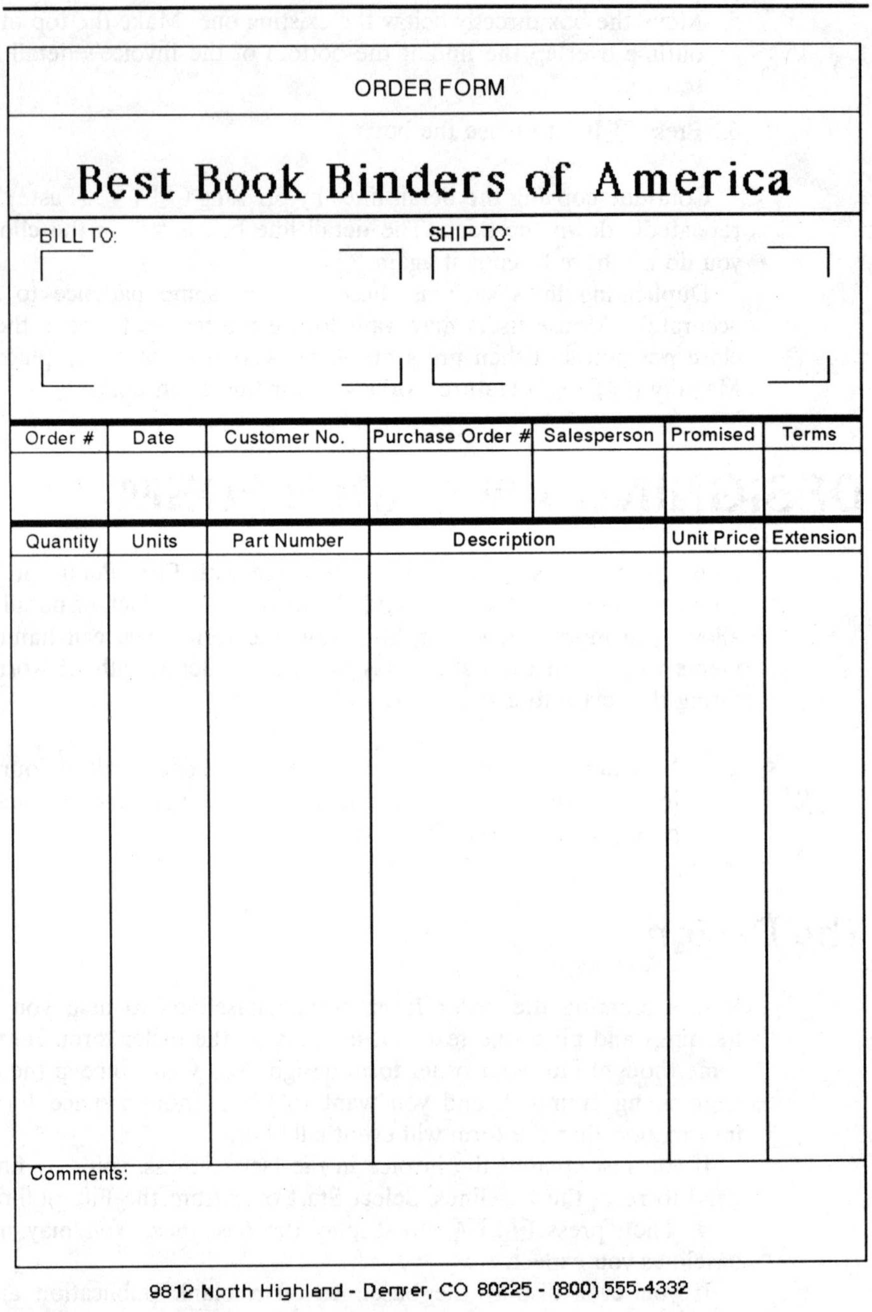

ORDER FORM

Best Book Binders of America

BILL TO:

SHIP TO:

Order #	Date	Customer No.	Purchase Order #	Salesperson	Promised	Terms

Quantity	Units	Part Number	Description	Unit Price	Extension

Comments:

9812 North Highland - Denver, CO 80225 - (800) 555-4332

≡≡≡ **FIGURE 11-9.** An order form to create

number 1 to reset the baselines to a single column of baselines down the page. Version 2 users will have to select Define page from the Page pull-down menu and press (F1) at the Define Page screen to reset the baselines.

DRAWING THE BORDER The border around the order form is easy to draw. It is simply a box drawn at specific measurements on the page. The box serves as an outline for the order form and sits above the company's address. To add the box, follow these steps:

1. Press (ALT-L) to display the rulers.
2. Select the box-drawing tool.
3. Use (SHIFT-ARROW) or the mouse to move the cross to H1.0, V1.0.
4. Press (F10), or press and hold a mouse button, to anchor one corner of the box.
5. Drag the lower-right corner of the box downward until the cross rests at H7.5, V10.0.
6. Press (F10), or release the mouse button, to finish the box.
7. Press (CTRL-HOME), or point to the top of the elevator bar, to display the top of the publication.

DRAWING HORIZONTAL LINES Figure 11-10 shows you the measurements and fonts you'll use for the sample order form. The easiest starting point is drawing the horizontal lines. The line-drawing tool and the line-width tools will do the job. To add the lines, follow these steps:

1. Select the line-drawing tool. The thinnest line width should be selected.
2. Move the cross to H1.0, V1.5.
3. Press (F10), or press and hold a mouse button, to anchor the left end of the line.
4. Press the arrow keys, or move the mouse, until the cross ends up at H7.5, V1.5 (the right side of the border).
5. Select the second line thickness. Draw another line from H1.0, V2.25 to H7.5, V2.25.
6. Select the widest line thickness. Draw the third line from H1.0, V3.75 to H7.5, V3.75.
7. Select the thinnest line width again. Draw a fourth line from H1.0, V4.0 to H7.5, V4.0. Your screen will look like the one in Figure 11-11. (The first line will have scrolled up out of view.)

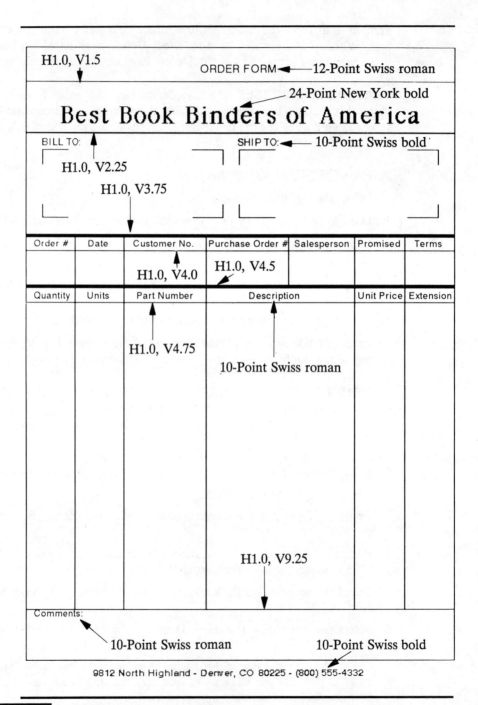

FIGURE 11-10. The measurements and fonts of the invoice

8. Select the widest line width again. Draw a fifth line from H1.0, V4.5 to H7.5, V4.5.

9. Select the thinnest line width again. Draw a sixth line from H1.0, V4.75 to H7.5, V4.75.

10. With the thinnest line width still selected, draw a final line from H1.0, V9.25 to H7.5, V9.25.

The Form's Text

The order form's title ("ORDER FORM") is 12 points high. You learned in Part I that 72 points equal an inch. Since the title goes inside one-half inch, you know that the box that holds the title is 36 points tall. To place an 18-point title, you have to place it about three quarters of the way down the box.

This is too technical for most applications, but it gives you an idea of what designers consider. Since First Publisher's ruler lines are marked in quarter-inch measurements, it is difficult to split them and place the title at exactly

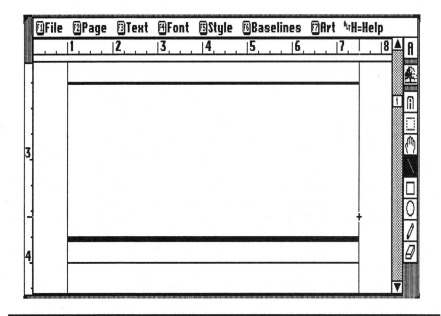

FIGURE 11-11. Adding horizontal lines

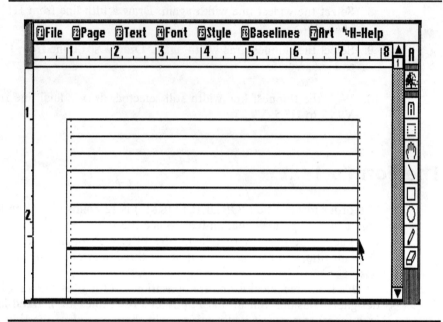

FIGURE 11-12. Viewing the order form's baselines

three-quarters of the way down the box. That is why you will "eyeball" a lot of the placement of your text and graphics. This is fine—if you are off, First Publisher will let you correct your placement quickly and easily.

You probably are better off, however, if you add baselines to the order form to hold the text. There are several reasons for this. The title and the heading ("Best Book Binders of America") are centered, and baselines will help with the centering. Also, the horizontal boxes across the detail area should each have titles placed on the same baseline to keep them even.

ADDING BASELINES Select Adjust column from the Baselines pull-down menu. The baselines will appear as shown in Figure 11-12. You will notice in the figure that the baselines are not centered within the order form's border. Therefore, the first thing you must do (if this is the case for your baselines as well) is to center them so that text can be placed accurately within the order form boundaries.

Follow these steps to center the baselines:

1. Select the top baseline by pointing to it and pressing ⬛F10⬛ twice or by clicking the mouse button.

2. Point to the left handle.

3. Pull the baseline handle to H1.0 (to align it with the left edge of the border). Then press (**LEFT ARROW**) three more times (or drag it just a little further with the mouse) to center the baselines on the order form. Figure 11-13 shows the results.

 As you can see, the baselines are slightly wider than the lines of the form. This is an advantage, as it would be difficult to tell them apart otherwise.

Now it is time to pull the top baseline down to the title's position. After pulling the baseline down, you will set it up for centering the text. Follow these steps:

1. Select Adjust below from the Baselines pull-down menu.

2. Point to the top baseline.

3. Press (**F10**) twice, or click the mouse button, to display the handles on the top baseline.

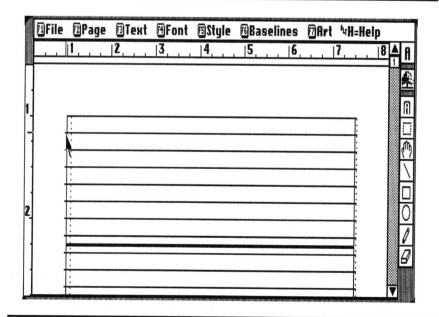

FIGURE 11-13. Centering the baselines

4. Drag the middle handle upward by pointing to it and pressing (F10), or by pressing and holding down a mouse button.

5. Pull the baseline until it rests between V1.25 and V1.50.

6. Press (F10) or release the mouse button to adjust the baselines. Figure 11-14 shows your screen at this point. Even though the lines look messy, be sure you keep them apart by looking at the sides of the order form.

7. Press (ALT-A) to select Adjust single from the Baselines pull-down menu.

8. Press (F10) to select the top baseline.

9. Press (ALT-X) to center all future text that will go on the top baseline.

You need to pull the rest of the baselines down to start at the heading's line (the company name). Do so by following these steps:

1. Select Adjust below from the Baselines pull-down menu.

2. Point to the second baseline and display its handles.

3. Pull the second baseline downward until it rests between V2.0 and V2.25.

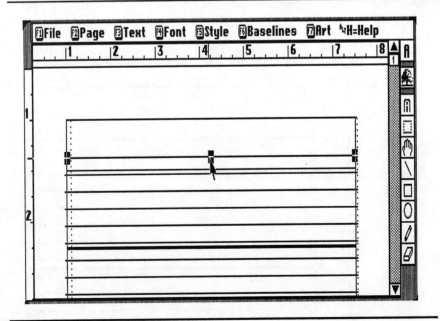

FIGURE 11-14. Pulling down the baselines

4. Press (**ALT-A**) and (**F10**) to select Adjust single from the Baselines pull-down menu.

5. Select the top baseline by displaying its handles. Press (**ALT-X**) to center future text on this line.

The small titles within the horizontal boxes should have baselines to keep them aligned across the page. Adding them is just a continuation of what you have been doing. Add the baselines by following these steps:

1. Select Adjust below from the Baselines pull-down menu.

2. Display the third baseline's handles by pointing to it and pressing (**F10**) twice, or by clicking the mouse button.

3. Point to the middle handle.

4. Drag the baseline downward until it rests on the V4.0 mark. Then raise the baseline slightly (about four (**UP ARROW**) keypresses).

5. Anchor the baseline by pressing (**F10**) or by releasing the mouse button. Your screen will look like the one in Figure 11-15.

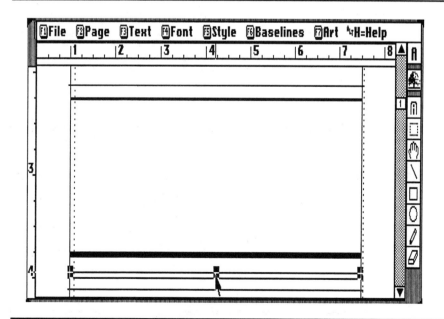

FIGURE 11-15. Moving several baselines

Scroll your screen downward until you see the V5.5 mark. This will give you more room to see what you are doing for the next baseline. Repeat the above five steps to pull the fourth baseline (and all others below it) to slightly above the V4.75 mark (three (UP ARROW) keypresses).

ADDING VERTICAL LINES   Scroll the screen to the top of the publication. You are now ready to add the vertical lines that run through the body of the order form. All of these lines are drawn with the thinnest line width. Select the line-drawing tool and the thinnest line width, and then follow these steps to draw the vertical lines:

1. Move the cross to H1.75, V3.75. Press (F10), or press and hold a mouse button, to anchor the beginning of the line.
2. Drag the line downward until it rests at H1.75, V9.25.
3. Press (F10) to anchor the line.
4. Repeat the above steps to draw lines starting at H2.5 and H3.75.
5. Draw a shorter line from H5.0, V3.75 to H5.0, V4.5.
6. Draw two more long lines starting at H6.0 and H6.75. When you are through, the middle of your publication screen will be similar to the one in Figure 11-16.

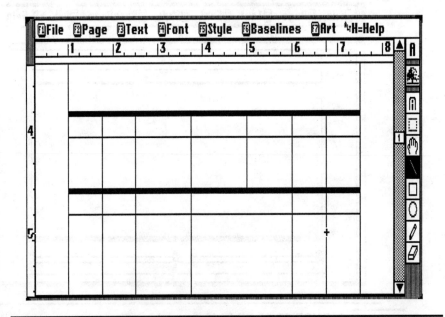

FIGURE 11-16.   Drawing the vertical lines

ADDING TEXT Press (**SHIFT-F9**), or point to the top text tool with the mouse, to activate the baselines for text. To add the text, follow these steps:

1. Make sure the cursor is at the top baseline (you might have to press (**SHIFT-HOME**) or point to the top of the elevator bar to get it there).
2. Select the 12-point Swiss roman font.
3. Type **ORDER FORM**. Since you set the baseline for centering, the title will be centered as well.
4. Press (**ENTER**) to move the cursor to the next baseline.
5. Select the 24-point New York bold font.
6. Type **Best Book Binders of America** and press (**ENTER**).
7. Select the 10-point Swiss roman font for the titles inside the horizontal boxes.
8. Press (**SPACEBAR**) 4 times, then type **Order #**.
9. Press (**SPACEBAR**) 7 times (to move to the second box) and type **Date**.
10. Press (**SPACEBAR**) 9 times and type **Customer No.**.
11. Press (**SPACEBAR**) 9 times and type **Purchase Order #**.
12. Press (**SPACEBAR**) 4 times and type **Salesperson**.
13. Press (**SPACEBAR**) 6 times and type **Promised**.
14. Finally, press (**SPACEBAR**) 5 times and type **Terms**, then press (**ENTER**). Your screen should look like the one in Figure 11-17.

If you get off a space or two while typing the text, you can back up with the arrow keys or the (**BACKSPACE**) key and type the letters again. The lines will not be interrupted when you change the text, because you are using baselines for the text and the lines are on the art overlay.

 When you design a form to fit your own needs, the placement of text and art takes a lot of trial and error.

The second set of horizontal text is needed. Type it as shown here:

1. Press (**SPACEBAR**) 4 times and type **Quantity**.
2. Press (**SPACEBAR**) 6 times and type **Units**.
3. Press (**SPACEBAR**) 10 times and type **Part Number**.
4. Press (**SPACEBAR**) 26 times and type **Description**.

5. Press (SPACEBAR) 22 times and type **Unit Price.**

6. Press (SPACEBAR) 4 times and type **Extension.**

Figure 11-18 shows the result of your work up to this point. The last two lines of text will have to be graphics text. The "Comments:" line was not worth rearranging a baseline for, since it can be typed very easily. It is typed with the same font as that used for the horizontal box titles. The name, address, and phone number at the bottom of the page have to be typed with graphics text because the baselines will not extend that far down the page. Type them in the Swiss 10-point bold font.

Select the graphics text tool (the second tool from the top), point to the location of these two lines, and then type them. You may have to select and move the name, address, and phone number line to get it centered.

Although in this book the vertical lines are added before the text, you may find it easier to type the labels at the top of each column, then center the lines around it. As long as you understand what you are doing and where you are headed with your publication, you can add text and art in the order you are most comfortable with.

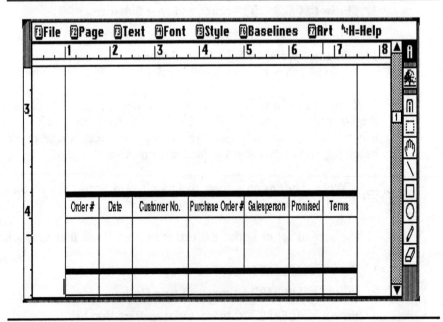

FIGURE 11-17.   Filling in the title boxes

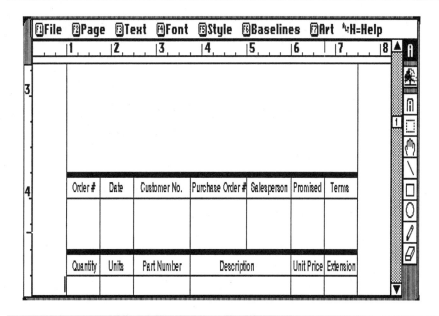

═══ **FIGURE 11-18.** Typing the title box text

Finishing the Order Form

You are almost through with the order form. You only need to add the "BILL TO:" and "SHIP TO:" areas. The corners for these areas can be drawn freehand; however, you may find it easier to keep the alignment if you draw a box first and use the eraser to erase what is not to be included. To ensure that the corners are evenly placed, draw one large box first, by following these steps:

1. Scroll to the top of the order form.

2. Select the box-drawing tool.

3. Position the cursor at H1.25, V2.5.

4. Press **F10** to anchor the upper-left corner of the box.

5. Drag the upper-right corner of the box to H7.25, V2.5.

6. Drag the lower-right corner of the box to H7.25, V3.5.

7. Press **F10** or release the mouse button to anchor the large rectangle. Your screen should look like the one in Figure 11-19.

FIGURE 11-19. Creating the "BILL TO:" and "SHIP TO:" spaces

8. With the cross at the lower-right corner of the box, press (**F10**) again or press and hold a mouse button. Drag a new box, overlapping the old one (on some monitors, the lines will almost disappear when they overlap), until the upper-left corner rests at H4.5, V2.5.

9. Press (**F10**) or release the mouse button to anchor the box.

10. Repeat steps 8 and 9 to overlap the left-hand box. Start the box at H1.25, V2.5. Trace a new box over the old one, to H4.0, V3.5. Your screen should now look like the one in Figure 11-20.

11. Select the eraser tool and erase the column that was formed by the sides of the two boxes.

12. Erase most of each box so that only the eight corners remain.

All that you need to do is select the graphics text tool and the 10-point Swiss bold font, then type **BILL TO:** and **SHIP TO:**. When you are through, you will have a finished screen that looks like the one in Figure 11-21.

Your order form is now finished. You can make slight modifications by changing the form to include your own titles or even a company logo.

FIGURE 11-20. Aligning the eight corners

FIGURE 11-21. The top of the form is complete

Be sure to save this form. It can be customized to fill many different form needs, and it would be easier to change the text on the form you just made rather than re-creating it at a later date.

When designing other forms, always determine what titles and data you will need on the form before going to the keyboard. It is wise to draw a thumbnail sketch of what you want the form to look like. You might ask yourself the following questions: What information do I want to collect with the form? Who will use the form? How will it be used?

Determine what titles on the form change with each copy of it. You do not want these individual titles to be printed with First Publisher, since the creation of each order form would be too slow. You are creating the form to be filled in later by inventory clerks, order clerks, front-line personnel, or customers.

 If you use a laser printer, you may find that the supplied laser fonts that you can add to First Publisher (APLASER.FNT and HPLASER .FNT come with the system) make your form titles clearer.

Summary

In this chapter you learned how to create a detailed invoice and order form using First Publisher's line- and box-drawing tools. You practiced

- Placing text

- Drawing and placing lines and boxes

- Designing your own template

- Drawing a border

chapter **12**

CREATING
LETTERHEADS AND
BUSINESS CARDS

Creating Your Logo
Creating a Business Card

You can create stationery and business cards with First Publisher. By producing your own letterhead, you can save printing costs. Once you create your letterhead, you can save it in an art file and load it into almost any publication.

If you have a company logo, you should incorporate it into your letterhead and business cards. Try scanning it into First Publisher instead of drawing it with the drawing tools. Although the image may have to be touched up when you bring it into First Publisher, you will still save time by scanning it first.

If you do not have a scanner, more and more printing services will let you use their scanner and microcomputer for a small fee. Once you scan and save the image, you can enlarge or shrink it from within First Publisher without having to scan it again. See Chapter 4 for some scanner guidelines.

CREATING YOUR LOGO

If you are creating your own logo, make sure that it fits the image you want for your company. Always keep in mind that customers will see your logo almost every time they read a company document. Do not include art if you do not need it, although it certainly helps increase logo recognition. You want a logo that people remember.

 Most company logos are trademarked, so do not copy a logo you've seen in print.

Do not let the art overwhelm the rest of the logo, or it will make the text look too small by comparison. When creating stationery, keep your logo streamlined so that the reader can focus quickly on the words printed in the body of the text.

You can create many interesting logos with First Publisher even if you choose not to get extra fonts or clip art. BUSINESS.MAC is a good place to start. Figure 12-1 shows a printout of BUSINESS.MAC. As you can see, there are many graphic elements that you can combine to create interesting-looking logos such as the ones in Figure 12-2.

Drawing the Logo

Using First Publisher and its graphics files, you now will create the third logo in Figure 12-2, for Surveys Unlimited. If you have read the first part of this book, you should have little trouble with the following steps. To create the Surveys Unlimited logo:

1. Select Get art from the Art pull-down menu. Version 2 users will have to select Get graphics from the File pull-down menu.

2. Type **BUSINESS.MAC** when prompted for the graphics filename. Select the dotted-box side tool since you want to clip some of the art.

3. Move the cursor to the third set of people, about halfway down the screen. Point to the left corner just above the third set of people.

4. Press **F10** or press and hold a mouse button to anchor the selection box. Do not include any more white space than you have to in order to get the entire image.

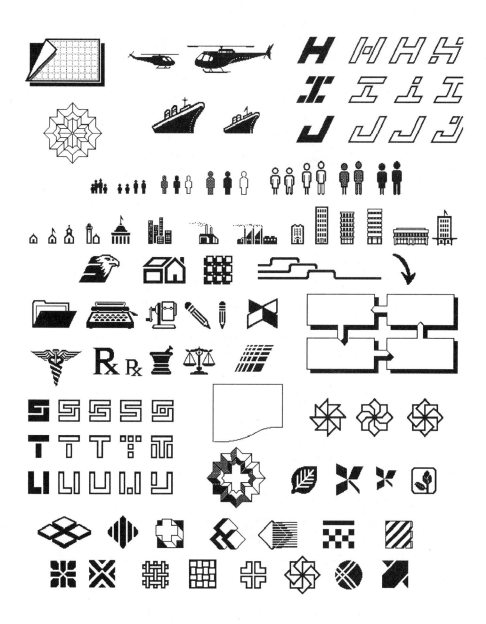

FIGURE 12-1. The BUSINESS.MAC clip art file

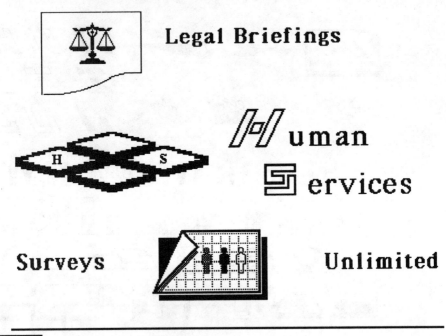

FIGURE 12-2. Sample logos

5. Drag the selection box to the right and just below the people image, and then press **(F10)** or release the mouse button. Your screen will look something like the one in Figure 12-3.

6. Select the hand tool.

7. Move the hand tool over the art you just selected; then press **(F10)** or press and hold a mouse button.

8. Drag the selected image up so it is centered over the graph paper image in the upper-left corner of the screen.

9. Press **(F10)** or release the mouse button to anchor the people over the graph image. Figure 12-4 shows the correct placement.

You now need to save the image to an art file so it can be loaded into a blank publication. Follow these steps:

1. Select the entire graph paper and people art image you just created.

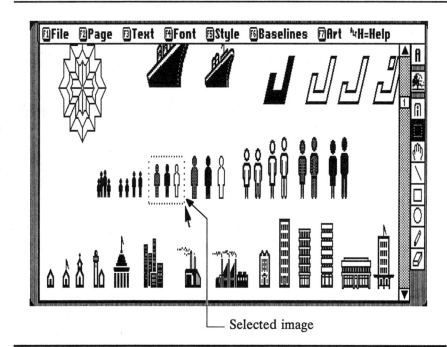

—— Selected image

FIGURE 12-3.   Selecting the people clip art

2. Select Save art from the Art pull-down menu.

3. Type **PEOPLE** at the filename prompt. The extension .ART will be supplied by First Publisher for you. The image will then be saved.

Now you can go to a blank publication screen and finish the logo. Select Start over (⟨**ALT-Y**⟩) from the File pull-down menu. Press ⟨**F2**⟩ at the "Save filename" prompt so that the modified graphics file will not be saved.

 If you modify a .MAC file and save it at the "Save filename" prompt, First Publisher saves it as a .PUB file to keep the original .MAC file intact.

At the blank publication screen, follow these steps to finish the logo:

1. Select Get art from the Art pull-down menu.

2. Type **PEOPLE.ART** when prompted for a filename.

Overlapping art

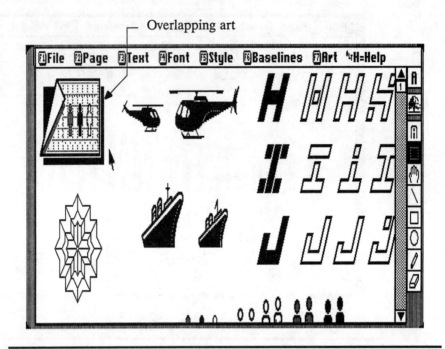

FIGURE 12-4. Positioning the people image over the graph art

3. When the hand tool appears, press **F10** or press and hold a mouse button to see the outline image of the graph paper and people. Place it in the top center of the page, as shown in Figure 12-5.

Now you are ready to add the company name. You should always use graphics text for logo wording so you can place the text exactly where you want it. To add the text, follow these steps:

1. Select the graphics text tool (the hollow *A*).

2. Move the pointer to a clear area on the page, well *below* the art. You will type the first word there and then move it to the left of the art.

3. Press **F10** twice or click the mouse button to move the cursor to the pointing arrow.

4. Select the 18-point New York bold font.

5. Type **Surveys**.

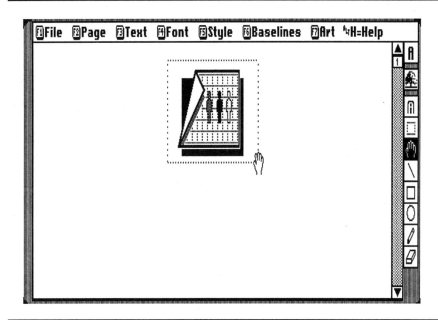

≡ **FIGURE 12-5.**   Placing the logo in the center of the page

6. Select the entire word you just typed.

7. Select the hand tool. Position it over the word, and then press (**F10**) or press and hold a mouse button to grab the text.

8. Move the text to the left of the art image so that it appears at about the same location as shown here:

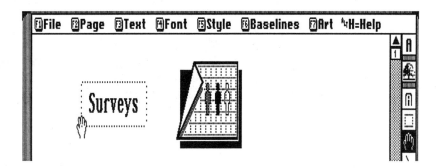

9. Type **Unlimited**. Repeat steps 6 and 7, and then move the word to the right of the art so that the logo is balanced.

10. The last step is to draw the lines on the three sides of the art. You might want to display the grid (**ALT-U**) to help you keep the lines uniform. Use the line-drawing side tool (the slanted line) to draw the bottom line first, then the side lines.

11. Select Save publication from the File pull-down menu, and type **LOGO** as the filename.

After you create a logo, it can be resized to fit any publication. When creating business cards, the logo will have to be made smaller. When using the logo on advertising fliers, you may have to increase its size. The Surveys Unlimited logo will be used for the next few sections; be sure to save it so you can use it in the following examples.

Producing Stationery

You will probably want to put your logo and return address on your stationery. If you have a large, bold logo, such as the one you just created, there is little room for the return address. Therefore, you may want to put the address directly below the logo in a very small font size.

Another option is to place the return address at the bottom of the stationery. This might keep the logo and address from dominating the body of the letter written on the stationery. In following sections you'll learn how to produce stationery with the address and logo together, and with the address at the bottom of the stationery.

COMBINED LOGO AND ADDRESS An example of a logo with the return address directly below it is shown here:

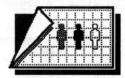

Surveys   Unlimited

931 E. Skelly Drive, Suite 600, Miami, Florida 98912 (991) 555-6543

Creating this type of letterhead is easy, especially if you have created the publications in the previous chapters. Follow these steps:

1. Select Start over from the File pull-down menu.

2. Press (**ALT-L**) to display the ruler lines.

You should get into the habit of displaying the ruler lines before pulling art into a blank publication; they will help you center the art better.

3. Select Get art from the Art pull-down menu.

4. Type **LOGO** when prompted for an art filename.

5. Position the hand placement tool at the top center of the publication, then press (**F10**) or press and hold a mouse button to display the logo.

6. The logo you created in the last section is approximately 6 inches wide. Therefore, you should center the logo between the 1-inch and the 7-inch horizontal ruler lines.

7. Press (**F10**), or release a mouse button, to anchor the logo.

You might want to get a preview of the document by pressing (**ALT-Z**). As you can see from Figure 12-6, the logo is fairly centered. When looking over

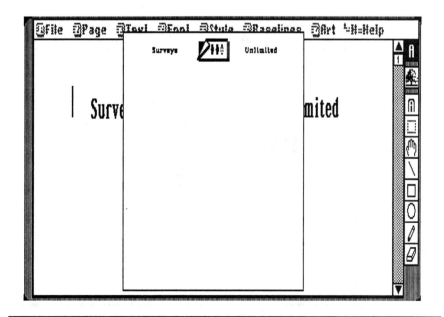

FIGURE 12-6.   Displaying a preview of the printed publication

a logo's placement, keep in mind that there needs to be plenty of white space on the stationery for the text. Your screen's normal display measurements are not as accurate as your page preview (especially if you are using a CGA graphics adapter) or your printer.

Add the address as graphics text so you can place it exactly where you want it. Select the 12-point Elite normal font, then select the graphics text tool. Type the following address and telephone number on one line: **931 E. Skelly Drive, Suite 600, Miami, Florida 98912 (991) 555-6543**. Since it is typed as graphics text, you can center it under the logo. Figure 12-7 shows your screen after this is done.

ADDRESS AT BOTTOM Instead of putting the address just below the logo, you can place it at the bottom of the page. Keep the address in the 12-point Elite font. You might choose to type it in boldface this time, since it will not stand out as well as it did when combined with the logo.

The process of adding the address at the bottom of the page is exactly like that of putting it below the logo. Be sure to type the address as graphics text so you can change its placement if you need to. Figure 12-8 shows a printout of this type of stationery. Your logo design will dictate the placement of your address.

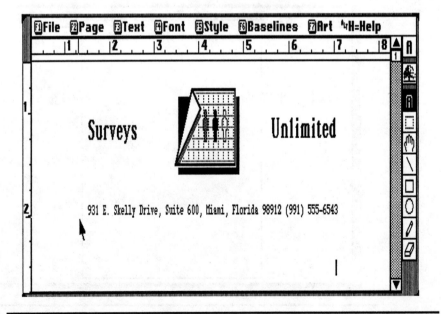

FIGURE 12-7. Placing the return address

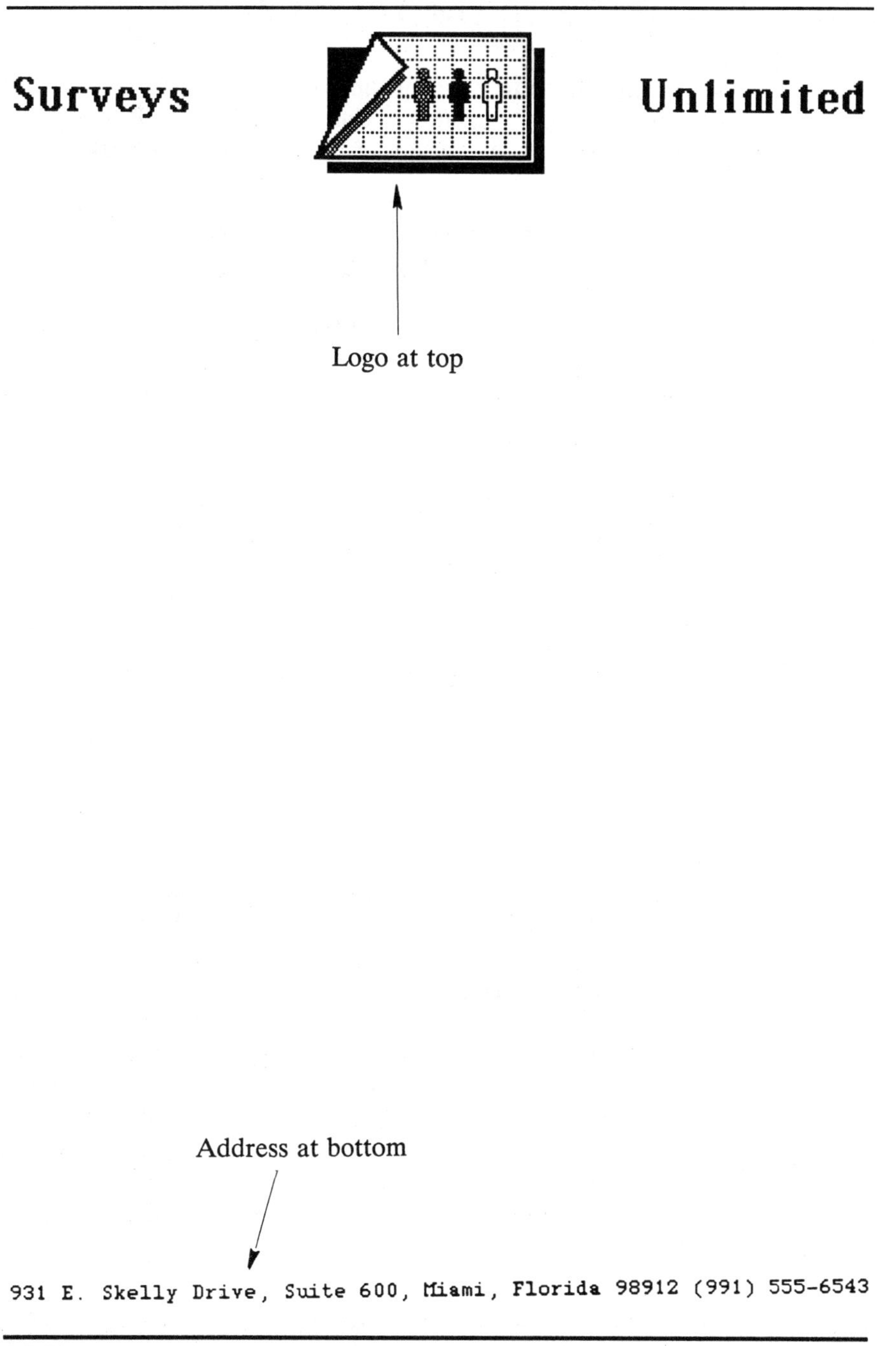

Surveys   Unlimited

Logo at top

Address at bottom

931 E. Skelly Drive, Suite 600, Miami, Florida 98912 (991) 555-6543

FIGURE 12-8. Stationery with the return address at the bottom

Using the LETTER.PUB Template

If you do not want to take the time to create your own logo design, First Publisher supplies a template file called LETTER.PUB that gives you a head start on a letterhead. A printout of LETTER.PUB is shown here:

```
┌─────          ─────┐          Company name

          Logo                  Company address

└─────          ─────┘
```
───────────────────────────────────

You must draw the art or clip it from one of the clip art files, resize it to fit the corners, and type the company name and address.

 You might not want to keep the underline that appears on the template under the letterhead. Sometimes, an underline offsets the letterhead nicely; other times, it creates a separation that does not look right with a large logo. You will have to print out your letterhead with and without the underline to decide which looks best.

CREATING A BUSINESS CARD

You can create business cards with First Publisher. Figure 12-9 shows a screen that has the text and art for a finished business card on it. You may want to shrink your entire logo to fit a business card. However, a very detailed logo may not look good when shrunk to a very small size. You might want to keep the general form, but blacken in some of the detail.

The biggest problem with producing business cards on the computer is that many printers cannot handle the heavier stock of paper needed. You may have to try different kinds of paper to get one thick enough to produce a card but thin enough to go through the printer.

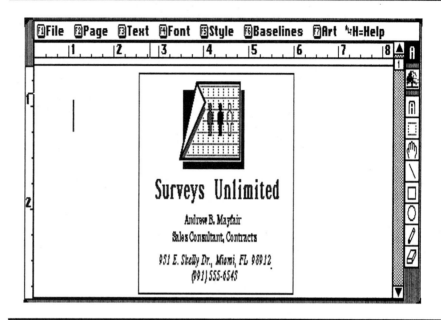

FIGURE 12-9. A finished business card

 If you own a laser printer, check with your supplier to find a heavy stock that has been certified to work with your printer.

When displayed on your screen, the business card may not look rectangular. The screen sometimes distorts squares and rectangles to make up for the graphics adapter's lack of resolution. You must go by the ruler lines or print the card out. Use the page preview (**ALT-Z**) feature frequently to keep your business card's shape in its proper perspective.

Before printing, you should duplicate the business card several times on a single page. Select the business card, press **ALT-D**) (or Duplicate from the Art pull-down menu); then place the duplicated text with the hand tool. You will have fewer copies to make if you put several cards on the same page, as shown in Figure 12-10.

Surveys Unlimited

Andrew B. Mayfair
Sales Consultant, Contracts

951 E. Skelly Dr., Miami, FL 98912
(991) 555-6545

Surveys Unlimited

Andrew B. Mayfair
Sales Consultant, Contracts

951 E. Skelly Dr., Miami, FL 98912
(991) 555-6545

Surveys Unlimited

Andrew B. Mayfair
Sales Consultant, Contracts

951 E. Skelly Dr., Miami, FL 98912
(991) 555-6545

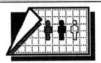

Surveys Unlimited

Andrew B. Mayfair
Sales Consultant, Contracts

951 E. Skelly Dr., Miami, FL 98912
(991) 555-6545

Surveys Unlimited

Andrew B. Mayfair
Sales Consultant, Contracts

951 E. Skelly Dr., Miami, FL 98912
(991) 555-6545

Surveys Unlimited

Andrew B. Mayfair
Sales Consultant, Contracts

951 E. Skelly Dr., Miami, FL 98912
(991) 555-6545

Surveys Unlimited

Andrew B. Mayfair
Sales Consultant, Contracts

951 E. Skelly Dr., Miami, FL 98912
(991) 555-6545

Surveys Unlimited

Andrew B. Mayfair
Sales Consultant, Contracts

951 E. Skelly Dr., Miami, FL 98912
(991) 555-6545

FIGURE 12-10. Duplicating the business card multiple times

Summary

In this chapter you used First Publisher's graphic files and skills you have learned in earlier chapters to create a logo for use on personalized stationery and business cards.

chapter 13

BUSINESS REPORTS

Creating a Report
Future Business Reports

B usiness reports consist of balance sheets, income statements, and year-end reports. All of these can be produced with a normal word processor. However, by combining text and graphics as well as your company's logo, you can do much more to enhance your business reports' appearance.

First Publisher's strength lies in its ability to lay out text and graphics in an appealing manner. First Publisher is *not* able to produce graphs using numbers. There are several spreadsheet and charting programs (such as Lotus 1-2-3) that can produce business graphs. Once the graphs are generated, you can use SNAPSHOT to bring them into your publication. Since business reports contain so much numerical information, you will need to let your spreadsheet program produce financial models for your publications.

CREATING A REPORT

Figure 13-1 shows the first business report that you will produce with First Publisher. You will find that First Publisher is not used for the creation of the report—only the layout. Most of the work is done in a spreadsheet

Surveys 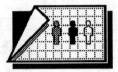 Unlimited

FINANCIAL HIGHLIGHTS
(In 1000's except Per Share & Employees)

Years ended June 30	1988	1989	1990
FOR THE YEAR:			
Revenue	$29,594	$48,840	$54,725
Net Income	$3,164	$4,366	$5,861
Net Income Per Share	$1.11	$1.25	$1.68
Average Shares Outstanding	2,854	3,485	3,486
NET MARGIN	10.7%	10.4%	10.9%
Total Assets	$17,060	$23,543	$31,548
Total Plant & Equipment	$6,626	$9,144	$12,253
Total Equity	$11,216	$16,339	$22,189
Number of Employees	263	363	487
RETURN ON EQUITY	28.2%	26.7%	26.4%

FIGURE 13-1. A business report produced with First Publisher

program. The steps that describe this report's preparation assume that you are using Lotus 1-2-3 or a compatible program that can save information to an ASCII text file. If you do not have access to a spreadsheet program, you might want to skip to Chapter 14 since the rest of this chapter assumes that you do.

First Publisher cannot import graphs directly from Lotus 1-2-3, so you have to take a SNAPSHOT image of the graph. See Chapter 4 for more details on using SNAPSHOT. Only the specific SNAPSHOT commands needed for the sample business report will be presented here.

Before starting your spreadsheet program, change to your First Publisher subdirectory (probably called PUB) and type **SNAPSHOT** at the DOS prompt. You will see the SNAPSHOT load message. You are now ready to start your spreadsheet program.

Creating the Spreadsheet Portion

Figure 13-2 shows the screen from Lotus 1-2-3 that was used to produce the sample Surveys Unlimited report. A spreadsheet program is used for putting numbers into a more meaningful format. If you are going to produce many business reports and you do not have Lotus 1-2-3 or a similar program, you should consider purchasing one.

A1: 'FINANCIAL HIGHLIGHTS   `READY`

	A	B	C	D	E	F	G	H
1	FINANCIAL HIGHLIGHTS							
2	(In 1000's except Per Share & Employees)							
3								
4	Years ended June 30				1988	1989	1990	
5								
6	FOR THE YEAR:							
7	Revenue				$29,594	$48,840	$54,725	
8	Net Income				$3,164	$4,366	$5,861	
9	Net Income Per Share				$1.11	$1.25	$1.68	
10	Average Shares Outstanding				2,854	3,485	3,486	
11								
12	NET MARGIN				10.7%	10.4%	10.9%	
13								
14								
15	Total Assets				$17,060	$23,543	$31,548	
16	Total Plant & Equipment				$6,626	$9,144	$12,253	
17	Total Equity				$11,216	$16,339	$22,189	
18	Number of Employees				263	363	487	
19								
20	RETURN ON EQUITY				28.2%	26.7%	26.4%	

17-Jul-90   04:28 AM

FIGURE 13-2.   A spreadsheet to be imported into the publication

Using your spreadsheet program, type in the chart shown in Figure 13-2. You must save the spreadsheet as an ASCII text file before you can import it into First Publisher. Almost every spreadsheet can be saved in the ASCII format. To save a Lotus 1-2-3 file in the ASCII format, follow these steps:

1. Press the slash (/) to display the Lotus 1-2-3 menu.

2. Select Print.

3. Select File to send the output to a disk file.

4. When you see the Lotus 1-2-3 pathname, (**BACKSPACE**) through the disk path before typing the filename. For this example, type **FINANCE.TXT** for the ASCII disk file and press (**ENTER**).

5. Select the range that will include the entire spreadsheet.

6. Select Go to send the file to the disk file.

7. Select Quit to leave the print menu.

Of course, if you use a spreadsheet program other than Lotus 1-2-3, the commands may differ greatly from those presented here.

 If you use MultiMate, you can import spreadsheets directly into First Publisher without saving them in an ASCII text file format.

Displaying the Graph

You now must produce the graph for the publication. The steps for creating a Lotus 1-2-3 graph are presented shortly. Most spreadsheet programs can create a graph such as this one. Once you create a graph, you must take a snapshot of it with the SNAPSHOT program you loaded into memory earlier in the book.

The Lotus 1-2-3 graph is created by selecting the Net Income figures and displaying them in a bar graph. Follow these steps:

1. Press the slash to display the Lotus 1-2-3 menu.

2. Select Graph to prepare for the graph.

3. Select Type to select a graph type.

4. The graph is a bar graph, so select Bar.

5. Select the X range and highlight the years 1988 through 1990.

6. Select the A range and highlight the Net Income row of numbers.

7. Select View to see your graph. Your screen may look like the following illustration at this point:

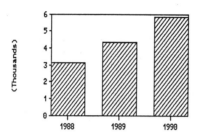

If you are using a spreadsheet other than Lotus 1-2-3, or a non-CGA monitor, your screen may look slightly different.

8. Press (**SHIFT-PRTSC**) to take a snapshot of the graph.

9. Press (**ESC**).

Now exit Lotus 1-2-3 and develop the SNAPSHOT image with SNAP2ART. At the DOS prompt, change to the First Publisher subdirectory and type **SNAP2ART** followed by **E** to save the file as SNAP.ART. You can then load SNAP.ART into your publication when you are ready for it.

If you get this message:

The file snap.art already exists, delete it or use a new name

you must delete SNAP.ART before running SNAP2ART. This is a file created earlier, and the system does not want to overwrite it. If you want to save what is already in SNAP.ART, rename it before running SNAP2ART.

Adding the Logo

Now that you have the text and graphics ready to load, start First Publisher and prepare for them. The top of the report contains the company logo you created in Chapter 12. To load the logo, follow these steps:

1. Load the First Publisher program.

2. Select Get art from the Art pull-down menu.

3. Type **LOGO** when prompted for the art file.

4. Move the hand tool to the top of the page and press (**F10**), or press and hold a mouse button, to display the logo.

5. Move the logo as high on the page as possible. If the logo's art image includes extra white space at the top, you should resize it using (**ALT-R**) to get it close to the top of the page and make room for the report. Press (**F10**), or release the mouse button, when you have the logo centered. Figure 13-3 shows the screen at this point.

Since you will be importing text, you must prepare the baselines. Although First Publisher will import the text a few lines down, moving the baselines now will keep the text from flowing over the art when you make adjustments to it. Follow these steps to lower the baselines below the logo:

1. Select Adjust below from the Baselines pull-down menu.

2. Point to the top baseline.

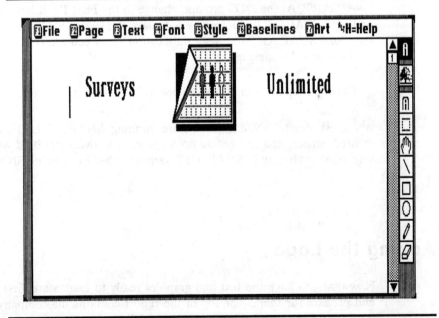

FIGURE 13-3. Centering the logo on the report

3. Press (**F10**) twice, or click the mouse button, to display the baseline handles.

4. Point to the middle handle. Press (**F10**), or press and hold a mouse button, and drag the handle down the page about an inch to give the top line of text ample room under the logo.

5. Press (**F10**), or release the mouse button, to anchor the baseline and all others below it. Figure 13-4 shows the screen after this is done.

Importing the Spreadsheet

You must now bring the text into your First Publisher screen. Once you import the file, you will convert it to the proper font size and style, as well as add an underscore after the year line.

To import the text from the spreadsheet, follow these steps:

1. Select the 12-point Geneva normal font. This is the font used when First Publisher imports the worksheet file.

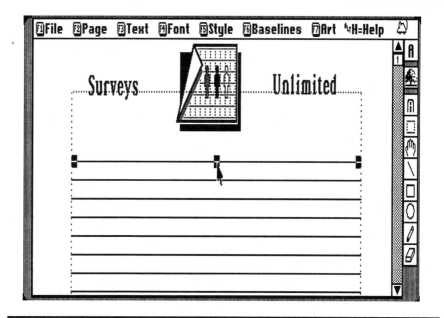

FIGURE 13-4. Pulling down the baselines

2. Select Get text from the Text pull-down menu.

3. Type **FINANCE** at the "Filename" prompt (or select it from the list of text files) and press (**ENTER**). First Publisher will supply the .TXT extension.

4. After a brief pause, First Publisher will ask for the file's format by displaying the following screen:

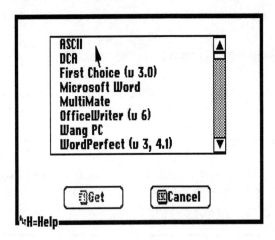

5. Select ASCII.

6. After a brief pause, First Publisher will import the text file. Your screen will look like the one in Figure 13-5.

The text may look messy, but importing it from the spreadsheet saves lots of time in the long run, especially after you get accustomed to First Publisher. You must now clean up the text so it looks good enough for the report.

 If you attempt to import a large spreadsheet, part of it may be forced into the page overflow area described in Chapter 3. You may have to jump to the next page in the publication, using (**ALT-J**), and place the overflow text there.

FIXING THE TEXT Any time you import tabular material, whether it is from Lotus 1-2-3 or any other program, you will lose the formatting of the

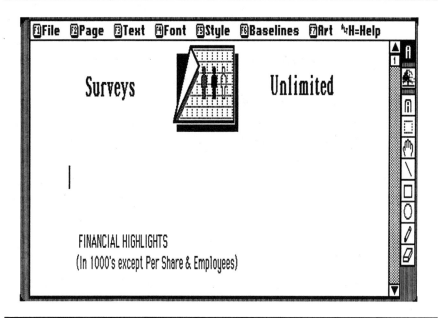

═══════ **FIGURE 13-5.** After importing the spreadsheet

columns. First Publisher imports the correct characters and numbers but cannot keep columns in their original placement.

There are three ways to incorporate tabular material into a First Publisher publication:

- Import and edit the table by hand (as done here).

- Use SNAPSHOT to capture the table as a graphic art image (you will, however, lose the ability to edit with the text tool and baselines).

- Import the table as an ASCII text file, and then save it under the .MAC file extension. The file will then be an art image that you can load and divide back into columns using the art-movement tools.

Before adjusting the table, you should change its fonts to their final sizes and styles. Otherwise, you may have to realign your text again. Select and change the font by choosing from the Font and Style pull-down menus as described here:

1. Mark the "FINANCIAL HIGHLIGHTS" text by pressing (F10) or pressing and holding a mouse button.

2. Move the highlight to the last letter and press (F10) again or release the mouse button. This will highlight the entire heading.

3. Select Bold from the Style pull-down menu. This will change the selected heading to a boldfaced one.

4. Repeat these steps for the remaining four headings (the ones in upper-case characters). Figure 13-6 shows what your screen should look like at this point.

The rest of the characters should remain in their existing font. You must use the editing and cursor-movement keys, listed for you in Table 13-1, to fix up the text. To match the sample, make sure there are nine spaces between the years in the text. Align the rest of the text with the years.

Delete the extra spaces between the logo and the first line so that the text starts just below the logo. Once done, your screen will look similar to the one in Figure 13-7. You are now ready to add the graphics elements to the publication.

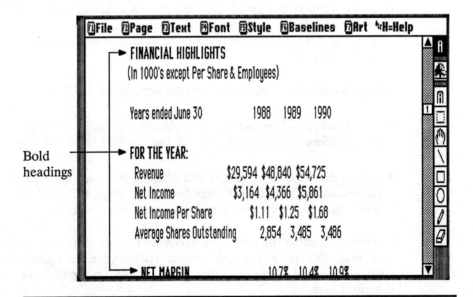

FIGURE 13-6. Boldfacing the report headings

Adding the Art

It is time to place the graph at the bottom of the page. You will have to edit the art a little before the publication is finished. To load the art, follow these steps:

1. Select Get art from the Art pull-down menu.
2. Type **SNAP** when prompted for a filename.
3. Move the hand tool below the text and press (F10) or press and hold a mouse button. Position the graph below the text and press (F10) or release the mouse button. Your screen will look like the one in Figure 13-8.

Keystroke	Cursor Movement
(UP ARROW)	Up one line
(DOWN ARROW)	Down one line
(LEFT ARROW)	Left one character
(RIGHT ARROW)	Right one character
(CTRL-RIGHT ARROW)	Right one word
(CTRL-LEFT ARROW)	Left one word
(PGUP)	Up one screen
(CTRL-PGUP)	Up a portion of a screen
(PGDN)	Down one screen
(CTRL-PGDN)	Down a portion of a screen
(HOME)	To the first column of the current line
(CTRL-HOME)	To the beginning of the page
(END)	To the last column of the current line
(CTRL-END)	To the end of the current page
(CTRL-N)	Right one column of text
(CTRL-P)	Left one column of text
(SHIFT- +) (on keypad)	To the next page
(SHIFT-MINUS) (on keypad)	To the previous page

TABLE 13-1. The Cursor-Movement Editing Keys

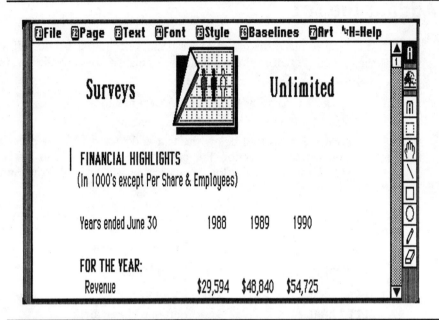

FIGURE 13-7. Cleaning up the report

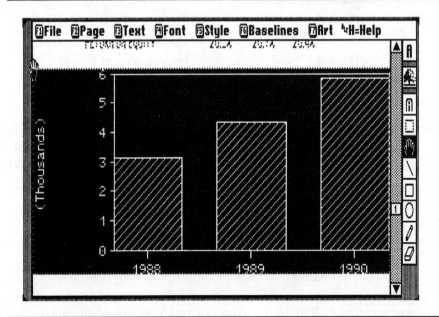

FIGURE 13-8. Positioning the spreadsheet graph

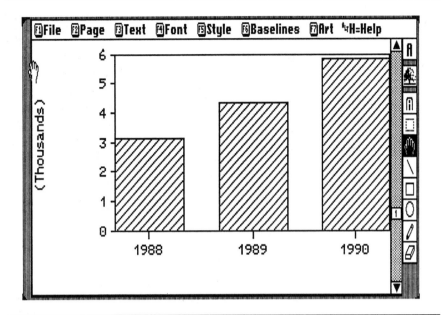

FIGURE 13-9.   Inverting the graph to match the rest of the report

The image will be inverted (white lines on a black background). Select Invert from the Art pull-down menu and fix this. Figure 13-9 shows the shading of the screen after the inversion takes place. The art now matches the text.

Press (ALT-R) to resize the image. Move the lower portion of the image up and away from the bottom edge of the paper. Bring the sides inward to align them with the body of the text. You might want to select the "(Thousands)" text and move it closer to the graph. Use page preview to see where the graph is in relation to the text. Leave enough room for the surrounding lines.

To add the lines to the report, select the widest line thickness. Select the line-drawing tool to draw the line shown in Figure 13-10.

The only line left to draw is the one under the title that starts with "Years ended June 30." Use the thinnest line width. Try page preview again. If it looks fine, print the report to the printer. The first time you print it, select the draft mode from the Print screen to see quick results. Once the report is final, you can print a smoothed version of it.

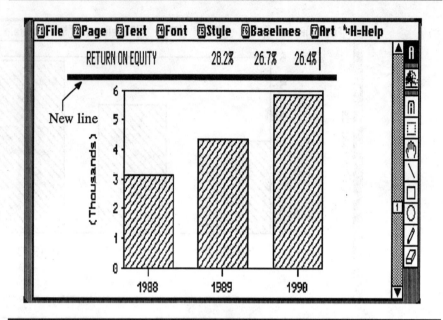

FIGURE 13-10. After drawing the separating line

FUTURE BUSINESS REPORTS

Your business reports may be good candidates for the special multiple-column formats available with the Choose layout option on the Page pull-down menu. Version 2 users can use the template files supplied with First Publisher, such as 1TOPBOT.PUB. You might want to look at these for future reference.

So far, the publications created in this book have been a single page in length. However, most business reports are longer. Annual reports typically have 10 to 20 pages. The Jump to page option (ALT-J) on the Page pull-down menu will take you from page to page in longer reports.

Summary

In this chapter you saw how to create business reports that incorporate graphic and spreadsheet data. You took advantage of First Publisher's layout and text formatting abilities to produce a professional-looking business report. This included

- Importing a graph from a Lotus 1-2-3 spreadsheet

- Importing the actual spreadsheet data directly from Lotus 1-2-3 as text in the report

- Adding effective lines and boxes to highlight key areas of the report

RESTAURANT MENUS

Restaurant menus can be fancy or plain; some have pictures, some do not. This chapter shows you how to create two different styles of menus. There are special considerations that have to be dealt with—how often the menu items change, how often the prices change, and whether or not art is to be incorporated into the menu.

This chapter walks you through the creation of a menu from scratch. Version 3 users can look at the SANDWICH.PUB template file supplied with First Publisher. Then, version 2 users can use the MENU.PUB template file supplied with the program to create a detailed menu. You will see how adding baselines at the proper places allows you to change price text easily while preserving the surrounding art.

A DAILY MENU

Figure 14-1 shows a printout of a daily menu, the first sample menu you will create. This type of menu can be handed out at reunions and church

Menu
for the hungry

Smith Reunion, Sept. 3rd

"Your bellies will be
as full as your hearts"

Menu

Chicken bits	**Cheese cake**
Smashed potatoes	**Fresh fruit**
Super salad	**Ice cream**
Golden corn	**Ice tea**

FIGURE 14-1.   Sample printout of a daily menu

gatherings. These menus inform the reader of the selection for the current meal without regard to prices. The menu selection changes almost every time it is used; therefore, you will want to put the food on baselines that can be easily changed.

Getting the Art

Before starting the menu, you must clip the art from the clip art file called LEISURE.MAC. You will resize it when you bring it into the publication. To get the art, follow these steps:

1. Select Get art from the Art pull-down menu. Version 2 users will have to select Get graphics from the File pull-down menu.

2. Type **LEISURE.MAC** when prompted for the graphics file. The clip art file will appear.

3. Select the eraser tool and erase the mouthpiece from the clarinet in the upper-left corner of the screen. This will make room for the selection of the bread basket next to it.

4. Use the selection box tool to select the entire bread basket image. Do not get any more surrounding white space than you have to. Figure 14-2 shows your screen after you have selected the image.

5. Select Save art from the Art pull-down menu.

6. Type **BREAD** when prompted for the art filename. First Publisher will save the selected bread basket to the art file called BREAD.ART.

7. Select Start over from the File pull-down menu to erase the screen. Do not save the LEISURE file; press (F2) when prompted to do so.

Laying Out the Baselines

Almost all of the text on this menu will change from event to event. Therefore, the text will reside on baselines. Also, all text above the food items will be centered on the baselines.

Use the Adjust below command to adjust all of the baselines on the page. Follow these steps to set them up properly:

FIGURE 14-2. Selecting the bread basket image

1. Press (ALT-L) to display the ruler lines.

2. Select Adjust below from the Baselines pull-down menu. First Publisher will display the baselines.

3. Point to the top baseline. Press (F10) twice or click the mouse button to display the baseline handles.

4. Point to the middle handle. Press (F10) or press and hold the mouse button to grab the top baseline. Pull the baseline down to V2.25. (You may have to use the arrow keys to hit V2.25 exactly.)

5. Press (F10) again, or release the mouse button, to anchor the top baseline. Your screen should look like the one in Figure 14-3.

6. Press (ALT-X) to select Center from the Baselines pull-down menu. All baselines below the top one will center any text typed on them since Adjust below is still selected.

7. Pull the second baseline to V2.75.

8. Pull the third baseline to V3.5.

9. Pull the fourth baseline to V4.75. You should scroll the screen so that you can see the rest of the vertical ruler line.

10. Pull the fifth baseline to V5.25.

11. Pull the sixth baseline to V6.25.

12. Pull the seventh baseline to V7.0. This is the first line of the items on the menu. These items should *not* be centered due to their special spacing. Therefore, select Left justify from the Baselines pull-down menu so that all of the remaining baselines will be aligned with the left column.

13. Pull the eighth baseline to V7.75.

14. Pull the ninth baseline to V8.5.

15. Pull the tenth baseline to V9.25.

16. Reselect the seventh baseline (at V7.0). Point to the left handle and move it to H1.75, V7.0. This will indent the menu items. Your screen should now look like the one in Figure 14-4.

17. Press ⌐**CTRL-HOME**⌐ to move the cursor to the top of the screen.

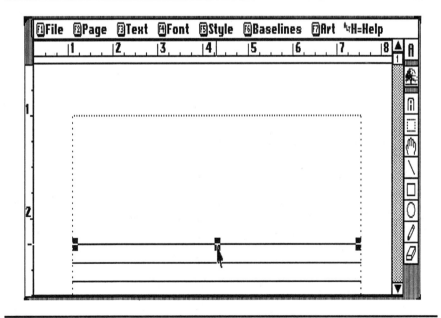

FIGURE 14-3.   Adjusting the baselines to start lower on the page

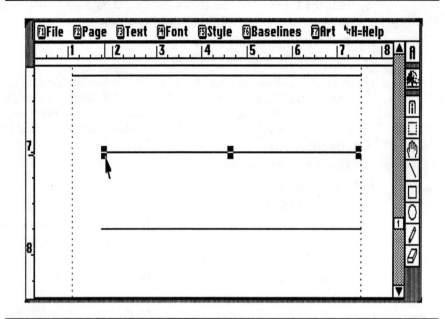

FIGURE 14-4.   Increasing the left margin size

Now that your baselines are set up for the text, select Adjust below from the Baselines pull-down menu again to hide them.

Drawing the Border

You now are ready to draw the border around the menu. It consists of a thick-lined box with a thin-lined box inside of it. First Publisher's box-drawing tool makes this easy, as you will see. Follow these steps:

1. Select the box-drawing tool.

2. Select the thickest line-drawing width.

3. Move the cross hair cursor to H1.0, V1.0.

4. Press (F10), or press and hold the mouse button, to anchor the upper-left corner of the box.

5. Move the cross to H7.5, V10.0 and press ⟨**F10**⟩, or release the mouse button, to finish drawing the box.

6. Press ⟨**CTRL-HOME**⟩ to see the top of the publication. It should look like the one in Figure 14-5.

The thin box is located one quarter-inch within the box you just drew. To draw it

1. Select the thinnest line-drawing width.

2. Since the box-drawing tool is still selected, move the cross pointer to H1.25, V1.25.

3. Press ⟨**F10**⟩, or press and hold a mouse button, to anchor the upper-left corner of the box.

4. Move the cross to H7.25, V9.75 to draw the box.

5. Press ⟨**F10**⟩ or release the mouse button.

6. Press ⟨**CTRL-HOME**⟩ to see the top of the publication. It should look like the one in Figure 14-6.

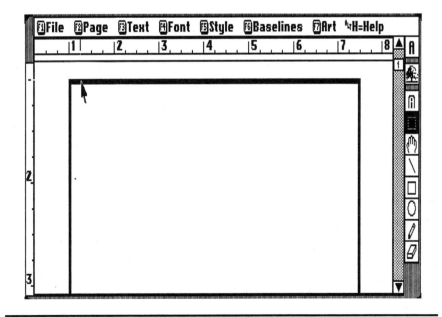

FIGURE 14-5.   A thick border drawn around the menu body

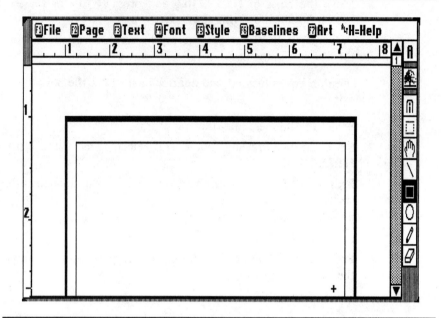

FIGURE 14-6. Enclosing the body in a second border

Positioning the Art

The bread image should be brought into your publication and resized at this time. On the final menu (Figure 14-1), the bread is positioned on the page in two places, each a mirror image of the other. You will anchor the left image; then duplicate and flip it for the other side. Follow the steps below to add the art:

1. Select Get art from the Art pull-down menu.

2. Type **BREAD** at the filename prompt.

3. When the hand appears, move it to the upper-left corner of the menu.

4. Press (**F10**) or press and hold the mouse button to display the bread.

5. Position it in the upper-left corner, just inside the thin border. Try not to overlap the border, but get the bread's outline as close as possible.

6. Press (**F10**) again, or release the mouse button, to anchor the art.

7. Press (**ALT-L**) to display the ruler lines.

8. Press (**ALT-R**) to resize the bread image. The bread should be about 1 3/4 inches wide and 1 3/4 inches tall. Once you have resized the bread, your screen will be similar to Figure 14-7.

The image should now be duplicated, flipped, and placed on the other side of the menu. Follow these steps:

1. Press (**ALT-D**) to select Duplicate from the Art pull-down menu. First Publisher will send a copy of the art to the art clipboard.

2. Move the hand tool to the other side of the screen.

3. Press (**F10**), or press and hold the mouse button, to display the art image.

4. Position the image just inside the thin border. Try not to overlap the border, but get it as close as possible.

5. Press (**F10**), or release the mouse button, to anchor the art.

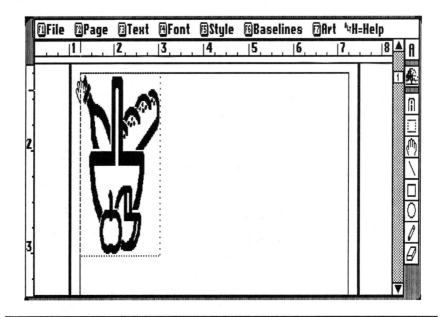

FIGURE 14-7.   Placing the bread basket art image

6. Select Flip horizontal from the Art pull-down menu. Since the image is still selected, it will be what is flipped (or made into a mirror image), as shown in Figure 14-8.

 If you overlap the thin-lined border, you may lose some of it when you place the art. If this happens, you can touch up the line with the line-drawing tool.

Adding the Text

The text is easy to add since you have already set up the baselines. You just position the text cursor at the top of the screen (on the top baseline) and type the menu's text as described here:

1. Select the text tool (the top tool).

2. Select the 36-point New York normal font for the main title.

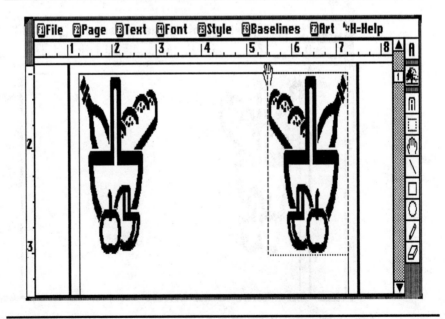

FIGURE 14-8. Duplicating and flipping the bread basket

3. Type **Menu,** and then press ⏎ENTER⏎. The word will center itself auto-matically on the baseline.

4. Select the 18-point New York bold font.

5. Type **for the hungry** and press ⏎ENTER⏎.

6. Select the 24-point New York normal font.

7. Type **Smith Reunion, Sept. 3rd** and press ⏎ENTER⏎.

8. Select the 18-point New York bold font.

9. Type **"Your bellies will be** and press ⏎ENTER⏎.

10. Type **as full as your hearts"** and press ⏎ENTER⏎.

11. Type **Menu** and press ⏎ENTER⏎.

Your screen will look like the one in Figure 14-9. You are now at the left-justified baselines, so the text will no longer be centered automatically. To finish the text:

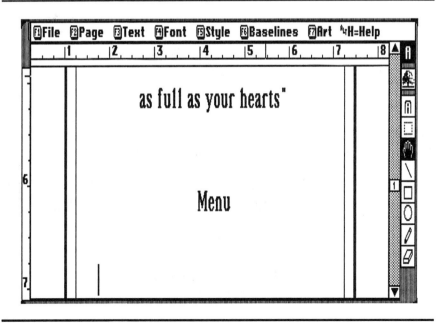

FIGURE 14-9. The text at the top of the daily menu

1. Type **Chicken bits** followed by 17 spaces. This number of spaces will place the two columns as evenly as possible.

2. Type **Cheese cake.** You can align the rest of the menu items as you type them with these two items. They all use the same font. Press <kbd>ENTER</kbd> at the end of each line.

When you are done, press <kbd>ALT-Z</kbd> to see a page preview like the one in Figure 14-10.

ADDING THE SEPARATING LINE   Save the file before going on. You are almost through with the menu, and this would not be a good time to lose the work you have done. Get into the habit of saving your publication every ten minutes or so. That way, in the unlikely event of a power failure, your work will be safely tucked away on disk. Select Save publication and save your file as **OURMENU.PUB**.

The only thing left to do is to draw the line that separates the top half of the menu from the bottom half. Follow these steps:

1. Select the line-drawing tool.

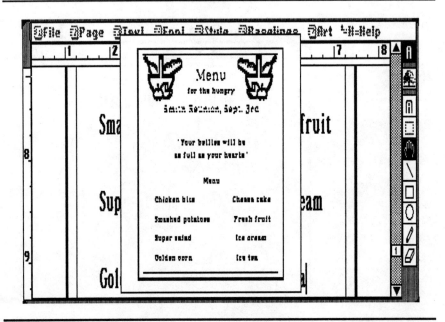

FIGURE 14-10.   Looking at a page preview of the daily menu

2. Select the second-thinnest line width.

3. Position the cross at H1.5, V5.75.

4. Press (**F10**), or press and hold the mouse button, to anchor the left end of the line.

5. Drag the right end of the line to H7.0, V5.75.

6. Press (**F10**), or release the mouse button, to anchor the right side of the line.

Your screen should look like the one in Figure 14-11. You are now done with the first sample menu; save it and print it out.

USING SANDWICH.PUB IN VERSION 3

Version 3 supplies a template file called SANDWICH.PUB, shown in Figure 14-12. This is a straightforward template file. All of the text is on a baseline,

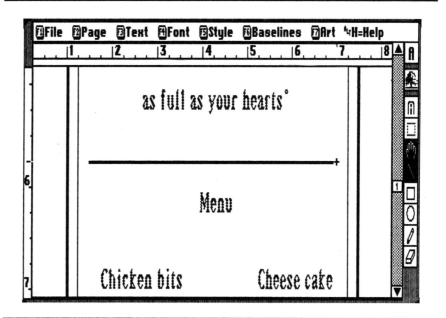

FIGURE 14-11. Drawing the separating line on the menu

THE SANDWICH SHOP

Fresh and delicious to go

Today's Specials

California Dreamin': Turkey, avocado, and sprouts on whole wheat.

Surf City: Seafood salad, lettuce, and tomato on a sourdough roll.

Mom's Memory: Meatloaf and ketchup on bakery white.

Zen Retreat: Monterey Jack, avocado, and sprouts in a wheat pita.

All sandwiches are $3.75.

Soup of the day: Brazilian black bean. Cup: $1.50. Bowl: $2.25.

Special combo: 1/2 sandwich plus a cup of soup for $2.75.

Try our delicious sandwiches!
The Sandwich Shop is in the Quito Shopping Center
at the corner of Cox and Quito in Saratoga.
Our hours are 10 to 8, Monday through Saturday.
To order, call (555)866-2770.

FIGURE 14-12. The SANDWICH.PUB template file

including the title, "THE SANDWICH SHOP." You can, therefore, change the text very easily to suit your own needs.

"THE SANDWICH SHOP" was typed in 24-point Dutch roman font. The body text (where each special is listed) was typed in 12-point Zurich roman font. This font is not included in MASTER.FNT; you can add it or substitute the 12-point Swiss roman font. The "Today's Specials" subtitle was typed in 18-point Dutch bold font as graphics text. The inverted text beneath the name of the shop is typed in 12-point Geneva bold font. You will find this information useful if you want to change the text.

USING MENU.PUB IN VERSION 2

Version 2 of First Publisher supplies a menu template file called MENU .PUB. The rest of this chapter describes this template file and its use. More can be accomplished with the MENU.PUB template file than with SAND-WICH.PUB in version 3; it is a two-column menu providing much more room for menu items and descriptions. Before starting, load MENU.PUB and print it out for reference. The following sections take the template file and use it to produce the menu shown in Figure 14-13. Most of the text on the menu will be typed on the baselines that are already set up in the template.

Since the menu's sections are so similar, the following examples will walk you through the steps to create just the first section. You will then be armed with the tools to finish the menu if you like, or you may want to re-create it to suit your own needs.

Clipping the Art

All of the art in the Midtown Diner menu is clipped from the graphics file called LEISURE.MAC. As with the previous chapters, you will find it best to clip all of the necessary art *before* beginning the menu. To clip the sandwich art image:

1. Select Get graphics from the File pull-down menu. Type **LEISURE.MAC** at the filename prompt.

2. Scroll the screen down until the entire sandwich image is clearly displayed.

Menu

Meat Items

Fresh Baked Ham
This succulent dish has been a
favorite of our customers for
many years. You will find it is
your favorite too.
$6.95

Catfish Delight
Our catfish comes fresh from area
lakes. The fish will be filleted and
cooked to your satisfaction.
$7.95

Fruit Dishes

Apples
Home-grown apples, baked to a
golden brown, served in cinnamon
sauce.
$1.95

Fresh Fruit Dish
Try this sampling of at least five
in-season fruits to make your
mouth water.
$1.95

Vegetables

Carrots and Peas
Cooked like Mom used to make
them.
$1.70

Fresh Spinach Salad
Grow up strong! Eat our delicious
spinach salad.
$2.20

Breads
Our bread will melt in your
mouth. Ask for the rolls or
biscuits.
Included with meal

Desserts

Homemade Ice Cream
Our peach ice cream is famous for
repeat business!
$1.95

Cheese Cake
If you ate as much as you will
want, we will have to carry you
home!
$2.95

Drinks

*All the usual tea, coffee, and soft drinks
of your choice.*
$0.75

FIGURE 14-13. A menu produced using the MENU.PUB template
file

3. Point to the upper-left corner of the image with the selection box tool.

4. Press (**F10**), or press and hold the mouse button, to anchor the selection box.

5. Drag the lower-right corner downward until the rest of the sandwich is selected. Do not select any more of the surrounding white space than you have to.

6. You will have to resize the image (and, later, all of the other art images used in the menu). Press (**ALT-L**) to display the rulers.

7. Press (**ALT-R**) to display the resizing handles.

8. Resize the image to about 1 1/4 inches wide and 3/4 inch tall. The image will look small, as shown in Figure 14-14, but it is the right size for the printed menu.

9. Select Save art from the Art pull-down menu and type **SANDWICH** when prompted for the art filename.

In the same fashion, select and resize the other sample menu art images from LEISURE.MAC. Keep track of the filenames you save them under as

FIGURE 14-14.   Resizing the sandwich art image

you will need to reload them into the menu. Be sure to get the spice shelf art that appears at the bottom of the menu.

Modifying the Title

Load the MENU.PUB template file (with $\boxed{\text{ALT-G}}$) and immediately save it under the filename MENU2ND. This will give you an intact copy of the template file for future use.

The template's title, "Green St. Bar & Grill," will be changed to reflect the new name, "Midtown Diner." This title is typed with graphics text so that you can place it wherever you want and invert the letters. You should first erase the old title. Follow these steps:

1. Highlight the selection box tool and point just above and to the left of the first letter, *G*.

2. Press $\boxed{\text{F10}}$, or press and hold the mouse button, to anchor that corner of the selection box.

3. Drag the selection box down and to the right so it surrounds the complete title.

4. Press $\boxed{\text{F10}}$, or release the mouse button, to finish selecting the title.

5. Press $\boxed{\text{DEL}}$, the speed key for Cut, from the Art pull-down menu. The title will disappear, leaving a blank space, as shown in Figure 14-15.

 If you delete too much of the awning that the title sits on, you can touch it up later.

The original restaurant name was typed with the 12-point Chicago bold font. This font comes from the EXTRA.FNT file. Since you may not have copied any of these fonts (as described in Chapter 7) to MASTER.FNT, this example uses the 12-point New York bold font. To place the new title:

1. Select the graphics text tool (the hollowed *A*).

2. Select the 12-point New York bold font.

3. Point to a blank area below the first line of text (under the first and fourth food groups).

4. Press $\boxed{\text{F10}}$ twice, or click the mouse button, to move the graphics text cursor there.

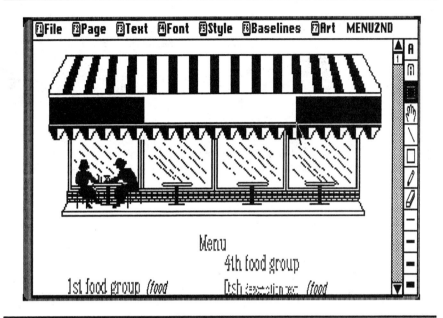

FIGURE 14-15.   Getting rid of the template's original restaurant name

5. Type **Midtown Diner**. Figure 14-16 shows what your screen should look like. Now that you have typed the text, you can select it and move it to the blank spot in the awning.

6. Choose the selection box tool and select the text. Do not get any more white space than you have to.

7. Select Invert from the Art pull-down menu to reverse the image (make it have white letters on a black background).

8. Select the hand tool.

9. Position the hand over the selected text and press (**F10**), or press and hold a mouse button, to grab the new title.

10. Drag the new title to its location at the top of the screen.

11. Press (**F10**), or release the mouse button, to place the text. Figure 14-17 shows your screen at this point.

You can fill in the white spaces around the new name with the line-drawing tool. You may have to magnify the image to fill in every detail.

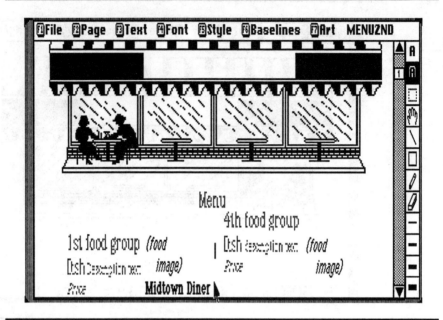

FIGURE 14-16. Typing a new restaurant name

The Menu Text

Adding the text for the menu is easy because the baselines are provided. The menu is in a two-column format after the title. Remember that (CTRL-N) moves your cursor to the next column (to the right), and (CTRL-P) moves it to the previous column (to the left). To get you started, here are the steps for adding the first menu item:

1. Select the text tool.

2. Move the text cursor to the beginning of "1st food group."

3. Press (DEL) until this text is fully deleted.

4. Select the 14-point New York bold font. Type **Meat Items**. Do *not* press (ENTER) at the end of the line. If you do, you will force part of the first column into the second, and lose the alignment.

5. With the cursor-movement keys, position the cursor at the start of the line that begins "DISH Description text."

6. Press (DEL) until this text is erased.

7. In the same manner, erase the "Price" text.

 For this template, do *not* press (ENTER) after any line of text. Otherwise, you will lose the second column's alignment.

The food description must have ample room, so it should start two lines down from the heading, not directly underneath it. This will make room for the art that will go next to the title. Type the name and description as described here:

1. Move the cursor two lines below "Meat Items." There should be one blank line between the cursor and the heading.

2. Select the 12-point New York bold font and type **Fresh Baked Ham**.

3. Move the cursor to the beginning of the next line using the arrow keys or the mouse.

4. Select 12-point New York normal.

5. Type the following:

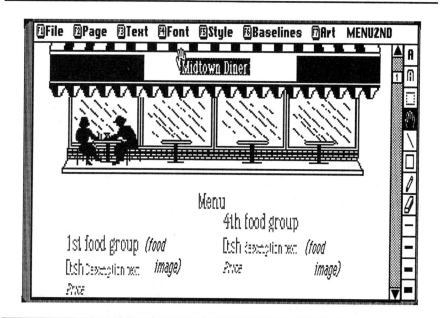

FIGURE 14-17. Inverting and moving the new name

This succulent dish has been a favorite of our customers for many years. You will find it is your favorite too.

As you type, notice that the second column is pushed downward. First Publisher always inserts text as you type. Press ⬚DEL⬚ enough times to put the second column's "4th food group" back in its original location in the template MENU.PUB. Although it may seem tedious, you must do this every time the text in the second column is moved over. Otherwise, you will lose the placement of the rest of the template.

Last, you must add the price of the item. Since the price may change, it should be on a baseline by itself.

1. Move the cursor to the line directly below the ham description.
2. Select the 10-point New York italic font.
3. Type **$6.95**. After you press ⬚DEL⬚ to adjust the second column (if necessary), your screen will look like the one in Figure 14-18.

Skip a line and repeat these steps for the Catfish Delight. If you want to finish the menu, you can. You may find that you have to adjust the menu periodically to make up for an extra line.

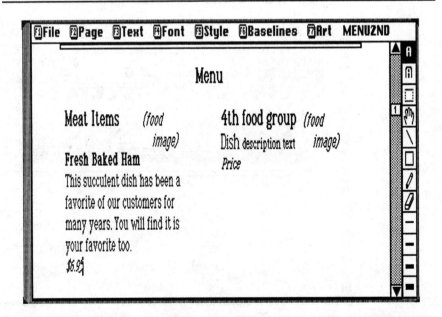

FIGURE 14-18.   The first item on the menu is nearly complete

Inserting the Art

The only thing left for you to do is insert the art over the area marked "(food image)." Before doing this, you must select the food image message and press (DEL). Use the selection box tool for this, since it is graphics text.

Once the food image has been deleted, follow the usual procedure of selecting Get art from the Art pull-down menu and typing the filename that you saved the graphic image under.

Summary

In this chapter you saw how to create two types of food menus. The first menu is a general listing of meal items for gatherings such as picnics and socials. The second menu is more formal and lists descriptions and prices of the items served. To create these menus, you

- Collected food art from the supplied clip art files of First Publisher

- Added the baselines for the text in the menu

- Used the SANDWICH.PUB template file, a two-column menu template with room for descriptions and prices

APPENDIXES

Installing First Publisher
Supplied MASTER.FNT Fonts
Clip Art and Template Files
Desktop Publishing Glossary
DOS Directories

In the last section, you got lots of hands-on experience using the First Publisher desktop publishing system. You are now ready to create you own publications, either using the template, art, and font files supplied with the program, or by developing your own from scratch.

Part III incorporates appendixes that tell you about installing First Publisher on your system. The font, template, and clip art files that come with First Publisher are each shown for your reference, and a glossary of desktop publishing terms is supplied.

You will find that this book has taken up where the *First Publisher User's Guide* left off—giving you useful and functional hands-on examples and explanations that will get you started on your desktop publishing endeavors.

Midtown Diner

Meat Item

Fresh Bake
This succulen...
of our custom...
will find it is...
$6.95

Catfish Del
Our catfish co...
lakes. The fis...
cooked to your...
$7.95

Vegetable

Carrots and
Cooked like M...
$1.70

Fresh Spin
Grow up stron...
spinach salad...
$2.20

Breads
Our bread wil...
for the rolls o...
Included wit...

Surveys  Unlimited

FINANCIAL HIGHLIGHTS
(In 1000's except Per Share & Employees)

Years end...

FOR THE
Revenue
Net Incor
Net Incor
Average

NET MAR

Total As
Total Pl...
Total Eq
Number

RETURN

(Thousands)

ORDER FORM

Best Book Binders of America

BILL TO:

SHIP TO:

Order #	Date	Customer No.	Purchase Order #	Salesperson	Promised	Terms

Quantity	Units	Part Number	Description	Unit Price	Extension

Comments:

9812 North Highland - Denver, CO 80225 - (800) 555-4332

INSTALLING FIRST PUBLISHER

Making Backups
Installing the Program
Running the Printer Program
A Note to Mouse Users

F irst Publisher is very easy to install. The process involves copying the program disks to your hard disk under a directory name you specify. Then you tell the program about your system's configuration by running the PRINTER.EXE program. Once you run the printer program, you do not need to worry about the printer configuration again unless you change printers.

MAKING BACKUPS

Before going any further, make a copy of every disk that comes in your First Publisher package with the DOS DISKCOPY command. The disks are not copy-protected, but you must be properly licensed before you can copy the program legally.

If you are using a 5 1/4-inch disk drive, you should have the following seven disks:

- Program Disk 1
- Program Disk 2
- Program Disk 3
- Fonts Disk
- Sampler Disk
- Utility Disk
- Laser Support Disk

If you are using a 3 1/2-inch disk drive, you should have the following disks:

- Program Disk 1/Fonts Disk
- Program Disk 2/Program Disk 3
- Laser Support/Sampler Disk
- Utility Disk

INSTALLING THE PROGRAM

This book assumes that you use a hard disk system. First Publisher is very cumbersome to use on a floppy disk system, since a publication can easily grow to a size larger than will fit on a disk.

Before copying the program disks, you must name the First Publisher subdirectory where the First Publisher program files will reside. Usually, this is called "PUB." Create the subdirectory by typing the following command from the DOS prompt:

MD C:\PUB

As with all DOS commands, you can type uppercase or lowercase letters. At the end of this and every DOS command, press (ENTER). If you want to call the First Publisher subdirectory something other than "PUB" (not recommended), type another name after the backslash. If you are using a hard disk other than drive C for your subdirectory, type the appropriate drive letter. For example:

MD D:\PUB

If you want to keep publications in more than one subdirectory, you should make the subdirectories at this point. By keeping your publication in a separate subdirectory from the program files, you will not have to search through long directory file listings when looking for a specific publication. However, you *will* have to type the complete subdirectory pathname every time you load a publication file.

Now change to the program subdirectory and copy the program files. Type the following command at the DOS prompt:

CD C:\PUB

You are now located in the PUB subdirectory and are ready to copy the program disks. For every disk that comes with your First Publisher system, follow these steps:

1. Insert the disk into the A drive.

2. Type **COPY A:*.*** at the DOS prompt. You will see a list of files being copied as DOS transfers them from the floppy disk to the hard disk's current directory.

3. Take out the disk and get the next one. Continue copying the First Publisher disks until all are located on the hard disk. If you do not have a laser printer, do not copy the Laser Support Disk.

 Now that you have copied the programs to your hard disk, store the original disks in a safe place, even though you have backups.

RUNNING THE PRINTER PROGRAM

Chapter 1 showed you how to start First Publisher. Before starting it for the first time (and any time you change your printer hardware), run the program called PRINTER.EXE that came on the First Publisher system disks. Follow these steps:

1. Change to the First Publisher subdirectory by typing **CD\PUB**.

2. Type **PRINTER**. The screen shown in Figure A-1 will appear. This is the list of printers that First Publisher supports.

3. Find your printer in the list and type the number to the left of it after the printer number prompt. If you do not see your printer listed, continue pressing (**ENTER**) without typing a printer number to see more printers listed. There are 74 printers supported in version 3.

4. Press (**ENTER**).

5. Type **y** or **n** (in uppercase or lowercase letters) after the "Scale output (Y/N)?" prompt. If you are unsure about the scaling, read the section in Chapter 5 on scaled output. If you do not want to worry about the scaling at this time, type **y**. You can run the PRINTER.EXE program again if you change your mind at a later time. (The scaling prompt will not appear if you have a PostScript printer.)

6. Press (**ENTER**).

7. The "Pause between pages (Y/N)?" prompt will appear. If you have a manual single-sheet feeding printer, type **y**. Otherwise, type **n** to indicate that you have a continuous form printer or a laser printer with an automatic sheet feeder. Press (**ENTER**) when you have answered this prompt.

8. Type the number that is to the left of your printer port after the "Printer port" prompt, and then press (**ENTER**).

You will be returned to the DOS prompt, where you may start First Publisher.

 If you do not see your printer in the list, you should pick the printer most similar to yours. You may have to consult your printer manual to find out if your printer emulates another model.

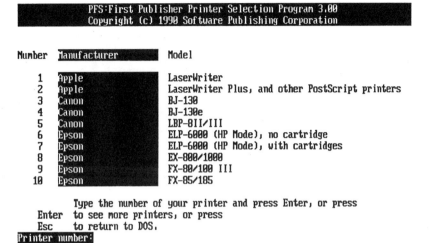

```
     PFS:First Publisher Printer Selection Program 3.00
     Copyright (c) 1990 Software Publishing Corporation


Number  Manufacturer           Model

   1    Apple                  LaserWriter
   2    Apple                  LaserWriter Plus, and other PostScript printers
   3    Canon                  BJ-130
   4    Canon                  BJ-130e
   5    Canon                  LBP-8II/III
   6    Epson                  ELP-6000 (HP Mode), no cartridge
   7    Epson                  ELP-6000 (HP Mode), with cartridges
   8    Epson                  EX-800/1000
   9    Epson                  FX-80/100 III
  10    Epson                  FX-85/185

        Type the number of your printer and press Enter, or press
Enter   to see more printers, or press
Esc     to return to DOS.
Printer number:
```

══════════ **FIGURE A-1.**　The opening screen of PRINTER.EXE

A NOTE TO MOUSE USERS

First Publisher supports all computer mice that are compatible with the following:

- LOGIMOUSE
- Microsoft Mouse
- Mouse Systems' PC Mouse

SUPPLIED
MASTER.FNT FONTS

Cairo 18-Point normal

Dutch 10-point bold
abcdefghijklmnopqrstuvwxyz1234567890!@#$%^&*()
ABCDEFGHIJKLMNOPQRSTUVWXYZ

Dutch 10-point italic
abcdefghijklmnopqrstuvwxyz1234567890!@#$%^&*()
ABCDEFGHIJKLMNOPQRSTUVWXYZ

Dutch 10-point roman
abcdefghijklmnopqrstuvwxyz1234567890!@#$%^&*()
ABCDEFGHIJKLMNOPQRSTUVWXYZ

Dutch 12-point bold
abcdefghijklmnopqrstuvwxyz1234567890!@#$%^&*()
ABCDEFGHIJKLMNOPQRSTUVWXYZ

Dutch 12-point italic
abcdefghijklmnopqrstuvwxyz1234567890!@#$%^&*()
ABCDEFGHIJKLMNOPQRSTUVWXYZ

Dutch 12-point roman
abcdefghijklmnopqrstuvwxyz1234567890!@#$%^&*()
ABCDEFGHIJKLMNOPQRSTUVWXYZ

Elite 12-point bold
abcdefghijklmnopqrstuvwxyz1234567890!@#$%^&*()
ABCDEFGHIJKLMNOPQRSTUVWXYZ

Elite 12-point italic
abcdefghijklmnopqrstuvwxys1234567890!@#$%^&*()
ABCDEFGHIJKLMNOPQRSTUVWXYZ

Elite 12-point normal
abcdefghijklmnopqrstuvwxyz1234567890!@#$%^&*()
ABCDEFGHIJKLMNOPQRSTUVWXYZ

Geneva 10-point bold
abcdefghijklmnopqrstuvwxyz1234567890!@#$%^&*()
ABCDEFGHIJKLMNOPQRSTUVWXYZ

FIGURE B-1. MASTER.FNT fonts

Geneva 12-point bold
abcdefghijklmnopqrstuvwxyz1234567890!@#$%^&*()
ABCDEFGHIJKLMNOPQRSTUVWXYZ

Geneva 12-point italic
abcdefghijklmnopqrstuvwxyz1234567890!@#$%^&()*
ABCDEFGHIJKLMNOPQRSTUVWXYZ

Geneva 12-point normal
abcdefghijklmnopqrstuvwxyz1234567890!@#$%^&*()
ABCDEFGHIJKLMNOPQRSTUVWXYZ

Goudy Old Style 14-point italic
abcdefghijklmnopqrstuvwxyz1234567890!@#$%^&()*
ABCDEFGHIJKLMNOPQRSTUVWXYZ

Goudy Old Style 14-point roman
abcdefghijklmnopqrstuvwxyz1234567890!@#$%^&*()
ABCDEFGHIJKLMNOPQRSTUVWXYZ

New York 18-point bold
abcdefghijklmnopqrstuvwxyz1234567890!
ABCDEFGHIJKLMNOPQRSTUVWXYZ

New York 24-point bold
abcdefghijklmnopqrstuvwxyz1234
ABCDEFGHIJKLMNOPQRSTUVWXYZ

New York 24-point normal
abcdefghijklmnopqrstuvwxyz1234
ABCDEFGHIJKLMNOPQRSTUVWXYZ

New York 36-point norm
abcdefghijklmnopqrstuv
ABCDEFGHIJKLMNOPQR

Pica 12-point bold
abcdefghijklmnopqrstuvwxyz1234567890!@#$%^&*()
ABCDEFGHIJKLMNOPQRSTUVWXYZ

Pica 12-point italic
abcdefghijklmnopqrstuvwxyz1234567890!@#$%^&()*
ABCDEFGHIJKLMNOPQRSTUVWXYZ

Pica 12-point normal
abcdefghijklmnopqrstuvwxyz1234567890!@#$%^&*()
ABCDEFGHIJKLMNOPQRSTUVWXYZ

Swiss 10-point bold
abcdefghijklmnopqrstuvwxyz1234567890!@#$%^&*()
ABCDEFGHIJKLMNOPQRSTUVWXYZ

Swiss 10-point italic
abcdefghijklmnopqrstuvwxyz1234567890!@#$%^&()*
ABCDEFGHIJKLMNOPQRSTUVWXYZ

Swiss 10-point roman
abcdefghijklmnopqrstuvwxyz1234567890!@#$%^&*()
ABCDEFGHIJKLMNOPQRSTUVWXYZ

Swiss 12-point bold
abcdefghijklmnopqrstuvwxyz1234567890!@#$%^&*()
ABCDEFGHIJKLMNOPQRSTUVWXYZ

Swiss 12-point italic
abcdefghijklmnopqrstuvwxyz1234567890!@#$%^&()*
ABCDEFGHIJKLMNOPQRSTUVWXYZ

Swiss 12-point roman
abcdefghijklmnopqrstuvwxyz1234567890!@#$%^&*()
ABCDEFGHIJKLMNOPQRSTUVWXYZ

FIGURE B-1. MASTER.FNT fonts (*continued*)

CLIP ART AND
TEMPLATE FILES

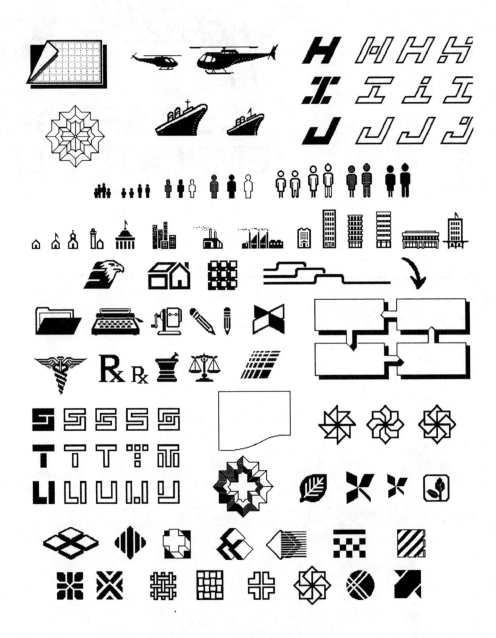

FIGURE C-1. BUSINESS.MAC clip art

═══ **FIGURE C-2.**   HOLIDAYS.MAC clip art

FIGURE C-3. LEISURE.MAC clip art

FIGURE C-4.   PERSONAL.MAC clip art

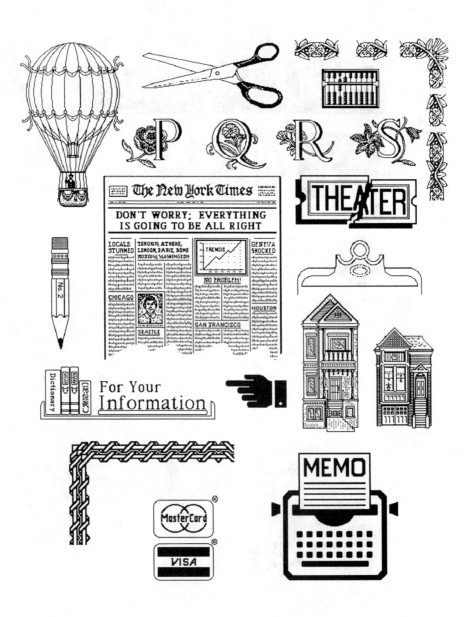

FIGURE C-5. PUBLICAT.MAC clip art

Inside of card

Inside of card

Your message goes here.
After typing graphics text
and placing art right-side
up, use Flip Horizontal and
Flip Vertical to rotate the
message to face the correct
direction.

Your message can take
up both inside panels.

←⤸ Fold card in half on this line first.

Back of card

Front of card

Fold card in half on this line second. ⟶⟶

Card credits

FIGURE C-6. CARD.PUB template

House and trees

Hotel name

Hotel address

Hotel description

FIGURE C-7. CIRCULAR.PUB template

Company name

Company address

Logo

FIGURE C-8.   LETTER.PUB template

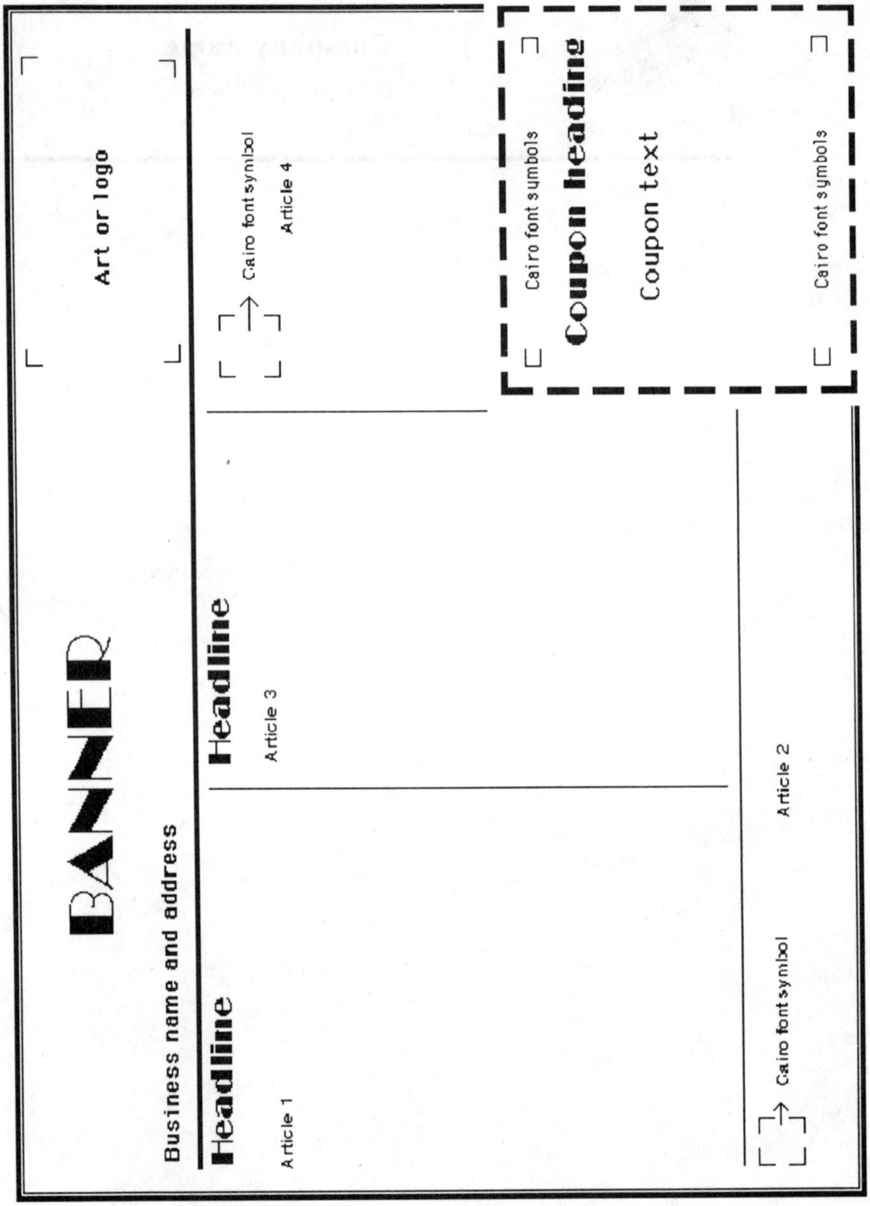

FIGURE C-9. MAILER.PUB template page 1

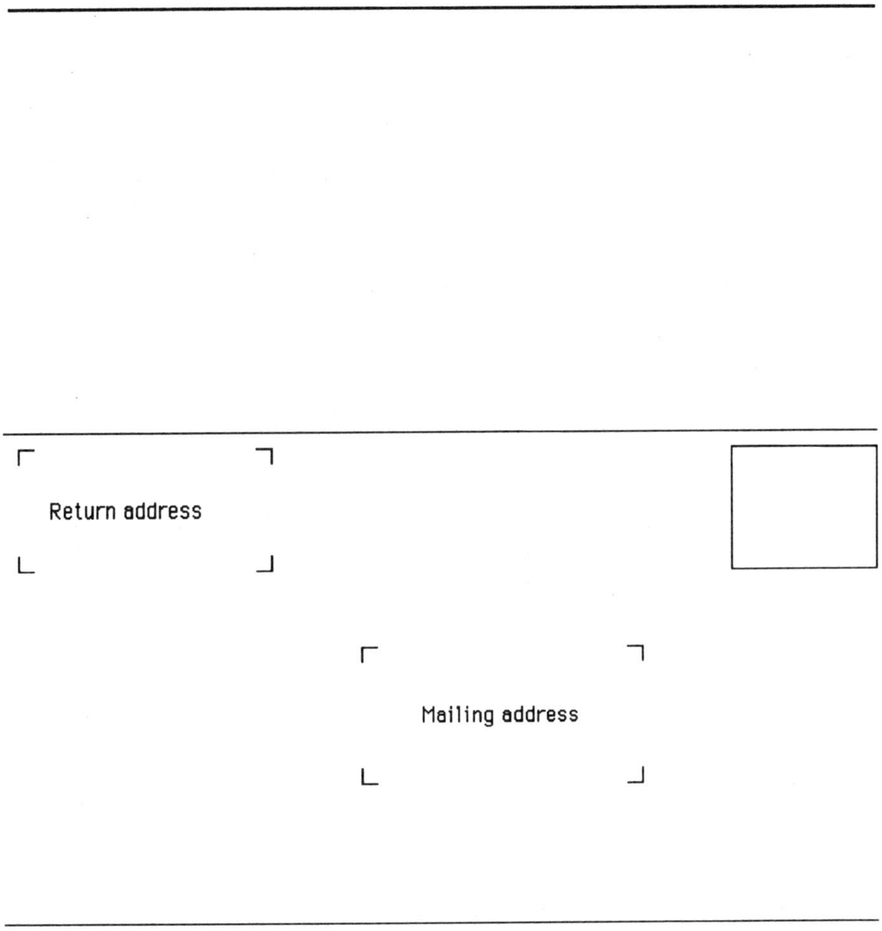

```
┌        ┐                                              ┌──────────┐
                                                        │          │
  Return address                                        │          │
                                                        │          │
└        ┘                                              └──────────┘

                          ┌              ┐

                            Mailing address

                          └              ┘
```

FIGURE C-10.   MAILER.PUB template page 2

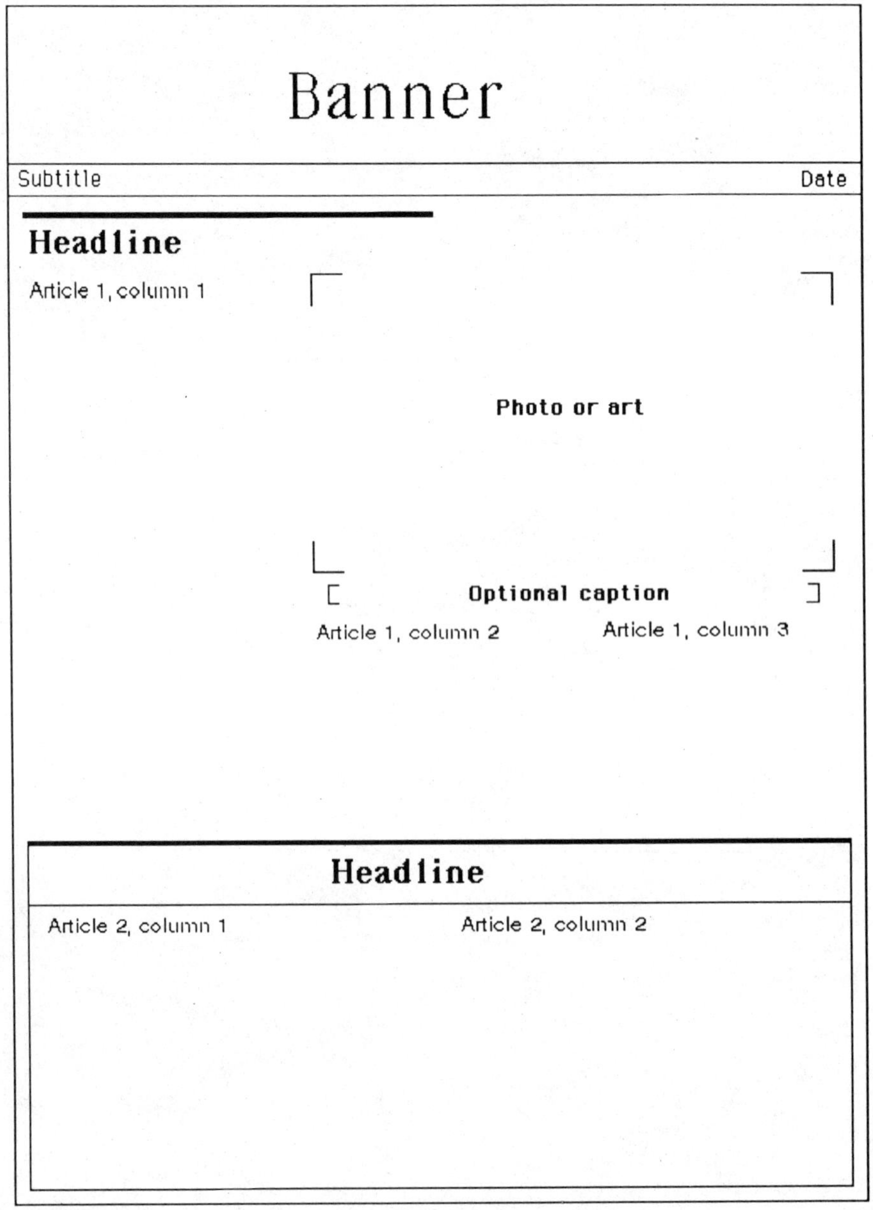

Banner

Subtitle   Date

Headline

Article 1, column 1

Photo or art

Optional caption

Article 1, column 2   Article 1, column 3

Headline

Article 2, column 1   Article 2, column 2

FIGURE C-11. NEWS.PUB template

THE SANDWICH SHOP

Fresh and delicious to go

Today's Specials

California Dreamin': Turkey, avocado, and sprouts on whole wheat.

Surf City: Seafood salad, lettuce, and tomato on a sourdough roll.

Mom's Memory: Meatloaf and ketchup on bakery white.

Zen Retreat: Monterey Jack, avocado, and sprouts in a wheat pita.

All sandwiches are $3.75.

Soup of the day: Brazilian black bean. Cup: $1.50. Bowl: $2.25.

Special combo: 1/2 sandwich plus a cup of soup for $2.75.

Try our delicious sandwiches!
The Sandwich Shop is in the Quito Shopping Center
at the corner of Cox and Quito in Saratoga.
Our hours are 10 to 8, Monday through Saturday.
To order, call (555)866-2770.

══ **FIGURE C-12.**   SANDWICH.PUB template

DESKTOP PUBLISHING GLOSSARY

Art overlay   The section of the screen where art is placed. There are two kinds of art overlays: the standard art overlay and the high-resolution art overlay. The art overlays act as transparencies that are placed over the screen so you can see text and graphics at the same time.

Baselines   Nonprinting horizontal lines that text sits upon when you type it.

Box-drawing tool   The seventh tool of the side tools, used for drawing boxes of various line widths.

Circle-drawing tool   The eighth tool of the side tools, used for drawing circles and ovals of various line widths.

Clipboard   There are two clipboards in First Publisher: a text clipboard and an art clipboard. When you copy, cut, or paste text or art, the text or art is placed on the corresponding clipboard.

Cursor   The text cursor lets you know where the next character will be typed. The graphics cursor takes on the shape of the graphics tool you are currently using.

Drag   When you press the (F10) key, or press and hold a mouse button, you can drag (move) whatever element is under the cursor to another location on the screen.

Elevator   The white box that moves up and down the elevator bar as you scroll your screen.

Elevator bar   The thin vertical bar that runs the full length of the screen to the left of the side tools. The elevator moves along this bar to give you an idea of how far down or up a publication your screen is.

Eraser tool   The tenth side tool, used for erasing graphics text, lines, and art.

Font   The typeface, size, and style of a text character.

FONTMOVE   A program supplied with version 2 of First Publisher that moves fonts to and from your font files.

Graphics text tool   The third side tool, which lets you use the keyboard to type characters that can be treated as art.

Grid   Horizontal and vertical rows of dots that let you place art and text exactly where you want them on the screen.

Gutter   The amount of space, measured in inches, between the columns of text in a publication.

Hand tool   The fifth side tool, which appears when you place or drag an art image.

Handles   The three black boxes that appear on a selected baseline, or the four that appear on a graphics image when you resize it.

Justified text   Text that aligns with the extreme left or right margin or with both margins of a column.

Landscape   Printing from left to right across the longest edge of the paper (so that the page is 11 inches wide and 8 1/2 inches long, for example).

Layout   The organization and placement of the art and text on a page.

Leading   The spacing from one baseline to the next (rhymes with "bedding").

Line-drawing tool   The sixth side tool, used for drawing straight lines on the standard art overlay. (Also called straight line tool.)

Magnify   This option lets you expand a small portion of the screen so you can edit the fine details that make up graphic images.

MASTER.FNT   The file that First Publisher looks in when searching for the particular font you request. All fonts used in your current publication must reside in this file.

Pencil tool   The ninth side tool, used for freehand drawing. The pencil tool is also used for touch-ups to magnified art.

Picturewrap   The ability of First Publisher to flow text around an art image.

Point   A publishing measurement that defines the height of a character or leading. There are 72 points in an inch.

Sans serif   Typefaces without small dots and cross lines on the ends of the characters.

Scanner   A hardware device that electronically converts printed text and art to a graphic image on your screen.

Selection tool   The fourth side tool, used for capturing all or part of a standard art image.

Serif   Typefaces that have small dots and cross lines on the ends of the characters.

Template file   A file supplied by First Publisher, or created by you, that contains the layout and unchanging art and text for a specific publication.

Text overlay   The section of the screen where text is placed when it is typed with the text tool (the first side tool). The text overlay acts as a transparency placed over the screen so you can see text and graphics at the same time.

WYSIWYG   Stands for "What You See Is What You Get," and refers to the ability to get a preview of the printed document's appearance on the video screen.

DOS DIRECTORIES

The DOS Directory
Subdirectories
DOS Commands for Subdirectories

An important concept of microcomputer operating systems, subdirectories, was introduced with PC DOS version 2.0. Computer users will find that manipulation of files is easier with subdirectories.

Although this appendix is not intended to replace a good text for PC DOS, it should give you an overview of PC DOS subdirectories and their use with First Publisher.

THE DOS DIRECTORY

Every file added to the disk is given a name, called the *filename,* when it is created. When you issue a command to retrieve a file, the operating system looks for the filename in the directory. There is at least one directory on every disk.

Looking at the Directory

There are several ways to view the contents of the directory on your disk. The DOS command, DIR, displays a list of the contents. For instance, if you issue the command, **DIR A:**, from the DOS prompt and press (ENTER), the operating system will give you a listing of all the files located in the directory of the disk in drive A. A sample result of this command is shown here:

```
C:\>DIR A:

 Volume in drive A has no label
 Directory of  A:\

MYDATA   DOC    72064 10-10-87  8:25a
SALES    JAN    23210  3-07-85  1:43p
SALES    FEB     2688 11-17-89  1:25a
SALES    MAR   117783  6-19-89
EMPLOYEE DAT    35737  6-19-89
ACCTG    DAT     8603  6-19-89
PUBNEWS  PUB    54805  6-19-89
        7 File(s)    44032 bytes free

C:\>
```

The directory command displays important information about the files listed in the directory: the filename, the extension, the size of the file in bytes (in computer jargon, a *byte* is equivalent to one character of information), and the date and time the file was last saved to disk. The operating system also keeps track of the location of the file on the disk. This location information is not shown in the directory listing, but the operating system must know where to look when you request a file.

If you do not specify a drive name after the DIR command, you will see a directory listing of the files on the current drive—usually C if you work from a hard disk. You can change the default disk drive by typing a new drive name followed by a colon (:) at the DOS prompt, and then pressing (ENTER).

SUBDIRECTORIES

Every formatted disk has at least one directory, called the main or root directory. The root directory is designated by a backslash (\) with nothing to the right of it. C: is the full name of the main directory on drive C. If you store a file called ABCDEF.DAT in this main directory, its full name would be C:\ABCDEF.DAT.

A hard disk with 20 to 30 megabytes (that's approximately 20 to 30 million characters of information in computer lingo) of storage can hold many files—enough, in fact, that one directory listing would become so long, it would be hard to find a specific file. When a directory becomes too full, it can be hard for you to find files.

There is a limit to the number of files that can be stored in a directory. This limit is 112 files per root directory for DOS versions below 3.3. Although this limit is large, you should get into the practice of storing your files in subdirectories instead of keeping all of them in the main directory.

Working with Subdirectories

You should group your files together by function in subdirectories. All of your First Publisher programs are probably saved in the directory called PUB. You might save all of your spreadsheet files in a subdirectory called SHEETS. Your graphics files could be stored in a subdirectory called GRAPHICS.

Subdirectories are named just as files are: a first name consisting of one to eight characters, with an optional extension, or last name, of one to three characters. The first name and extension are separated by a period.

Subdirectory names are listed with filenames in a directory. If you created a subdirectory called SHEETS and requested a directory listing of the main directory, you would see an entry called SHEETS. The full drive, directory, and filename (called the *path* and filename) would be C:\SHEETS. If you created a file in this subdirectory called INCSTMT.WK1, its full path and name would be C:\SHEETS\INCSTMT.WK1.

A directory listing distinguishes between regular files and subdirectories with the label <DIR> after the subdirectory's name. The following illustration is an example of a directory listing, from the operating system, that includes subdirectories:

```
C:\WORD5\SAMPLE>DIR

 Volume in drive C has no label
 Directory of  C:\WORD5\SAMPLE

.            <DIR>      7-18-90   1:19p
..           <DIR>      7-18-90   1:19p
DEMO    TXT  135142     7-04-86   1:23a
DATA    CNF     265     7-04-86   1:23a
DATA    DYN   11157     8-05-86   1:23a
GLEN         <DIR>      7-18-90   1:21p
JAYNE   DAT    7680     1-01-87   1:43p
MYSUB        <DIR>      7-18-90   1:20p
BETTYE       <DIR>      7-18-90   1:20p
FEATURES DOC 114362     7-04-86   1:23a
        10 File(s)   1294336 bytes free

C:\WORD5\SAMPLE>
```

You can perform directory listings of subdirectories by adding the full path of the subdirectory to the DIR command, such as typing **DIR C:\PUB**.

In addition to files, a subdirectory can hold other subdirectories. For example, two people, Glen and Bettye, may share a First Publisher program. If so, they might have a subdirectory called PUB that holds two more subdirectories called GLEN and BETTYE. GLEN would hold all of Glen's publication files and BETTYE would hold all of Bettye's. Figure E-1 shows what such a directory structure might look like. The full path and filename for a file called FEBNEWS.PUB in Bettye's subdirectory would be

C:\PUB\BETTYE\FEBNEWS.PUB

Whenever you get a graphics or text file from First Publisher, the program displays a list of files from the current subdirectory. If the file you need is in another subdirectory, you must type the full path and filename at the filename prompt.

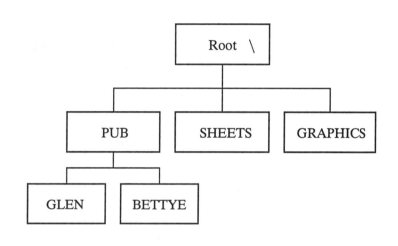

═══════ **FIGURE E-1.** The subdirectory structure

SUBDIRECTORY CURRENCY If you are currently logged to the C drive (that is, have set C as the current, default disk drive) and perform a directory command, you will get a list of all files in the main directory. If you changed to the First Publisher subdirectory, PUB, and then executed a directory command, you would see a listing of files in the PUB subdirectory and no files in the main directory.

This concept of *currency* is important. Whatever subdirectory (or main directory) you are in is the directory on which all commands, including file saves and directory listings, will be performed. You can easily change subdirectory currency through DOS.

DOS COMMANDS FOR SUBDIRECTORIES

Now that you are familiar with the concept of subdirectories, you are ready to learn how to work with them. There are only three commands that you will ever use with subdirectories. These commands let you create a subdirectory, change to another subdirectory, and remove a subdirectory.

Creating a Subdirectory

Before you can copy files to or from a subdirectory, the subdirectory must exist on the disk. You must create subdirectories with the operating system command MKDIR ("MaKe DIRectory"). MD is the shortcut for the command. When you create a subdirectory, it is made from within the current directory. If you are in the main directory and type **MD DATABASE**, a subdirectory called DATABASE will be created off the main directory. Then, if you type **DIR** from the main directory, you will see an entry for DATABASE in the list of files. To make this subdirectory current, you need to change to C:\DATABASE.

Changing to a Subdirectory

Once a subdirectory is created, you need to be able to change to it. You can change to a subdirectory with the DOS command CHDIR (or CD for short). To change to a subdirectory, give the full pathname of the subdirectory.

To change to Bettye's subdirectory, which resides in PUB, you would type **CD \PUB\BETTYE** at the DOS prompt.

Removing a Subdirectory

If you create a subdirectory and then later decide you do not want it, you can easily remove it from the disk. You must delete all files from the subdirectory before you can remove it. Also, there can be no subdirectories left inside the subdirectory you are removing.

One last item to be aware of before removing a subdirectory: You cannot be in the subdirectory you are trying to remove. You must change to another subdirectory or to the main directory first.

The operating system command RMDIR (or RD for short) removes the subdirectory you specify. Give the full path of the subdirectory to remove. To remove BETTYE from PUB, type **RD C:\PUB\BETTYE**.

As long as BETTYE contains no files or subdirectories, and as long as you are currently in another subdirectory (such as SHEETS), this command works fine.

This appendix was not intended to replace a good text on operating systems. For more complete coverage, read *DOS: The Complete Reference, Second Edition,* by Kris Jamsa (Berkeley, CA: Osborne/McGraw-Hill, 1990).

You should now have a good feel for using subdirectories. Some people use a computer for years and know nothing about subdirectory usage. Since you are now familiar with subdirectories, you can better organize your files, and understand more about DOS.

INDEX

A

Add fonts option, 184-187
Adjust above option, 149
Adjust below option, 149
Adjust column option, 149
Adjust single option, 146, 149, 160
Arrow keys, emulating mouse with, 38
.ART files, 92-93, 98
Art menu, 48-50, 98, 119
Art
    capturing, 21, 122-129, 306-307
    combining with text, 115-118,
       165-168, 280
    files, 92-93, 120
    high-resolution, 92, 118-121
    importing, 18-19, 120, 122-129
    modifying, 21, 48, 97-105
    moving, 98-99
    outlining, 213
    placing, 147, 165-166, 171-174, 198,
       199-200, 295
    saving, 112, 120, 291
    scanning, 21, 120, 129, 287
    selecting, 96, 202, 237
    separating, 239-241
    sizing, 259
    standard resolution, 92, 97, 120, 127
    touching up, 268, 328, 337
    See also Clip art; Drawing; Graphics text
ASCII files
    importing, 13, 85, 86

ASCII files (*continued*)
    saving spreadsheets as, 306, 311
    saving text as, 80, 83, 86

B

Backup disks
    making, 29, 345-346
    storing, 347
Backups, font file, 188-189
Baselines menu, 47-48, 146-147, 149, 159
Baselines, 146-147
    adding, 274-278
    centering, 274-276
    defined, 17, 369
    displaying, 146
    extending, 159-161
    hiding, 146
    moving existing, 216-217, 308-309
    placing, 149, 151, 171, 173, 208
    resetting, 269-271
Batch file, for startup, 30-31
Beep signal
    when inputting text, 67, 80-81
    when scrolling, 56
    when using SNAPSHOT, 123
Bitstream scalable fonts, 15-16, 23, 179
    adding, 186-187
    in .FNB files, 181-182
    on Font menu, 180
    and printer installation, 348
Blocks, 46, 65
    working with, 74-80

Microsoft Paintbrush, importing from,
18-19, 122
Microsoft Windows Paint, importing from,
18-19, 122
Microsoft Word, importing from, 13, 85
Mirror image. *See* Invert option; Inverting
images
Monitors, 24, 26-27
Mouse
compatible types, 25, 349
driver program, 29
installation of, 26
moving cursor with, 69, 71-72, 73-74
placing text and art with, 200, 269
use of, generally, 26, 37-38, 40
Mouse symbol, 38
Move command, 65
Moving
art images, 98-99
text, 77
MultiMate, importing from, 13, 85
Multiple page publications, 316

N

NEWS.PUB, 220-222
Newsletters
design of, 12, 115, 206, 255
multiple-column layout, 220-230
single-column layout, 202-220
templates for, 230-231
Normal type, 47

O

Office Writer, importing from, 13, 85
Operating system. *See* DOS
Orientation, page, 87-88, 148-150
and elevator bars, 54
in version 2.1 and below, 132
Overflow
area, page, 81, 310
text, 80-82
Overlays
defined, 64-65, 369-371
high-resolution, 118
rulers on, 174

Overlays (*continued*)
standard art, 119, 171
text, 146
using, 116-117

P

Page menu, 42-45
Pages
creating, 81
number of, 42
Paintshow Plus, importing from, 18-19, 122
Paper
for business cards, 298-299
size, 87, 148-149
Paste options, 46, 48
Pasting
images, 100-102, 268-269
text, 77-79, 82
Pathnames, specifying, 41, 59-60, 376
PC Paint Plus, importing from, 18-19, 122
PC Paintbrush, importing from, 18-19, 122
Pencil tool, 57, 106-107, 251, 371
PFS:First Choice, importing from, 13, 85
PFS:WRITE, importing from, 13, 85
Picturewrap, 165-168
and baselines, 145, 147
defined, 371
Picturewrap option, 43
Pixel, defined, 49
Point size, 47, 371
Popup programs, 32
Portrait mode, 87-88, 132, 149
Previewing publications, 45, 131-134, 299
Prices, 340
Print
modes, 139
options, 136-143
resolution, 29, 139, 179-180
Print option, 41
Printer, 27-29
default, 136
and fonts, 179-180, 182
installing, 347-348
laser, 139, 299
selecting, 136, 138
Printer program (PRINTER.EXE), 347-348

The manuscript for this book was prepared and submitted to Osborne **McGraw-Hill** in electronic form.
The acquisitions editor for this project was Roger Stewart, the technical reviewer was John Levy, and the project editor was Judith Brown.

This book was designed by Stefany Otis and John Erick Christgau, using Times Roman for text body and Swiss boldface for display.

Cover art by Bay Graphics Design. Color separation and cover supplier, Phoenix Color Corporation. Screens produced with InSet, from Inset Systems, Inc. Book printed and bound by R.R. Donnelley & Sons Company, Crawfordsville, Indiana. Command card printed by Schmidt Printing Inc., Rochester, Minnesota.

PFS:First Publisher 3 Command Card

Function	Command Keys
TEXT OVERLAY CURSOR CONTROL	
Character left	LEFT ARROW
Character right	RIGHT ARROW
One line up	UP ARROW
One line down	DOWN ARROW
Left one grid unit	SHIFT-LEFT ARROW
Right one grid unit	SHIFT-RIGHT ARROW
Up one grid unit	SHIFT-UP ARROW
Down one grid unit	SHIFT-DOWN ARROW
Word left	CTRL-LEFT ARROW
Word right	CTRL-RIGHT ARROW
Left end of line	HOME
Right end of line	END
Top of current page	CTRL-HOME
End of last text on page	CTRL-END
Up partial screen	CTRL-PGUP
Down partial screen	CTRL-PGDN
Left of landscape screen	CTRL-L
Right of landscape screen	CTRL-R

Function	Command Keys
TEXT OVERLAY CURSOR CONTROL	
Jump to a page	ALT-J
Next column to right	CTRL-N
Next column to left	CTRL-P
Next page	SHIFT-+ (on keypad)
Previous page	SHIFT-MINUS (on keypad)
Simulate a mouse press	F10
SIDE TOOL SELECTION	
Highlight next tool	F9
Highlight top tool	SHIFT-F9
Highlight previous tool	ALT-F9
MOUSE COMMANDS	
Move mouse	Point to screen item
Click a mouse button	Select item
Press and hold a mouse button	Drag an item
Click on horizontal elevator left arrow	Move to left of landscape screen
Click on horizontal elevator right arrow	Move to right of landscape screen

PFS:First Publisher 3 Command Card

Function	Command Keys
CONTEXT-SENSITIVE HELP	
Display help on current function	ALT-H
(F1) FILE	
Get a publication	ALT-G
Save a publication	ALT-S
Print a publication	ALT-P
Status of publication	ALT-T
Start over	ALT-Y
Exit to DOS	ALT-E
(F2) PAGE	
Picturewrap	ALT-W
Show rulers	ALT-L
Use grid	ALT-U
Jump to page	ALT-J
Show page	ALT-Z
(F3) TEXT	
Cut selected text	DEL
Copy selected text	ALT-C
Paste selected text	ALT-V

Function	Command Keys
(F6) BASELINES	
Adjust single column	ALT-A
Center selected baseline	ALT-X
Realign text on baseline	ALT-T
(F7) ART	
Cut selected art	DEL
Copy selected art	ALT-C
Paste selected art	ALT-V
Duplicate selected art	ALT-D
Rotate selected art	ALT-O
Resize selected art	ALT-R
Crop	ALT-K
Magnify art	ALT-M
Set line width	ALT-HYPHEN

© 1990 Osborne McGraw-Hill

PFS:First Publisher 3 Made Easy